SEX AND THE BRAIN

Jo Durden-Smith
and Diane deSimone

SEX AND THE BRAIN

ARBOR HOUSE New York

Library of Congress Catalogue Card Number: 83-70492

ISBN: 0-87795-484-4

Manufactured in the United States of America

10 9 8 7 6 5 4 3 2 1

This book is printed on acid-free paper. The paper in this book meets the guidelines for permanence and durability of the Committee on Production Guidelines for Book Longevity of the Council on Library Resources.

Portions of *Sex and the Brain* originally appeared in Playboy Magazine.

*For Jack, Joan and Adele, a father
and two mothers: and for Lewis
Mumford, the father of us all*

ACKNOWLEDGMENTS

We should like to thank all those scientists whose voices are heard in this book: for their generosity with their time, their enthusiasm and their kindness to us. We have tried to be as accurate as possible in their accounts of their own work and attitudes and of the work of others. Any mistakes—in fact or in view taken—that remain in the text are, of course, ours.

We should also like to thank all the other scientists who, although not quoted in the text, helped to make this book possible through the encouragement and help they gave us at various stages of the research: Huda Akil; Richard Alexander; Monte Buchsbaum; Martin Daly; David de Wied; Marian Diamond; Klaus Döhler; Bernard Dufy; Robin Fox; Albert Galaburda; Ruben and Raquel Gur; Mark Gurney; David Margules; Catherine Mateer; Bruce McEwen; Fred Naftolin; Agu and Candace Pert; Philip and Mary Seeman; Roger Short; Barry Smith; Roger Sperry; Julian Stanley; Larry Stein; Lois Verbrugge; Stan Watson; George Williams; Margo Wilson and Eran Zaidel. Our thanks should also go to three people who helped provide us with essential research materials: Gene Cone and Bard Bardossi

7

of The Rockefeller University and Richard Thomas of WNET-TV in New York.

Some of the material in this book appeared, in a different form, in Playboy Magazine. We should especially like to thank four people there: Jim Morgan, for believing in us and in the importance of the subject; Eileen Kent, for always being ready to help; Mary Zion, for doggedly checking every fact; and Arthur Kretchmer, for jumping in with a crucial suggestion in the fifth month of the series.

Finally we should like to express our gratitude to two people who kept us going and egged us on. Our tireless agent, Christine Tomasino; and a good friend, Richard Hess. Friendship is a difficult art. But he, in this way, as in others, is an artist.

CONTENTS

The Brain

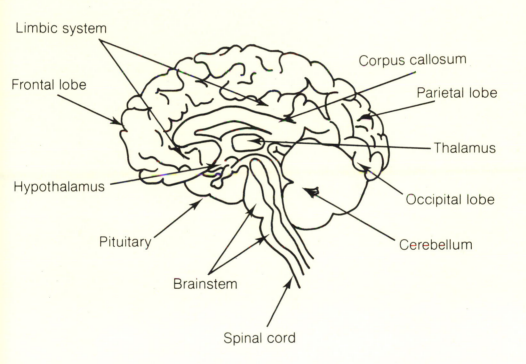

Limbic system

Frontal lobe

Hypothalamus

Pituitary

Brainstem

Spinal cord

Corpus callosum

Parietal lobe

Thalamus

Occipital lobe

Cerebellum

INTRODUCTION

THE CUTTING EDGE

THIS BOOK IS a detective story. The detectives are scientists. And the body in question is ours: differently sexed, differently brained, differently male and female.

This book is the story of a science in the making—of a trail of clues gradually coming together into a new picture of what it means to be a man or a woman. Like most detective stories it gives an account of the problems to be solved, the detectives' methods and the accidents that undercut old assumptions. Unlike most detective stories, it remains unfinished, since it is about the most fundamental of all searches—the search deep within the male and female body and brain for an answer to the essential questions of our own being: where we came from, why we are here and who we are.

Science, as the Nobel Prize biologist, Sir Peter Medawar, recently wrote, "begins as a story about a possible world—a story which we invent and criticize and modify as we go along, so that it ends by being, as nearly as we can make it, a story about real life." But science is much more than a story. It is also the destroyer of myths. It is the knife with which we cut open our future. And it inexorably changes the way we are forced to think about the world and about each other.

This is true of the revolution of Copernicus, who proclaimed that this whirling rock, the earth, was not after all the center of the universe. It is true of the successive revolutions of Darwin and Freud. And it is true of the revolution now being made by scientists who are opening new avenues into the male and female brain. This science is already challenging all our modern, fondly held beliefs about sex and gender. It is threatening the deeply entrenched attitudes and institutions of psychology and psychiatry. And it is undermining, above all, the notion that we are beyond nature—freed by our technology, our culture and our possession of mind into some stratosphere above the animal kingdom.

For the past eighty years or so men and women of the west have progressively arrogated to themselves an increasingly greater freedom from all biological and ecological constraints. We have technologized the planet and industrialized our own bodies. We have separated sex from reproduction and have increasingly devoted ourselves to a democratic mechanics of arousal and orgasm. We have stuffed ourselves with pills and stoked ourselves with hormones.

We have been encouraged in this by a medicine that has presumed that the human body is a machine that can be tinkered with at will; by a science that has announced that an incorporeal substance, the mind, is the true director of all human affairs; and by a politics that has declared that men and women, as creations of this mind, should ignore the different biologies of their bodies and aspire to sameness.

All of these assumptions, as well as the institutions and careers that have been built upon them, are now under attack from a new science of the male and female brain.

The human brain is a forest of a hundred billion nerve cells in the bone case of your skull, the branches of which, if laid end to end, would stretch to the moon and back. It is two pinkish-gray handfuls of custardlike tissue, whorled like a walnut, turned in upon itself, hungry for oxygen and chemical energy, and driven by enough electricity to light a small lamp bulb. It is also who you are.

Man, woman or child, it is your brain which rules your behavior, the way you respond to your environment, the way you plan and think and dream. Interfere through drugs with the working of these hundred billion cells, and your behavior and your perceptions will be changed. Damage these cells, with strokes and tumors, the bullet or the knife, and your abilities will be impaired. Transplant these cells to another body—the stuff of science fiction—and your identity, your history, will go with them. The body they will go to will be the donor, not the recipient. And the body they will leave behind, now useless, will be what it always was from the beginning: a container, brilliantly designed by nature to meet the brain's needs and aspirations, given the kind of world it lives, learns, moves and wants to reproduce in.

The container, we all know, is differently sexed before birth; it flowers at puberty into the full expression of maleness and femaleness. But what of the seat of its personality, its brain? What if that too is born into the world set, like the body, into a male or female pattern—ready to develop as it confronts the world into a male or female configuration of abilities and skills, drives and disorders, appetites and aversions?

This is what the new science of the human brain is beginning to tell us, as it finally bends toward the central enigma of our humanity all the techniques and technologies that have been developed in other disciplines in the past quarter century. It is telling us that there may well be, after all, one overriding constraint on our ability to intervene in our bodies and change the world for our present purposes—the constraint of our maleness and femaleness, wired before birth into the chemistry and circuitry of the male and female body and brain.

This notion flies in the face of all the beliefs and prejudices into which we in the west have been conditioned over the past twenty-five years. We have come to accept, all too blithely, that medicine and science are all-knowing—surely one of the cruelest hoaxes of this century—and that gender is an accident confined simply to the machinery of the body. We take for granted that it is our minds that are all-important and that we are shaped after birth into irreducibly unique psychologies *solely* by our contacts with the culture in which we find ourselves. Given this, we have bought wholesale the idea that differences between men and women *must* be caused by the environment. To suggest otherwise is to be guilty of a kind of sexual inegalitarianism.

Early on in researching the material that was to lead to this book we went to visit Richard Alexander, a leading evolutionary biologist at the University of Michigan in Ann Arbor. He told us with some amazement of a class he had recently given. He had asked his students to make a roster of the differences between men and women. After much argument they had come up with two: men produced sperm and women produced eggs; and women had the further ability to make and then feed babies. This did not surprise Alexander. What did surprise and puzzle him was the considerable bad blood caused by the exercise, the animus shown especially by the women. Only later did a colleague suggest an explanation. The women were angry, perhaps, because they thought that to admit even these differences was to deny themselves power—power as defined by the society. If true, Alexander regretted it. "Men and women *are* different," he said, "variously different, much more different than the class could obviously imagine. And to cut ourselves off from these differences, to deny them, is to cut ourselves off from nature and from something very remarkable about the legacy of our human inheritance."

The members of Alexander's class are the children of the nurture determinists. The notion that *nature* too might be at work in us seems foreign to them—as it is to most others today. And yet such is precisely what the new science of the brain is quietly announcing. Variously fed by the tributaries of different disciplines—ethnology, anthropology, evolutionary biology, neurology, immunology and endocrinology—it is saying that nature is every bit as important as nurture in the manufacture of our personalities: who we are, our brains. We are not as new or as self-made as some current scientific orthodoxies claim us to be. In fact, we are old. We are animals. And in our brains, male and female, is written the long history of the paths we have taken through other species to arrive at this place.

The result is a considerable difference between human males and females, a difference that has been progressively shaped by evolution since our earliest beginnings in the first multicellular organisms. We are all of us the children of children—of fathers and mothers coming together for the purpose of successful reproduction. And bred into our bodies and brains over hundreds of thousands of generations, whether we like it or not, remain the separate qualities necessary to the task. A separate inheritance.

This book, then, is a detective story that travels backward in time through our evolutionary past but begins with the assumptions, myths and orthodoxies of an *immediate* past that must be cleared away and learned from. It is *also* a detective story set in the present—a story that brings together the latest work done by brain scientists in laboratories around the world and tells of the controversy that often surrounds them. And it is finally, too, a detective story about the *future*—a future that this science is even now beginning to create. Science, as we have said, is the knife, the cutting edge that carves out our future. But it is, as we have seen so often in the past, a knife that cuts both ways. One way the new science of men and women may cut is toward a future in which we will be forced to overhaul some of our institutions, to reconsider our newly acquired liberations and to reappraise our most cherished belief about ourselves—our assumed "civilized" position above the rest of nature. But the other way in which it may cut is toward a future in which we will be encouraged to mechanize and industrialize our bodies even further through the new chemical and genetic technologies that science is now beginning to offer us.

We are living today at a revolutionary point in evolutionary time. Brain scientists are digging at the roots of creativity and learning, of sleep and sex, of pleasure and pain. And they will soon be ready to supply men and women with new instruments by which they can alter the way they experience, interpret and engage the world. There will be new means to control addiction, appetite and memory; a new approach, through the brain, to contraception and sexual dysfunction; and new treatments for the depression, senility, schizophrenia and stress that are the apocolyptic four horsemen of the modern age. We are fast moving toward a time in which we can change the world by changing the brain that perceives it, a time in which concentration, protection from stress, memory, freedom from anxiety, pleasure and even orgasm will be easily, instantly, chemically available.

At the same time scientists are taking the first steps toward intervening directly in the evolutionary processes that have produced us, male and female. They have within their grasp the ability to rewrite the genetic scripts of human fetuses while they are still in the womb. And it is not too fanciful to imagine a time, not unlike that of Aldous Huxley's *Brave New World*, in which favored germ cells are selected and stored, test tube babies are routine and a basic redesign of the human stock is made possible. If these things happen, the maleness and femaleness of our future descendants will have become an irrelevance, as will the inborn legacy of the male and female brain. We will by that time have done away with the messiness of our own humanity and

have become merely the modifiable products of our own bi-
otechnology.

This book has no easy answers. But both such futures are
being prefigured by the new science of men and women. And we
have a responsibility to our children and to their children to
learn to choose between them. We cannot do this simply by
relegating science to the back pages of our minds, where small
fears meet large ignorances. We cannot do this by taking for
granted old scientific orthodoxies and worshiping new science
from afar. We can only do it by attempting to understand how
far the science of men and women has already come in *its* understanding of our place in nature and of the differences between
us, and in its ability, slowly gathering, to override them. Such is
the subject of this book.

Much of its material is, we acknowledge, controversial. For
even to suggest that there are fundamental differences between
men and women is still to provoke an inchoate anger, a conviction that an injustice, a slight against social health, is being
committed. To further suggest that these differences are innate,
inscribed before birth in the finite organ of the brain, is to
compound, in the view of many people, the crime. It is considered illiberal, and it runs counter to what is seen as the revealed
truths of the mainstream of science, the massive institutions of
psychology and sociology.

All of which means that many of the scientists we shall be
meeting in these pages have often been obliged to face attacks
on two fronts. They have been denounced as biology-obsessed,
anti-psychological mavericks. And they have been dismissed as
illiberal, as either virulently anti-feminist or militantly feminist,
depending on who is doing the attacking. This has had a considerable effect on the acceptability of their work, even at a scientific level. A number of scientists—many of them women—have
told us of the difficulties they have had with grants and with the
publishing of articles in professional journals. One internation-
ally known woman researcher told us of a grant proposal being

turned down, not on the grounds that it was a poor proposal—it was highly rated—but on the grounds, in the words of just one referee, that *"this work ought not to be done."* It was perceived as anti-humanist.

Such a view is a pervasive one. It is our modern climate of opinion. But it also persists in ignoring that what we have assumed to be the science of men and women is essentially a makeshift, jerrybuilt structure erected out of the prejudices of the past. It is this structure that a truly modern science of the brain—with all its implications for us as men and women—is now quickly if quietly replacing.

PART ONE
NATURE/NURTURE

1
THE DEATH OF THE OLD, THE BIRTH OF THE NEW

A HUNDRED AND twenty-five years ago, a scientific orthodoxy was being slowly spatchcocked together to provide for *its* age a climate of opinion that was to linger long after. At the time virtually nothing was known about the human brain, according to the contemporary first edition of Gray's *Anatomy,* except that people of intelligence had heavier and more capacious brains than idiots. This was not a lot to go on. But it encouraged a pride of brain scientists, among them Samuel George Morton in Philadelphia and Paul Broca in Paris, to scurry through morgues and infirmaries and collections of old bones and to measure there, with seeds and shot and rule and ribbon, a wide variety of human skulls. They arrived, virtually to a man, at the same sonorous, reverberating conclusion. Women had a good deal less native intelligence than men. In a pecking order achieved through the measurement of brains, and even the hat sizes of dead geniuses, white Anglo-Saxon Protestant males led the field, followed by other northern Europeans, then Slavs, then Jews, and, a long way further back, Negroes and savages bringing up the rear. White females, from their brain size, were found to be on a level with Negroes and savages, and certain of their cranial arrangements suggested a similarity to white male children.

This discovery chimed happily and precisely with the notion of "nature's ladder," the ascending scale of perfection, implicit in creation, of which man, with his immortal soul, was the crown. It also sat easily with Darwin's revolutionary new ideas about evolution and the origin of species. For natural law could comfortably be applied to the differences that had been found, and extra rungs in the ladder could be scientifically demonstrated. European males, with their superior technologies and larger brains, were clearly, according to the new language, more *evolved* than their benighted, instinctual cousins on other continents. They were also more evolved than the females in their own midst. All the signs and portents collected by inquiring Victorian science pointed the same way. If women looked more like their own white children than hairy, muscular men, then that, according to Ernst Haeckel's theory of recapitulation, was another reason for believing that they had stopped developing at an early stage of human evolution. If men were more variable than women—with more idiots and more geniuses, for example, as Havelock Ellis pointed out—then this proved once more that men were the essential engine behind human evolution, the source of the species' differentiation and the origin of all progress: women were nonvarying because they were merely reproductive. If women's brains were like those of children and savages, then they were clearly also more innocent, more instinctive and more in need of protection than men. And if they were less like their partnering males than the women of their savage forebears were, then the differences between them had obviously been favored in the progressive march upwards of the human race. Women, wherever the evidence came from, were the evolutionary vehicle which carried mankind forward in its struggle for self-improvement. But men were the drivers. It was their destiny to carry the responsibility of their larger brain. And it was the destiny of women to reproduce. To refuse to do so was to deny the species further advancement.

The scientific orthodoxy that was shaped and fattened on these synthetic raw materials sputtered on, in one form or another, in one place or another, until the period after World War I. The fact that it was based on an utter garbling of what Darwin had actually written was neither here nor there. It justified the political and social dispensations of the times. European males dominated continents, businesses and households by the divine right of their evolutionary inheritance. And their women, more uterine than cerebral, found their natural place in the delivery room, the nursery and the drawing room, where they bore and raised children and preoccupied themselves with all the psychosomatic ailments that male doctors increasingly found in them.

If this particular scientific orthodoxy now seems to us antique and illiberal, a product of the ignorant, bigoted, bad old days, we should nonetheless pause to remember that some of the most illustrious scientific names of the period were involved in its making. For better or worse it *was* the science of its time, with every appearance of being rigorous, logical, objective and internally coherent. We should also remember that, despite its early dethronement as science, it has loitered on in the public mind —and even, to some extent, in science—until today. Until the 1960s, indeed, it provided most of the weather in the climate of the collective opinion. Put crudely, after all, the orthodoxy maintained that nature and biology were all-important. Operating through Gregor Mendel's units of inheritance, christened "genes" by Wilhelm Johannsen in 1909, they uniquely determined the intelligence of men and women, their status in life and the degree of achievement of which they were capable. Since this was so, sex differences and social hierarchies were both the result and the expression of natural forces in action. To tinker with them would be to fly in the face of nature, to adopt an unnatural course.

The argument from nature is no longer a popular one. And people who still hold such views as the above are commonly considered throwbacks, conservatives, obstacles to egalitarianism and the creation of a better society. We consider them so —those of us who do—because we, after all, have the facts, facts which support a more enlightened point of view. We have the full force of a *new,* modern scientific orthodoxy behind us. This orthodoxy pronounces that the individual of either sex, of whatever race is the product not of biology but of the environment he or she is born into. Each human psychology is shaped not by genes but by the network of social influences and interpersonal relations found in this environment. And gender differences, among other things, are gradually learned from them. Culture, or to use a more emotive word, nurture is what is basic to the development of the human personality, its aims and aspirations, its faults and failings, its skills and abilities. Nature, that old bugbear, has nothing to do with it.

This orthodoxy is obviously a great deal more humane than the one it superseded; the incarnation in science not only of a chauvinist Adam and a compliant Eve, but also of the sons of Cain cursed forever into slavery. It is also democratic. It implicitly contends that differences between people, being social artifacts, can always be eliminated. It holds out the possibility of equal postbirth influences for all. To this extent, then, it's expressive of the idealism fundamental to the founding of the country which brought it to birth. The old orthodoxy—ideology, rather—was the child of an expansivist, colonial Europe, obsessed by class and with the continuities of birth and money. The new orthodoxy, on the other hand, was the child of the New World. It was as liberal and progressive as the New World had always aspired to be—free from history, free from class, free from the need to dominate and free, finally, from the crippling burden of race and sex prejudice. This, of course, is something to be applauded. But it doesn't mean that the new orthodoxy, now our modern climate of opinion, is any less an ideology than the one that preceded it. Nor does it mean that it has not served and helped create, equally well, new political and social arrangements in America and elsewhere.

It does not mean, above all, perhaps, that the orthodoxy, however much we take it for granted, however much we see it enshrined in the institutions and attitudes of our culture, is a final, clear and shining truth from God. Scientific orthodoxies, as we know very well from the world of physics, are constructed out of the materials—information, tools and technologies—that are available at any given time. They often make the world coherent at the expense of having to leave much of it out. They can always, then, be demolished by the emergence and acceptance of new techniques, new discoveries and new fields of study. For they represent not only knowledge and security but also compromise, ignorance and roads not taken.

To see this more clearly—to see how the science of men and women has become a constant fretting about individual psychologies and the effects of culture, and to see why there is often so much hostility to the work of the brain scientists we shall be meeting in the pages of this book—we have to go back and see how the new orthodoxy was built upon the ruins of the old, and where it has led us.

The monument to male and bourgeois certainties that was Victorian anthropology's contribution to the theme of the differences between us crumbled away for a variety of reasons. It crumbled, for one thing, because brain science, after its first fine flurry of measurement, had really nothing much else to contribute to it. It did spend time comparing a few subdivisions of the brain in men and women, with results that predictably favored the higher mental processes of men and the "perception"—this was allowed them—of women. But it was soon confronted with the awful truth that, though it had a crude geography of brain function for them all, it had no idea of how the brain of any of them—man, woman or savage—actually worked. So it slunk from the public eye back to its laboratories, to spend the next thirty or forty years trying to learn the language the male and female nervous system used. This left the field to the anthropologists proper, and to evolutionists who were progressively more circumspect in their interpretations of Darwin. It was they who finally scuppered the Eurocentric and androcentric view of man's history.

First, it soon became plain to them that the savages they encountered were hardly the homogeneous subhumans that skull-toting academics had pictured. They were as different from one another as they were from northern Europeans and no less, for all their primitive methods of production, human. Second, since it was increasingly clear to them that sophisticated cultures had arisen rather early in human history, it was no use believing that Victorian culture was at the top of some uniformly ascending ladder. And third, a less wish-fulfilling reading of Darwin confirmed that evolution was indeed no ladder at all, climbing rung over rung towards London and Paris. It was a branching tree. Men, women and savages, wherever they were, were all on the same branch. They were one species, one biology, one primate.

This conclusion might have led to the beginnings of a science based on man's place in the animal kingdom. It might have placed men and women firmly back in nature. But this would have been to deny the Victorian conviction of the baseness of instinct, the intolerable neural itch of the flesh. It would have flown in the face of human discomfort at being reduced from being the proud possessor of an immortal soul to being no more than a hairless, bipedal, big-brained, two-sexed ape. More than that, though, it would have been to override the insistent imperatives of racism. For if all men were brothers beneath the skin, how could the obvious superiority of some of them be explained?

The answer, of course, was culture. Culture is what separates man from other animals and makes one group of men superior to another. Men and women are first and foremost creators of, and products of, societies. The nature and biology that they share, then, is irrelevant. This was a convenient way out of the wood; it allowed men a dominant role in the making of culture and it kept savages in their place, as primitives. It rapidly congealed, then, into a conventional wisdom of science, one that was to have important effects. For it successfully split biological evolution from cultural evolution, and it divided anthropology into two essentially separate disciplines, physical anthropology and cultural anthropology. For the next seventy years or so, especially in the New World, the cultural twins, evolution and anthropology, were to occupy the grandstand, wearing stars like Margaret Mead and Bronislaw Malinowski in their caps; while their poor relatives, physical anthropology and biological evolution, were relegated to the cheap seats.

The period we are speaking of happened to coincide with the rise of an intuitive brain science that snatched up the mantle of succession from the physical brain science now so woefully in retreat. This new brain science, in the absence of any better way of going about things, looked at the brain, or mind, as a black box, with wires going into it (experience), and wires coming out (behavior). What was in the black box could be inferred by making connections between a faulty input and a deranged output (Sigmund Freud, the father of psychoanalysis), or it could be declared merely an unknowable, and therefore rather uninteresting, bridge between stimulus and response (John B. Watson, the father of behaviorism). Either way, little value was given to what was in the black box before it arrived on the human scene at birth. Learned behavior was all that counted, according to John Watson, from whose extreme environmentalism even thought and consciousness were banished. And its opposite, unlearned behavior or instinct, though not rejected by Freud, was still seen by him as a dangerous force in dire need of socialization. This may seem a little unfair to Freud who argued, after all, for the primacy of sexual drives and saw the unconscious as a battleground between instinct and culture; who therefore saw that there was an inherited biology of the brain, perhaps different in men and women. But it was precisely this element in his thought that was most bowdlerized by his often socialist and feminist disciples in what was to become the American school of psychoanalysis. In any case, the point is not that instinct was not important to Freud, but that it was seen by him as morally suspect. It was culture and the progressive civilization of the individual and the society that tamed, according to Freud, the potential anarchy of instinct. And so culture, for him as for Watson, was the critical determinant of the individual personality.

Culture, then—nurture; experience; learned, conditioned or acquired behavior, call it what you will—became, in the first three or four decades of the twentieth century, the cynosure of virtually every anthropologist worth his or her salt and at the same time the King Charles's head of the two main schools of psychological thought that the century produced. To the heady brew of this consensus—the makings of the dish of the new orthodoxy—should now be added the flavor of one further discipline that was going to exert considerable power in the years to come: sociology. In the period before World War I, sociology was little more than the fledgling child of cultural anthropology. It busied itself with primitives and prehistory. It earnestly debated such issues as the age—believed young—of the human family, and the possibility—believed likely—of a matriarchal phase in human evolution. The evidence for each was, to say the least, patchy, but the enthusiasm for both, among radical intellectuals, was high. But then, in the 1920s, the profession was called to order.

Under the clipped instructions of such men as Emile Durkheim and Charles Horton Cooley sociology now took on its modern form. From now on evolutionary theory and speculations about history were to be abandoned as useless and unprofitable. Generalities were to be sent packing. Instead, the bailiwick of the new toddler science was to become the network of relations—interpersonal and institutional—that shaped the male or female individual. The individual, after all, was the vehicle of society's culture. He was little more than the process of his own socialization. For any understanding of the society, then, the individual—as child, as student, as urbanite, as parent, as social product—had to be put under the glass and intensively studied. His or her motives and feelings—let alone instincts, of course—were irrelevant to the terms under which sociology set up the shop of its responsibility. What mattered were the influences, healthy or unhealthy, of family, school, city and so on.

Out of the ruins of the old orthodoxy, in other words, rose, by way of stopgap theories of the brain and a road not taken, the three "modern" sciences of men and women—committed to precisely the same world view, embarked on essentially the same project and based on the same presuppositions. Evolutionary theory, to all three of them, was useless when applied to human behavior. Behavior was never biologically but always culturally determined and caused. To apply evolutionary theory to it was like applying the laws of interplanetary attraction to the ups and downs of the stock exchange. Evolutionary theory, then, was inapplicable. Biology was immaterial. And history was simply a place of ignorance in the past where mistakes were made. Men and women were prisoners of none of them. Instead, they came into the world brand new and potentially free, and were made healthy or unhealthy by the cultural dispensations to which they were then exposed.

It was this idea of health that ultimately brought the three disciplines together into one science. Health—change, cure and the prevention of damage to both individuals and the society— became fundamental to the role each of them played in the 1930s, 1940s and 1950s. Cultural anthropology scoured the world for patterns of child care, parenting and, above all, sexual behavior to bring back, as advice, to an America declared in the 1940s one of the three societies on earth in which sex was taboo. Sociology poked about in families and stalked the corridors of schools, analyzing and judging and suggesting more hygienic methods of raising and educating children. And psychology—as psychiatry and psychotherapy—got used to thinking of itself as the picker-up of the pieces of the society's errors, the treater of its male and female walking wounded and the potential corrector, too, of its collective ailments. All three disciplines, then, gathered about themselves an aura of immense importance as their pronouncements were taken more and more seriously. They became the professions of the "experts," the diagnosticians and repair mechanics of the individual psyche and the doctors of the body politic. And between them they created the central ideology of our time.

2
TRUTH OR CONSEQUENCES

THE IDEOLOGY, WHICH has now permeated every corner of our society, maintains that for every psychological disorder or failing there is a social explanation, and vice versa. It maintains that men and women come into the world like blank sheets of paper—virgin psychologies—to be written on and bent into the shape of personality by the cultural institutions and social arrangements that they find there. It is an ideology because it has implicitly redefined for our modern era what freedom and equality mean. Freedom is now increasingly seen in the west as freedom from all psychological damage caused by unhealthy social influences or unnatural social limitations and restraints. And equality has now been effectively recast as sameness, or an equal opportunity for psychological health for all.

The ideology is the rationale behind the psychological rehabilitation of prisoners, the massive bureaucracies of welfare and social work and the hundreds of different forms of psychotherapy now available in the west. And it also dictates, backed with the full force of scientific orthodoxy, how men and women think about themselves and about each other. Through the me-

33

dium of the so-called sexual revolution and the rise of feminism, it has progressively touched and colored all our relationships and responsibilities—as workers, as lovers, as spouses and as parents.

The sexual revolution and the rise of feminism were at bottom simply the extension into sex and gender of the ideology promoted by the social sciences as health-giving or "helping" professions. For the period of the 1960s and 1970s, when it began to take hold as an instrument of social policy, coincided with the period when women of all classes and ages began to emerge into the marketplace in large numbers, and new forms of fail-safe female contraception became widely available to them. They were now seeking many of the same jobs as men. They were now free to indulge what many of them saw as a long-suppressed, male-like sexuality. Suddenly biology, which had been the traditional basis of their differential treatment in society, was irrelevant, it was plain, to who they were and who they aspired to be. And they demanded the sort of equality and freedom held out by the ideology. For if biology was irrelevant and women were exactly the same creatures of culture that men were, then any differences between them—in attitude and expectation, skill and ability—had to be culturally imposed. They had to be the result of psychological damage, an unnatural limitation and restraint imposed by society.

Like all other differences between humans, then—differences of class, intelligence and personality, for example—*gender* differences were finally, publicly exposed for what they were: environmental ones, the effects of a differential upbringing and a biased educational system. They were plainly unjust and inequitable. In a true democracy of men and women they could and would be eliminated. In such a democracy Jenny would be free to play with trucks and Johnny with dolls, both blissfully unaware of the long imprisoning history of what is "right" for boys and girls. In such a democracy men and women, freed from definition, freed from nature and the orthodoxies of sexual preference, would be able to have sex when and where and with whom they wished. Sex would become a full and fair exchange between healthy individuals, an expression of their health. And equality would at last reach from bank to boardroom to bedroom.

This seductive equation of sexual freedom and equality with social justice and health made the passage of the sciences of men and women from orthodoxy to ideology to full-blown climate of opinion a quick one. For in this form it finally covered all the comings and goings of human life, every private and public arena. It reached across *all* political and social divisions of race and class to the most fundamental division of all—gender. It reached through all the teeming variety of human action to the most basic action of all—sex. Some of the other protean forms of the ideology may still be matters for argument, perhaps. Is it the most important job of the school to protect and provide psychological health? Is the criminal *merely* the deranged product of his environment? But of this, at least, we are in the west more and more convinced: Men and women are equal and the same, rather than equal but different. Yes, they have inherited different sexual and reproductive equipment. And yes, women risk and must face the inconvenience of pregnancy and gestation. But these things too are irrelevant—they can be changed and protected against, they can be shut off or shut down.

As long as brain science remained quietly in the wings, as long as physical anthropology went on hoeing its narrow row and evolutionists maintained their distance from man, this view of men and women, as culture-creatures and mind-creatures, untrammelled by biology, was fine. Indeed, the news from almost every scientific front has managed to keep the orthodoxy in place, protected by the stockade of public acceptance. Outside the stockade ethologists may continue their time-consuming work on gulls and geese and chimpanzees and monkeys. But these are instinct-driven, cultureless creatures that offer at best mere parodies of the complexities of man. Outside the stockade endocrinologists may usefully tinker with the hormone systems that in dogs and rats control such things as blood pressure, glucose metabolism and the sexual cycle of the female. But these, to say the least, are hardly germane to the grander issues of the human mind and the influences of culture; they are to do with the entirely separate domain of the body. No, inside the stockade, the proper study of mankind is man—and mind. And the news that rings around it is almost always good. Men and women can change the sex of their bodies, to bring them into line with the gender orientation they feel as adults. The only help they need is psychotherapy and a few hormones. Children born with ambiguous genitals can be assigned to whatever gender the surgeon thinks appropriate. All they require, as they grow up, are the same few hormones for the body and the correct gender-upbringing and education for the mind. Human beings, as culture-mind creatures, can learn anything with the right help. They can learn to eliminate their own disorders, deviations and abnormalities. They can learn to take on and make their own fate. All they need to do is to submit themselves to the orthodoxy—its assumptions, its procedures, its professionals.

For the past twenty years, in other words, the orthodoxy has remained secure, immune from attack. For it can plainly deliver the goods. It can free women from the inconvenient inheritance of their portable plumbing. It can free transsexuals and anomalous children from thralldom to their genitalia. Its therapies and analytic methods can cure madness, neurosis and unhappiness. And its polls, surveys and studies of behavior can show the society where it needs the nips and tucks of alteration. Dug in, fortified, and protected on every side, then, the orthodoxy has in the past two decades ruled the way the science of men and women has gone about its business: where it has looked, how it has looked and what it has looked for. It has directed the sorts of conclusions it has come to and the way it has applied them. The organic remains out of court, outside the stockade. Fundamental differences between male and female lie beyond its pale too. So the mainstream, both of science and society at large, preoccupies itself with the transient statistics of marriage and divorce and with the effects of culture on anxiety and aggression, child-rearing and education and cocktail-party and jelly-bean-selection behavior.

For the past twenty years, then—as at the Brussels grand ball before the Battle of Waterloo in Byron's *Childe Harold*—all things have gone merry as a marriage bell. But now, quite suddenly, in the 1980s, just when the orthodoxy and its ideology have reached the full heights of general influence and prestige, the strands of brain science have finally come together into a new vision of what it means to be human. Scientists who have long toiled in the slow and wearisome vineyards of its various disciplines have suddenly found that they have a good deal to say to each other and to the public, if it will hear them. They have new techniques and technologies to share and a new story of men and women to tell. Slowly at first, but now with gathering speed, brain science is marching into the modern era, side by side with a new science of evolution. And all the little backwaters of both these disciplines have begun to come together into a broad stream that is flooding the orthodoxy's defenses and damaging beyond repair three of the "scientific" ideas that currently dominate the way we think about ourselves as men and women: the idea of psychological states as products of mind, the idea of the separation of mind and body and the idea that gender is not inborn but is learned and can be changed.

In the nineteenth century, on the basis of a general ignorance and a stopgap hypothesis about the human brain, science dictated the "correct" way to think about ourselves as men and women. In the twentieth century it has done the same. Given shape and direction by Freud and by the social and sexual reformers they attracted—sociologists like Charles Horton Cooley, anthropologists like Edward Sapir and feminist psychoanalysts like Karen Horney—the twin projects of psychology and sociology have come to dominate all our thinking about what it means to be human. They have elevated to our attention mind and culture. And they have ignored and left out of consideration everything that is inconvenient to these two categories

—genes, biology and, above all, the sex and finite chemistry of the human brain.

The result is that, under the aegis of what we take to be good science, we have learned to flinch from and reject any suggestion of inborn differences, including gender differences, between us. We have difficulty making sense of the headlines a new science is now yielding up almost daily. Instead, we voraciously consume every ephemeral report from the statistical and psychological front, as if that were the only science of men and women there was—"seventy-two percent of males . . . sixty-three percent of females . . . are stressed" . . . "want romance" . . . "are unfaithful" . . . "dislike the idea of a woman President" . . . "and do or don't do the laundry." We increasingly see ourselves as passive and potentially fragile psyches on the hoof —male and female halls of mirrors in which psychological and social explanations peep out from behind one another. Scratch a depression or an aggression—we believe—find an upbringing. Dissect an inability or a lack of ambition, find a faulty education. Identify a failing or an unhappiness or a sexual problem—find a culprit.

This way of thinking is so ingrained in us that it requires a considerable wrench for us to understand the full implications of what brain science is telling us. It is telling us that all these things—inability, education, failing, unhappiness and sexual problems—are etched into the structure and chemistry of the male and female brain. Everything that happens to us in the world is an event in our brain and is encoded in our brain in some way. It alters the electrical conductivity of nerve cells in different parts of the system. It alters the availability of or sensitivity to messenger chemicals in different pathways. Or it changes the way the nerve cells arc and branch and make contact with one another, each through thousands of synaptic connections. The brain may be enormously complex, and it may be very difficult to find points of entry into it, but it is physical, limited and bounded. And everything that happens in it and to it is reducible, in theory and in practice, to a seizable physical mechanism. Your memory is mediated by and contained within a physical mechanism, a reordering of molecules, a chemistry. So is your experience of pleasure. So is your sensation of pain. *Every* interface that you make with the world—every conversation you have, every action you take—is initiated, furthered, recorded, monitored and stored by electrical and chemical changes in the nerve cells and at the sites of contact between them.

The brain, again, is who you are. There is no mind where Descartes located it, in what Colin Blakemore of Oxford University has called "the enigmatic pimple" of the pineal gland. There is no controlling ghost or master puppeteer poised above the skull or else scattered, loose as metaphor, throughout the whole human organism. Instead there is only body and brain, male and female, an interdependent whole. In your brain—as it develops in contact with the world and its own body—lies every feeling and every failing. And in its chemistry—in the interaction in it between neurotransmitters, hormones and the chemical factories and transportation systems of its hundred billion cells—lies your ability, however gained, to play snooker, baseball, the great lover, Chopin or Shakespeare.

Nurture, then—culture—is in the brain. But so, of course, is nature: the unfolding genetic program by which our brains are made, the roots of all maleness and femaleness. If this thought makes you uncomfortable, if you are leery of the part that nature plays in us—if you believe that any fundamental brain differences between men and women should be ignored even if they exist and that the prevailing scientific orthodoxy is more enlightened, beneficial and humane than any other that might take its place—then you should consider this: the orthodoxy-cum-ideology that prevailed at the turn of the century pronounced that men were by nature brain-creatures and that women—with their smaller and less reliable amount of brain tissue—were by nature essentially womb-creatures. This was wrong, the product of bias and ignorance: in the compulsive study of brain size, no allowance was made for comparative body-mass and body-weight. But it did have—quite apart from its political and social effects—*medical* consequences.

In women, everything from depression to irritability to tuberculosis to "eating like a ploughman" was treated as if it was a dysfunction of the reproductive organs. Treatments were various at various times. Leeches were applied to the vulva and the neck of the uterus; the womb was washed out with infusions of milk and linseed tea or else cauterized—burnt into subjection—by chemicals. Clitoridectomy was for a time fashionable. And the removal of the uterus remained for a long time a last resort in particularly intractable cases. In 1906, a gynecologist estimated that one hundred fifty thousand women in the United States alone had lost their ovaries to surgery. Many, one assumes, were the victims of "hysteria"—womb-disease—which was of course *the* female disease of the times.

We are wiser now, it is true. But the orthodoxy-cum-ideology of *our* times has also had medical consequences, consequences we are only now just beginning to perceive. Thousands of would-be transsexuals, attracted by the liberation from gender that the orthodoxy promoted, have been physically marooned in a gender they aspired to be but were not; and the university clinics that provided their operations, under the orthodoxy's auspices, have been for the most part quietly closed down. An unknown number of children who were blithely altered at birth were corrected, it seems, in the wrong direction and are now, as adults, conflicted, uncomfortable and having difficulty in the gender they were assigned to. An unknown number of women, convinced by scientific pronunciamentos—by Kinsey's exploration with swab-like devices and by Masters's and Johnson's confirmation by machinery—that the vagina was insensitive and its capacity for orgasm nonexistent, had their vaginas altered for a better fit. It now seems likely that the tissue that was routinely removed was precisely the seat of the vagina's sensitivity and its capacity for orgasm.

For Masters and Johnson the body was a machine, a physical machine controlled by an inorganic mind fed on good and bad experiences. And the idea of the body as merely a sexual and reproductive machine, unconnected with mind, has flourished and continues to flourish elsewhere. In the 1950s and 1960s and up to the 1970s, for example, hormones were given as a matter of course in cases not only of difficult, but even of routine pregnancy. And they produced, it seems, a crop of children in whom the expression of gender, in both brain and body, has been affected. Meanwhile, the hormones given in the different forms of the birth control pill have been found to have side effects that affect not only the health of the body—phlebitis and heart disease—but the moods and sex drive of the brain—irritability, depression and loss of libido. There have been no long-term follow-up studies on the effect of the years of technical pseudo-pregnancy that the pill induces. And all too often its effects have been treated as if they were the result of a psychological rather than an organic disorder—a disorder brought on by the pill's hormones themselves. The same assumption—that psychological disorders are always psychologically caused—has condemned parents to take full responsibility for the inborn disorders of their children—autism and even schizophrenia were until recently laid at the door of cold, intellectual parenting. And it continues to condemn hundreds of thousands of people to the expensive rituals of the psychiatric confessional—obeisance to the various denominations of the church of Freud —when they are suffering from a seizable, treatable *organic* disease of the brain-body system.

All of these things are the legacy of an assumption that nurture, learning, upbringing and experience are all-important. Ignored is all the news that a new science of men and women is starting to bring us, everything that is the subject of the rest of this book. We are at the beginning, as we have said, of a new age, an age in which old assumptions must be overthrown. And to understand it, we must *begin* there, where Harvard professor Norman Geschwind always begins with his first-year medical students, "however much they think they know." At the beginning.

PART TWO
THE BRAIN

3
THE THINKING GLAND

CONSIDER YOUR BRAIN as you read this. Your eyes are now traveling along this line, to turn back again to the beginning of the next line. You are turning into words the symbols on this printed page. You are building them into sentences, coherent thoughts. You are aware of the people writing them in the past, their voice and their purpose. And you are conscious, aware of yourself. One hand holds these pages, between thumb and forefinger, perhaps, while the other rests and waits, ready to turn the page when it is needed. You note the end of the paragraph, as the time comes. And your eyes flick down and leftward to the beginning of the next.

You are now conscious of how your eyes are moving, and feel them in their sockets. You become aware of this act of concentration and then of your environment: the room you are in, the angle of the light, the presence of another person, the particular sound of a radio or a television playing. Your hand reaches out for a cup of coffee or tea, and you recognize it for what it is by the smell, the taste of the liquid and the memory of what you recently made for yourself. Your concentration now drifts outside the room you are in. You shift your position. And you wonder how long you will be addressed in this way: a real person in a real environment rather than an imaginary one.

In the last thirty or so seconds, if you have read these words straight through, and have responded to them, however marginally, you have been both audience and spectator of yourself. In your mind's eye, however fleetingly, you have moved through space and backwards and forwards in time. You have shifted between different modes of consciousness. You have made use of man's most important skill and all five (perhaps) of his senses. And in a sense, such is the power of words to evoke and direct, you have recapitulated his history. Language and the senses, followed in history by the extension of those senses—writing, paper, print, radio and television, all the paraphernalia you have available to you in this room—these are the things that define modern man.

All this, though, has not been done by you, as you ordinarily think of yourself. It has been done by your brain. For your brain is not an isolated organ; it is an integral part of what appear to be the outlands of your body. The retina, for example, that you have been using to read this, is one of your brain's ways of gathering information about its environment. The sensory nerves in your fingers, as you continue to hold these pages open, are your brain's ways of learning what the fingers are touching. And the nerves in your muscles, as you shift your arm and flex your leg, are no more than your brain's agents for making you move about. At one end of the scale of your life, as you sit or lie or loll here, is the world of the senses—information delivered to your brain by light (sight), chemicals (taste and smell) and mechanical forces and pressures (hearing and touch). At the other end of the scale of your life are your brain's responses to that world and its attempts to influence it: skimming a paragraph or reaching for a cup. And between the two stand thought, memory, pleasure, boredom, foresight, personality and gender identity: everything that makes men and women human—your brain.

Your brain, to repeat, is who you are. "You" is always a short-hand for "your brain"; "I" for "my brain." When you feel pain, it is your brain that feels it; when you use a drug to control it, it is your brain that you are treating. When you take a drink or a smoke or a mood-changing chemical, it is your brain that is seeking to alter and manipulate its own chemistry. And when you are sexually aroused, it is your brain that organizes the behavior that will lead to its own pleasure and fulfillment. Even when you die, it is your brain that does the dying, for lack of oxygen and nutrients. That is how your death, the end of your personality, is defined.

Your brain, then, is not a mechanical organ like your heart, your spleen, your liver and your kidneys. It is the seat of your personality, your aspirations and your drives. And in it lies the answer to the question: "How is my personality deployed, stored, regulated and expressed?" For in exactly the same way as, in creation, the human brain evolved for the survival of the species, so your own individual brain is progressively, plastically shaped by experience for the survival of yourself. A man or a woman with no memory of his or her past experiences, after all, and therefore no capacity for learning, will meet every circumstance, every letter of the alphabet, every street, every car, every source of heat or cold or pain, as if for the first time—and will have extreme difficulty surviving. A man or a woman with precisely your experience of these things, on the other hand—*your* memory and *your* capacity for learning—*is* you, a creature with a brain adapted for survival within the environment of your own particular life.

Your brain also, however, contains the answer to a much larger question: "What is there in the inheritance of my brain that sets me apart from the rest of creation?" Man, after all, is the creature of his genes. And your brain, as well as being the expression and record of your interaction with the world, is also the product of an individual genetic inheritance that stretches back in time across the tens of thousands of reproductively successful generations that have contributed to the stuff of your life, to the basic blueprint of your body and brain. As well as being an individual man or woman, you are also, in a sense, all men, all women. The number of brain cells that have been available to you in your life, for instance, was laid down three months before you were born, however much they later branched and grew in contact with the world. And the capacity for language was lateralized to one hemisphere of your brain before you ever saw the place in which you would speak it. Against the plasticity of your brain, in other words, is set its specificity—the processes, abilities and skills that are locked and prewired into its circuitry. Against our individuality is set our shared humanity, our shared maleness or femaleness. Against nurture is set nature. And it is this double aspect, finally, of the human brain—neither aspect easily separable from the other—that gives it its unique position in creation. For it brings together in the meeting ground of your brain both cultural and genetic evolution and the science that explores them. It brings together in one finite system—your brain—the answers to the two questions we have posed. And it brings within the reach of understanding—as we learn to read its meaning—not only the way in which an individual male or female brain learns and grows and fails and falls into madness, but also the way in which the collective brain of men and women is the expression, in flesh, of the long reproductive partnership that has brought us to the dominance of this planet.

For the past three or four years we have spent much of our time and energy following the road taken by scientists into what Nobel Prize-winner Charles Sherrington called "the enchanted loom" of the brain. We have visited laboratories on both sides of the Atlantic. We have attended otherwise closed meetings of scientists. We have watched experiments, have prowled through conferences and have sometimes almost drowned in the great outpouring of what scientists call "the literature." And so we have had a chance to see, at close quarters, some of the astonishing ingenuity of the circuitous pathways these men and women have followed into the complexities of man's essential organ. "By indirections find directions out," said Hamlet. And Hamlet's rule is the rule of brain science. Away out into the Pacific it goes, to study a slow-acting virus passed from brain to brain through cannibalism. In this indirection lay a Nobel Prize for Carleton Gajdusek and a new approach to some of man's most intractable brain disorders. Down into the nerve cells of a tide-dwelling mollusk it goes. In this indirection lie important clues to human learning and to the biological clock that governs many of our hormones. Into mathematics and the arcane world of algorithms it goes. And in this seeming indirection is a new understanding of how the brain must go about doing what it does and a prediction of necessary new groups of cells waiting to be discovered.

This is the first lesson in brain science that we learned in our wanderings: That it works, perforce, by indirection. Scientists cannot simply cut into the living human organism to see what is going on in it. And the direct paths into the human brain are strictly limited. Scientists can look directly, of course, at the physical effects of brain tumors, strokes and bullet wounds, and by studying how they impair a patient's abilities they can make maps of the sites in the brain that control these abilities. By applying electrodes to a patient's exposed brain during surgery, they can make similar—and sometimes more detailed—maps. (The brain has no pain sensors for its own tissue, and patients are often awake and responsive during brain surgery.) Then, too, in post mortems, they can distinguish the separate structures of the brain and analyze their size, their connections and their chemistry. But, apart from these few direct avenues, scientists are restricted—or were, until very recently—to indirect observations of the human brain from outside the skull and to work on the brains of animals.

One form of indirect observation is through the way the human brain responds to the world: its behavior. Another is through the skills and abilities it shows when confronted with controlled tasks in a controlled environment. These are the avenues taken by behavioral and cognitive research psychologists into the brain's mysteries. And to them can be added the indirections of electrophysiology—inasmuch as it concerns itself with the external recording of human brain waves and rhythms —and hemisphere studies—which investigate the responsibilities of the left and right brain in humans, by using as clues automatic eye movements, left- and right-handedness, the response to different visual cues and the differential sensitivity of the two ears. These techniques have recently been expanded by drugs and technologies that can shut down the operation of one hemisphere completely and can record the brain's energy use and blood flow while reading, talking, doing sums and so on.

As for the other main indirection—animal studies—this includes any number of different, as scientists call them, "models," depending on the problem being worked on: goats for sleep, cats for dreams and vision, primates for orgasm and the effects of sex hormones on brain development, for example; electric fish for the uniformity of their nerve cells; sea hares for the size and simplicity of theirs; and rats—always rats—for the convenient smallness of their brain and the comparatively large range of their behavioral repertoire. All of these models rest on the assumption that nature is economical; that nervous systems work on the same principles, however large or small they are; and that the brains of other mammals are enough like man's for conclusions about man to be drawable from them. And this has allowed scientists to perform in the brains of animals what they cannot perform in the human brain: to record the firing of a single cell in a kitten's cortex—most of our knowledge of how vision works comes from this approach—and to inject sex hormones into rats and monkeys to find out where in the brain they work to effect behavior. It has also allowed them to apply to animals the drugs that have been found, mostly by accident, to relieve human stress, depression, schizophrenia, pain and loss of libido. They can begin to uncover in their brains the way these drugs work: the chemicals and brain pathways involved by implication in man's addiction, anxiety, madness and sexual appetite.

Animal studies, though, are not very helpful when it comes to brain functions and abilities expressed only in man. And this is the second lesson in brain science that we learned as we worked: that brain science trades not only in indirections but also in abnormalities—because it is only through abnormalities, finally, that the normal workings of the human brain's higher functions can be arrived at. Someone who can talk and write and remember in a normal way can tell scientists very little about how these things work in the brain. But the man who, because of a brain lesion, can write but cannot read what he has written (*alexia* without *agraphia*) can tell them a great deal. The famous H.M. studied by Brenda Milner in Montreal—a man who, as a result of a brain operation to control his epilepsy, can no longer transfer his experience to any sort of long-term memory bank, and has to be reintroduced to his doctor whenever they see each other, even if the gap is no more than half an hour, is a very important research tool, too, for work on the processing and localization of memory. The same holds true for abnormal animals—mostly rats and mice—which have been specially bred to show congenital obesity, movement- and learning- and immune- and gender-disorders and the absence of particular hormones. And it holds true, too, for an astonishing variety of human behaviors and conditions. How do these behaviors and conditions differ from what is normal? Where, in the arcing and branching of the cells in the brain and the nervous system, in the pulse of electricity and the squirt of chemicals, can this difference be found? These are the questions.

Grist to brain science's mill, then, is every sort of deviation from the norm. There is the woman who, when tested at a New York clinic, had the highest pain tolerance and threshold ever recorded there—she had just returned from ten years as a nurse among the Eskimos—and within six months her tolerance and threshold were down to those of an average American woman. There is the young Canadian woman who had no sensitivity to pain at all, and who, because pain is man's friend, his early-warning system, chewed her tongue to a pulp as an infant, severely burned herself while calmly kneeling on a radiator at age two, and finally died, at twenty-eight, of unrecognized multiple infections. And there are the Greek villagers who, once a year, walk without pain on red-hot coals, to the honor of a local saint and to the considerable yearly curiosity of the German-based Max Planck Institute.

To their number can be added the blind man locked in a "day" of more than twenty-five hours, the spelunkers with a slowing cycle in the absence of daylight and the chronic insomniacs. The question is: What controls the biological clock and how is it connected to cyclical disorders like mania and depression? The children born to schizophrenic parents but adopted into separate, either schizophrenic or nonschizophrenic families: Is schizophrenia genetic or acquired from the environment? The man who successfully treated a supposedly incurable disease by subjecting himself to comic films and continuous laughter: What is the connection between the brain, health and the immune system? To their number can be added, too, the bizarre effects of head injuries, brain tumors and strokes in humans, of which we spoke before. For they can affect groups of cells only centimeters, or even millimeters, apart in the brain's general geography, and yet have dramatically different effects on the people who suffer them.

Thus there are people who cannot talk and people who can talk but make no sense when they talk; people who are paralyzed on one side and people who, though they can move their hand, for example, imagine that it belongs to someone else; people who cannot recognize faces, people who can't sleep, people who can't stay awake. There are histrionic boomers, compulsive diarists, sexual gannets, self-mutilators and otherwise upright citizens who become intermittently foul-mouthed, all of them suffering from recognizable damage to one or another structure in their brains.

In the days before modern brain studies, of course, these sometimes extreme changes of personality were seen as "psychological" in origin, or even as visitations from the devil. As recently as 1947, for example, there was the case of a young Maryland girl who spoke in strange voices, used obscene language, horribly twisted her features and had to be restrained from extreme violence towards herself and others. She was almost certainly suffering from a brain disease called Gilles de la Tourette's syndrome. And yet Peter Blatty based his best-selling book *The Exorcist* on her.

Tourette's syndrome, as it happens, affects males—usually children between the ages of two and fourteen—far more often than females. It tends to run in families; it has a genetic basis of some sort. And it has elements in common with three other disorders that also tend to run in families and also preferentially strike males: hyperactivity, autism and one type of learning disorder. This is the third lesson in brain science that we learned as we went from clinic to clinic and laboratory to laboratory: That in its ceaseless sifting of the natural world for the clues and models to be found there; in its relentless examination of all the oddities of human behavior, one major point of entry is the difference between male and female. At every level of its investigation, in other words, brain science uses males and females as "controls" for each other's behavior, skills, abilities, disorders, gene-expression and chemistry.

Are there differences between the male and female immune system, it asks, and what are they? This way lies an answer to the factors that influence the immune system's general effectiveness. Are there differences between the nonsexual behaviors of male and female animals, it asks, and can these differences be altered by sex hormones? This way lies an answer to the effect of sex hormones on the development of the brain and on behavior. Are there characteristic genetic abnormalities in males and females, it asks, and how are these expressed in the organization and chemistry of the brain? This way lies an answer to the gene-chemical pathways that govern the expression of normal maleness and femaleness.

"Look," says the remarkable young biopsychologist Jerre Levy, during one of our many visits to her laboratory at the

University of Chicago, "what we ultimately want to know, of course, is everything we can about the connection between genes, brain development, chemistry, hormones, the environment and behavior. Well, that's a pretty tall order, given that we have a brain of a hundred billion nerve cells, hundreds of thousands of genes, a varying environment and all kinds of behavior and all kinds of psychology to cope with. So we need a way of focusing. One important way of focusing is to compare and contrast different classes of individuals—left-handers and right-handers, for example. Schizophrenics and nonschizophrenics. Dyslexics—people who have a problem reading—and nondyslexics and so on. But the most important of these classes of individuals are males and females. They're important because sex is a *major* dimension of human difference, just as it's a *major* dimension of difference all the way across the animal kingdom. And we know that both genes and the sex hormones are involved in this difference, this basic difference in sexual functioning. If we find *other* differences between males and females, then —differences in behavior—we have a working hypothesis that we can test in both humans and animals, that these differences are an expression of genes and hormones in the development and function of the brain.

"Now we know quite a lot about how the genes—the sex chromosomes—influence the development of the male and female body and brain. We know quite a lot about how the sex hormones are deployed and how they work within cells. And we're beginning to know something about how the hormones interact with the brain's messenger chemicals—the neurotransmitters. At the same time, we know a good deal about the different behaviors, skills and abilities that males and females—human as well as animal—characteristically show. And we're beginning to know how and why these skills, abilities and so on are altered in certain abnormalities and disorders. We have information on several levels, in other words. And what we're now trying to do is to argue *between* the levels, to find as many connections as possible between them. This isn't easy. It's like trying to do a three-dimensional jigsaw puzzle of an unknown size, when all you've got to go on are different bits and pieces of the puzzle—from different levels and from different parts of the picture—arriving almost daily. It's going to take a long time to complete the whole puzzle, decades perhaps—even the little areas I'm working on are going to take five years at least. But already parts of it are beginning to come together. They're actually beginning to make some sense."

One of Jerre Levy's levels is obviously the gross anatomy of the male and female brain. But at this level the dead human brain—pickled or frozen, left whole or prized apart—can tell us very little about the differences between men and women or what they may mean. The brain of contemporary men weighs on average about 1,375 grams, almost three pounds. And it is both slightly heavier and slightly larger than the average contemporary female brain—a difference that can be largely accounted for by overall differences in body mass and body weight. The convolutions on the pinkish-gray surface of the brain—its cerebral cortex, or rind—may also be simpler and more regular in the brains of females than they are in males. But there the immediately observable differences end. The brains of men and women contain exactly the same structures, so far as is known, and present exactly the same general appearance.

If you approach the lifeless brain of a man or woman head on, so to speak, the first thing you notice is that the whorling of the cortex is interrupted at the midline. The brain, like a walnut meat, is divided front to back into two roughly symmetrical halves, the two cerebral hemispheres, each of which is responsible, by and large, for the sensory input and motor drive of the opposite side of the body. Information arriving from the periphery and the processes by which the various limbs and so on are moved are handled by the so-called parietal lobes of the two hemispheres, which stretch across the top surface of the brain. And the other lobes, or rounded divisions, have other responsibilities. The occipital lobes, at the back of the brain, control visual processing. The temporal lobes—above the ears when in the skull—are involved in memory, speech and hearing. And the frontal lobes have been implicated in learning, social behavior, intelligence and the stabilization of emotion.

Behind and below the cerebral hemispheres, as you turn the brain in your hands, lies the cerebellum, or small brain. The cerebellum is about the size of an apple. And it has its own cortex, its own convoluted and invaginated surface and its own bilateral symmetry of two halves. The cerebellum is one of the few structures of the brain to which a function can be clearly and certainly assigned. It is responsible for fine control of motor activity and muscular coordination. It ensures that the tiny actions of the body's muscles are tuned to the brain's intentions so that we do not, for example, when reaching for a fragile object or one that contains liquid, overshoot it, shake it, break it or spill it, as old people or those with cerebellar failure often do.

If you want to look any deeper into the brain of a man or a woman, you now have to pluck away the apple of the cerebellum to reveal the brain stem. The brain stem is the continuation of the spinal cord as it reaches the skull cavity that contains the brain. It is a thick white stalk, with nerve fibers carrying both incoming and outgoing information. And as it travels upward, beneath the vault of the cerebral hemispheres, it thickens and broadens. It receives input from facial nerves and nerve pathways governing vision, taste and smell. And then it ends in a surrounding cap of structures called the limbic system. The limbic system is responsible for many automatic bodily functions and for emotion and motivation. And its most important component is the hypothalamus which regulates what scientists fondly call "the four Fs"—feeding, fleeing, fighting and sexual activity.

Most of this rather sketchy information about the architecture of the human brain and the different responsibilities of its parts comes from two main sources: from work done on animals, by stimulating their brains with electricity or else cutting into them to see what effects will be produced, and from the evidence of brain damage in humans. Wars were the most important contributors to this second source. And indeed the heyday of the brain anatomists coincided, roughly speaking, with the period from the Franco-Prussian War to the aftermath of World War I. Two of the greatest brain researchers of their day, it is said, actually toured the battlefield of Sedan, augmenting their work on animals by attaching electrodes to the exposed brains of wounded and dead soldiers. There was no other way, until the invention of modern techniques and technologies, to study the human brain.

Or, rather, there was only one. And that brings us to another of Jerre Levy's levels: the view, not from the inside of (mostly male) brains, but the view from the outside; the record of how the normal male and female brain behaves and responds and solves problems in the world. This is the bailiwick of behavioral and cognitive psychology. And if we are to begin to see the threads of the connections between the dimensions of this new science, then it is their level of brain study that we should now introduce. First, they provide the simplest approach to the brain and to the complexities of the differences between male and female. And second, they provide the basis on which all the other approaches to the puzzle have been progressively built. In the beginning, there was observation . . .

Observations of the differences between men and women—in their behavior, skills and approaches to life—are nothing new, of course. In 1894, Francis Galton noted that women had lower touch and pain thresholds than men did. In the same year, Havelock Ellis documented what he thought to be sex differences in linguistic abilities. And at about the same time Joseph Jastrow, an experimental psychologist at the University of Wisconsin, found differences between men and women buried in lists of one hundred words that he asked his students to write out as rapidly as possible. On the basis of the words that were chosen at random Jastrow concluded that women were concerned with "attention to the immediate surroundings, to the finished product, to the ornamental, the individual and the concrete," while men were drawn to "the more remote, the constructive, the useful, the general and the abstract."

At the time there was no scientific framework into which such scattered and crude observations could be fitted, except one designed to demonstrate the natural inferiority of women. And in the years that followed it was no longer fashionable to undertake such studies except as demonstrations that sex differences were imposed by culture—parental treatment, upbringing and education, as we have seen. Not until some twenty years ago, in fact, with the emergence of a newly equipped brain science, did more than a handful of experimental psychologists begin to search out sex differences that might betray something deeper. By that time, numbers of researchers—among them a Vera Danchikova and a group led by the American William Young—had shown that the adult sexual behavior of certain animals could be switched from its normal gender-expression if they were given sex hormones before or just after birth. And through the 1960s it became clearer and clearer that the brain was the target organ involved; the brain was a gland, a thinking gland, but also a sex gland. It governed male and female sexual behavior.

"Finally, in the late 1960s," says Diane McGuinness one day in Palo Alto, California, "it became *absolutely* clear just what part of the brain was involved: the hypothalamus. The hypothalamus is the ultimate controller of the body's flow of hormones. And it's responsible for the way sex and reproductive behavior are organized—the estrus or menstrual cycle in females, for example, and the quite different pattern we see in males. The hypothalamus is almost certainly differently stamped by sex hormones before birth. It's like a photographic plate that is exposed before birth and then developed by a fresh rush of hormones at puberty. Well, this discovery couldn't be checked visually, of course—it wouldn't show up to the gross anatomist. But it raised all sorts of new possibilities. For if the hypothalamus controls sexual behavior, what other sorts of gender-related behavior does it control? And if one part of the brain is differently sexed, what about others? Are other parts of the brain differently sexed in males and females? And, if so, how might this show up in the different skills and abilities characteristic of men and women?"

Diane McGuinness is a research psychologist. A stylish and voluble woman who holds positions at both Stanford University and the University of California at Santa Cruz, she is one of the few scientists to work exclusively in the field of male versus female behavior, doggedly persevering in the face of criticism from mainstream scientists anxious about the implications of her work. Over the past decade, she and her Stanford colleagues, Eleanor Maccoby and Carol Nagy Jacklin, have separately observed and tested thousands of infants, preschoolers, high school and university students. And out of their studies—and the studies of others—has emerged a picture of quite wide statistical differences between human males and females in the brain.

"Some of these differences," she says, "appear extremely early in life. And others are more obvious after puberty. But the fascinating thing is that they seem to be *independent* of culture—as true in Ghana, Scotland and New Zealand as they are in America. First, women are more sensitive to touch. And they have better fine-motor coordination and finger dexterity—there may be cerebellar differences. Second, there are differences in the way information is gathered and problems are solved. Men are more rule-bound, and they seem to be less sensitive to situational variables: more single-minded, more narrowly focused and more persevering. Women, by contrast, are *very* sensitive to context. They're less hidebound by the demands of a particular task. They're good at picking up peripheral information. And they process the information faster.

"Put in general terms, women are communicators and men are takers of action. Because that's the implication of the most *important* difference between them, the one that's most widely accepted. Males are good at tasks that require visual-spatial skills, and females are good at tasks that require language ability. Males are better at maps, mazes and math; at rotating objects in their minds and locating three-dimensional objects in two-dimensional representations. They're better at perceiving and manipulating objects in space. And they're better at orienting themselves in space. They have a good sense of direction.

"Females, on the other hand, excel in areas that males are weak in, especially in areas where language is involved. They're not as good, in general, at anything that requires object manipulation and visual sharpness—they're less sensitive to light, for one thing. But they're much better at almost all the skills that involve words: fluency, for example, verbal reasoning, written prose and reading—males outnumber females three to one in remedial reading classes. Their verbal memory is also better. And they can sing in tune, six times more often than males can."

The usual explanation for these differences is that, in all cultures, boys are encouraged to be physical and exploratory, while girls are encouraged to be passive, verbal and musical—they gradually take on the shape that the culture imposes on them. But the usual explanation is undercut by the fact that the differences appear very early in life, as soon as researchers like Diane McGuinness are able to test for them. Male infants respond to what is visually catching in their environment, which for them is lights, patterns and three-dimensional objects. And they take on their physical environment more than females do. They are more curious about it. They play with the objects in it as often as with toys. And they tend to *draw* objects rather than people.

This is not what is found in female infants. Girls respond preferentially to the *people* in their environment. What is catching for them are faces rather than objects. They are also much more sensitive to sound. They vocalize more and are more comforted by speech than boys are. And they respond more to the social sounds around them, to tones of voice and music. Diane McGuinness believes this is a crucial difference. For sensitivity to sound is something that persists throughout life in women; as against men, sounds are likely to seem twice as loud to them, something that men would do well to remember. And it is almost certainly an important contributor to the female's early developing verbal abilities. Sounds and people, remember, as against objects in space. Communication versus action and manipulation. There is evidence to support the idea that tendencies in these directions are present in the male and female brain from the beginning. The language abilities of girls, for example, are not preferentially encouraged in them by their parents, studies have shown. And they are not affected by a traumatic early environment, as they are in boys. They are also a good predictor of later intelligence, as they are *not* in boys.

Diane McGuinness spreads her hands. "You know, I've been repeatedly told that it's somehow *improper* to do the sort of work that I do. I have a constituency of sorts among biologists, but none at all, really, in my own field of psychology. And that's because the conclusion of all this seems to me inescapable, and it rides against the whole direction most of science has taken over the past twenty or thirty years. These things are not culturally induced. They're *biological.* Just as the *capacity* for language is prewired into our brains before birth—as Noam Chomsky, among others, has shown—so, in females, is a special skill in it. So is the male's special visual and spatial skill. And so, perhaps, are all the other abilities and behaviors I've talked about. What comes easy to either sex is likely to be biologically programmed, like the hypothalamus: stamped, primed, waiting to be developed."

4
A TALE OF TWO HEMISPHERES

WE ARE BACK in Chicago. And Jerre Levy is sitting in her cluttered university office, one leg curled underneath her. She swoops periodically into a cup of coffee. "So you have these different abilities in males and females that scientists like Diane McGuinness, myself and others have found—communicative and manipulative, verbal and visual-spatial. And you have the not uninteresting fact that males and females also characteristically suffer from different disabilities: females from depression and hysteria, but also maybe from math disability, which is likely to be visual-spatial. And males from hyperactivity, but also from autism, dyslexia and stuttering—disabilities that affect language. Now we can't say with any absolute certainty that these differences are inborn, any more than we can for gender identity and sexual orientation. But we can say that whatever their origin, they're certainly expressed in the male and female brain.

"Having said that, there are two things, though, that you've got to remember about the differences. First, they're *statistical* differences—averages. And they're rather minor compared to differences between people of the same sex: of all the variations we observe among people, eighty to ninety-five percent of them are *within* men and *within* women. They're by no means cut and dried in every male and female. And second, the average sex differences that we *do* observe should never be allowed to have any effect on social policy, such as encouraging Jenny to give up math and Johnny to give up languages. If biological differences, after all, were to be made the basis of social policy, then the first thing we should do is to lock up all the *men,* since they're the ones who commit almost all the crime—murders, thefts, drunken driving and so on. They're more aggressive. And *they're* the ones at risk of being psychopaths."

Jerre Levy is a dark-haired woman in her early forties, whose dazzling talk is replete with the corkscrew vowels and sudden emphases of her native Alabama. And her way into the brain is the next level forward in the science of men and women: no longer *general* observation of the brain from outside—its behavior—but *particular* observation of the brain's two hemispheres and the skills and abilities for which each is responsible. In the late 1960s, in California, Drs. Joseph Bogen and Philip Vogel surgically separated the hemispheres of a number of epileptic patients in order to confine their violent electrical seizures to one half of their brains. And in doing so they produced a unique experimental group studied by 1981 Nobel Prize-winner Roger Sperry at the California Institute of Technology in Pasadena. Jerre Levy, along with Michael Gazzaniga, Eran Zaidel and Colwen Trevarthen, other leaders in the field, was a student of Sperry's.

The patients were cured of the whole-brain rampaging of their disorder. And they could get on with their lives without any noticeable difficulty. But their left brain could no longer communicate with its partner on the right, and vice versa. And although this did not show up as a problem in their daily comings and goings, it very quickly showed up in the tests that Sperry and his colleagues applied to them. One test, for example, required them to fix their gaze on a dot in front of them. They were then

briefly shown pictures of objects, either to the left or the right
of the dot. When an object was projected to the right of the dot,
they could easily identify it. But when it was shown to the left
of the dot, they could not *say* what they had seen, even though
they could correctly select the object with their left hand, by
touch alone, from a group of objects in front of them. In one
famous instance, a female split-brain patient, known in the literature as N.G., was shown the picture of a nude woman to the left
of the central dot. When asked what she had seen, she said,
"Nothing, just a flash of light." But she giggled and blushed,
responding *emotionally* if not verbally. And finally she said, "Oh,
doctor, you have some machine."

It was through tests like this that Sperry's group gradually
worked out the way in which the male and female brain is lateralized: the analytic left hemisphere specializing in language, by
and large, and the holistic right hemisphere—unable to use
language in the tests—specializing in the processing of emotion,
the recognition of faces and music, perhaps, but above all in the
performance of visual tasks and the perception of spatial relations. In most people, in other words, there was a general hemispheric division of labor between language skills and visual-spatial skills. And since these were the areas in which males and
females seemed to be superior to each other, it immediately
suggested a new way forward: to look at the differences in brain
organization between normal men and women. In the past ten
years, Jerre Levy, with others, has adapted the original tests and
devised a cluster of new ones to investigate the laterality patterns in normal people. And in doing so she has helped open
up a new avenue of inquiry into sex differences: not only in how
abilities differ, but in how these abilities are organized in the
brain.

"All right. What we're talking about is the selective *activation*
of one hemisphere or the other," Jerre Levy says. "Which hemisphere responds to what sort of stimulus in males and females.
Now the *left* hemisphere, as you know, controls and receives

messages from the *right* side of the body—and vice versa. But it is also activated by objects in the right visual field and by sounds perceived by the right ear. There is a crossover. All right. Now this means that we can broadcast directly to one hemisphere or the other. We can use a technique developed by Doreen Kimura of the University of Western Ontario, for example. We can present the two ears simultaneously with different sounds—sometimes verbal and sometimes nonverbal—and see which of the two sounds is reported by the hearer. Which *hemisphere,* therefore, specializes in processing and interpreting that sort of sound. We can also—for just a few thousandths of a second—flash in front of a subject pictures, words, digits, letters and dots and lines oriented to a central point *either* in the left visual field *or* in the right visual field *or* in both. And again we can see which hemisphere is faster and better at recognizing and processing which *sort* of information—verbal, nonverbal, spatial and so on. This will depend on the handedness of the subject. Almost all right-handers organize language on the left side and certain types of visual-spatial skill on the right side of the brain—left-handers are much more confusing. And it *also* may depend on the sex of the subject."

She pauses for a moment, as she must with students, to see if they are following her. "Look," she says, "there are only little pieces of evidence. This is a *very* young field; our techniques are crude; we're trying to become more sophisticated as we go along. But what evidence there is, from different approaches and different laboratories all over the world, indicates that the female brain may be *less* lateralized and less tightly *organized* than the male brain. In male right-handers, for example, language seems to be rather *rigorously* segregated to the left hemisphere, while their visual-spatial skills are as rigorously segregated to the right. This does not seem to be true in right-handed *females. Their* hemispheres seem to be less functionally distinct from each other and more diffusely organized. And switching between them seems easier. These differences—and one has to ask what is reasonable to believe, given the evidence we have—seem to be inborn."

In the early 1960s, about two and a half thousand miles from Roger Sperry's laboratory in California, Herbert Lansdell, a psychologist at the National Institutes of Health in Bethesda, Maryland, began to study another group of epileptics who had had part of their right hemispheres removed in order to control their seizures. And he gave a number of these subjects a test which required them to express a preference for one of a number of abstract designs. He expected them all to do quite poorly. But what he found instead was that it was only the *men* who did poorly. Intrigued, he went on to study patients who had had part of their *left* hemisphere removed. And he found a similar discrepancy. Though men performed badly on a number of the *verbal* tasks he gave them, women did not. Lansdell suggested, for the first time, that the organization of the brain might be different in the two sexes.

For a long time, Lansdell's suggestion remained just that—a suggestion. But then, in the mid-1970s, encouraged by the work of Jerre Levy and others, Jeannette McGlone of the University of Western Ontario in Canada looked at eighty-five right-handed adults who had been admitted to the neurology ward with damage to one or the other side of their brains. Going one step further forward, she established that only men showed specifically verbal deficits after left-hemisphere damage and nonverbal, spatial deficits after right-hemisphere damage. The women showed much less severe losses in both verbal and spatial ability. And only they showed loss of verbal abilities after right- *as well as* left-hemisphere damage. On the basis of this and other studies, Jeannette McGlone has argued that the male brain is more decidedly lateralized than the female brain, as Jerre Levy says, and more tightly organized. The female brain, by contrast, seems to have a more even distribution of verbal and spatial abilities. This conclusion has been hotly disputed. "Some scientists, as you know, seem to think this work shouldn't be done," Jeannette McGlone says. "And I've been attacked, sometimes very scathingly." But it has recently received dramatic confirmation from studies done elsewhere.

At Queen's University in Kingston, Ontario, James Inglis and J.S. Lawson approached the question from two different directions. First, they combed through thirty years' worth of scientific literature on the effects of brain damage on verbal and visual-spatial abilities—a wealth of research done without reference to sex differences. (Lansdell's suggestion had fallen on stony ground.) They then made a table of all the studies involved, depending on whether they had used all men, all women or a mixture of both. And they demonstrated that the confusion of the various results was entirely consistent with Jeannette McGlone's theory. The results *depended,* indeed, on precisely how many men and how many women had been included in each study. Second, they set up an investigation of their own. This time, they looked at a *hundred* brain-damaged right-handed patients and they found almost exactly what Jeannette McGlone had found—a pronounced lateralization of function in males and a quite different picture in females. Their female patients showed much less loss of function after damage to either hemisphere. But they *did* show some loss of *both* verbal and visual-spatial function after left-hemisphere damage.

At the same time, Jeannette McGlone began one further experiment herself. Patients facing brain surgery are often given a test named for neuroscientist Juhn Wada. "The surgeon," Jeannette McGlone says, as we sit in her office in University Hospital, "has to know in which hemisphere language is organized and how drastic, therefore, the surgery can afford to be. So the patient is given a shot of sodium amytal in one or the other of his carotid arteries, a shot which for a short time puts one of his hemispheres to sleep. The awake hemisphere is then given a number of language tests. Well, I haven't been able to do this with very *many* male and female patients yet. So my results are preliminary, though they're very striking and potentially very exciting, I think. I've been giving these men and women a simple language task—naming as many words beginning with the letter "d" as they can in thirty seconds—with both hemispheres intact and then with one or other of the two hemispheres out of action. And I've found that the men and women perform quite differently. The women perform best when they have both hemispheres available, and less well when *either* hemisphere is out of action. The men perform best when their right hemisphere is not available, less well when both hemispheres are intact and *very* much more poorly—worse than the women —when their left hemisphere is out of action. For language, in other words, the men seem to rely much more heavily on their left hemisphere. Language, and perhaps visual-spatial skills, are organized differently in them."

Yet more evidence that Jeannette McGlone is on the right track comes from near at hand, from people well known to her. One of them is Doreen Kimura, the professor of psychology at the University of Western Ontario with whom Jeannette McGlone originally studied. Doreen Kimura, a small, brisk woman in her late forties, is the inventor, as Jerre Levy says, of dichotic ear-listening, one of the indirect techniques by which the different responsibilities of the two hemispheres were originally assigned. Recently, though, she has found a more direct way of looking at the organization of language skills within the hemisphere responsible for it in almost all right-handers—the left. Here again, she has found differences between men and women.

"Well," she says, "I suppose it's taking Jeannette's work one step further, taking it within one hemisphere. The question here is whether men and women are differentially affected, whether they are made aphasic—lose language—as the result of damage to the same or different areas. And what we've so far found is that, if you divide the left hemisphere into front and back— anterior and posterior—then you can see that males become aphasic as the result of damage to *either* area. But females seem to become aphasic only if the damage is to the *anterior* area. In the posterior—the back—they seem to be unaffected. This suggests two possibilities. Either females have some language functions in their right hemisphere which remain in the left in males. Or their language functions are more focally and more economically organized in the left hemisphere than males' are. Either way, it shows, I think, that there are differences between men and women in the way language is deployed in their left hemispheres—there are intra- as well as inter-hemispheric differences. This has been confirmed by work done by another ex-student of mine, Katie Mateer, who's left Jeannette and me to work with George Ojemann at the University of Washington in Seattle."

George Ojemann is a neurosurgeon, a contemporary of Kimura's, tall, confident, spectacled. And for the past ten years he has been refining a technique by which electrical stimulation is applied to the exposed brains of patients before surgery. The aim is to make more detailed maps of brain functions, particularly language functions, than the Wada test alone can provide. Patients are given a number of language tests as they lie on the operating table. And if electrical stimulation at a particular site on the brain's surface interferes with their successful performance, then the site is marked down as an area important in one way or another to language—an area to be avoided, if possible, during surgery. For the past three or four years, in patient after patient, Katie Mateer has been studying the maps made in this way. And she has found that language does indeed seem to be more economically organized in the female's left hemisphere than in the male's. She has not found the exact pattern of back-front distribution of language Doreen Kimura has found in her aphasic patients, a pattern that has since been found to hold true in CAT scans of male and female aphasics. But she *has* discovered that in the female left hemisphere a much more restricted area, in *both* front and back, is given up to the basic language function being tested for—the naming of objects, expressions, pictures and words. And this suggests, once more, that the female's left hemisphere is either more space-efficient for language or that some of her language abilities lie elsewhere—in the right hemisphere.

We talk with Doreen Kimura through most of an afternoon about her own work and the work of Levy, Lansdell, McGlone and Mateer. And little by little the conversation widens to include all the little bits and pieces of evidence from other sources that combine to support the idea that the hemispheres of men and women are differently organized: the fact that men are more at risk from strokes in general and from stroke-related aphasia in particular; the fact that verbal and visual-spatial systems seem to overlap in women but not in men (K. Fukui in Japan); the fact that men may be able to do verbal and visual-spatial tasks simultaneously rather better than women, because their left and right brains operate more independently than women's (Sandra Witelson at McMaster University in Canada); the fact that men have more difficulty than women in doing two jobs that engage the right hemisphere—doing a visual-spatial test and operating the left hand, for example (Takeshi Hatta at Osaka University); and the fact that, by electrical measurements, women respond more to stimuli, generate more electricity in *both* verbal and visual-spatial tasks and learn to regulate their brain-wave frequencies *across* the hemispheres more easily than men do (Monte Buchsbaum at the American National Institutes of Health and Pierre Flor-Henry at the University of Alberta in Edmonton, among others). We also discuss the work of Ruben and Raquel Gur at the University of Pennsylvania. The Gurs are a young Israeli couple who spent many years linking rightward and leftward eye movements to the activation of the left and right brain in men and women. Now, however, they too have found more direct ways into the brain's activities, through new technologies tied to the brain's uptake of energy-emitting radioactive molecules. Their work is still in the early stages. But already they have shown that the brains of men and women are both differentially constituted and differentially supplied with blood. When women perform verbal and visual-spatial tasks, their left and right hemispheres seem to use larger amounts of energy than men's do.

Wherever you look—in every sort of study, using every sort of approach—scientists are finding differences in the way men and women organize their verbal and visual-spatial abilities. The studies do not always agree with one another exactly. But they *do* have a sort of coherence. The brain map for these abilities *is* different in men and women. The question is: Why?

Doreen Kimura is aware that the question is loaded and all possible answers steeped in controversy. "Well, we have to look at evolution, I think, at the separate evolutionary pressures on men and women. First, let's suppose that language was a relatively recently acquired skill. And let's assume that when the male and female of a species differ in the development of a skill there will be a different amount of brain space given up to that skill—this is true, we know, in birds. Now we *also* know that for ninety-nine percent of our history as emerging *Homo sapiens* we've been hunter-gatherers. And in a hunter-gatherer society there would be strong selective pressures on the males to be highly specialized, specialized as hunters. To hunt successfully —which meant survival, genetic and otherwise—they would need eye acuity, goal-directedness, good gross-motor control and the ability to calculate distance, direction and the essentials of a situation: exactly the sort of visual and spatial skills that scientists find in human males today. To achieve these skills, though, they would need to give up to them a good deal of brain capacity—neural space. And they would not have this space available for the abilities it became necessary for them to acquire later. Or—put another way—these later abilities would have to subserve the spatial and motor abilities they already had.

"Females, meanwhile—let us imagine—were subject to *different* evolutionary pressures and were being selected for *different* qualities from the males. And these qualities—maternal, social and cultural ones, let's say—required different motor skills, a different brain organization and better hemispheric integration perhaps. When language and its uses were acquired, then, they fitted rather differently into the architecture of the female brain. One suggestion is that they were free to be more flexibly expressed in *both* hemispheres, without having to be confined to the left, as in males. But more accurate, I think, is that they were slotted into motor systems that were already somewhat differently developed from the male pattern. The result, again, might be what we see: a different distribution of language in the left hemisphere and the different constellation of abilities with language that scientists find in women today. All this, you see, would be underwritten by evolution, directed by sexual selection and laid down in the male and female brain. It would still be there, waiting for us to find it."

Jerre Levy agrees. And she is prepared to go even further, to speculate about the different "maternal, cultural and social" qualities that may have been selected for, during human evolution, in women rather than men. Roger Sperry, when we visited him in Pasadena shortly before he won the Nobel Prize, called Jerre Levy "one of the most amazing assimilators of information I've ever met." And she reels off by rote all the studies, including her own, that have persistently demonstrated the abilities of females in particular areas: their superiority in certain important verbal skills; their better fine-motor coordination; their ability to pick up and respond to peripheral information and to read the emotional content of faces; their sensitivity to odors and their extreme sensitivity to the presence and variation of sound.

All these qualities, she suggests, make perfect sense in the context of a hunting and gathering way of life. Males in such a society, she argues, would have been loners. But females would have provided the essential, social core of the group, the glue that bound it together. Their roles in the group as gatherers and feeders would have selected for improved fine-motor coordination. And their roles as social mediators, caretakers, peace-keepers and protectors of their children would have selected for an increased emotional and social sophistication, superior communicational skills and an enhanced ability to react quickly to any source of threat in the environment. All of these qualities, she believes, survive, to one degree or another, in the women of today, subserved by the way their brains are organized. Collectively, she believes, they are at the root of "that ubiquitous anecdotal phenomenon," female intuition.

"The evidence, you see, is that the hemispheres of male brains are specialists—they speak different languages, verbal and visual-spatial. And it may be that they can communicate with each other only in a formal way, after encoding into abstract representations. The hemispheres of *female* brains, on the other hand, don't seem to be such specialists. And they *may* be able to communicate in a much less formal, less structured and more rapid way. If this is so, then it's entirely possible that females are much better than males at integrating verbal and nonverbal information—at reading the emotional content of tones of voice and intensities of facial expression, for example; at interpreting social cues such as posture and gesture; at quickly fitting all sorts of peripheral information—information in different modes— into a complete picture. This may be at the root of what we call female intuition, the ability of women, which *men* think illogical, to respond to a danger sensed rather than perceived—"My baby's in trouble"—or to produce a complete character analysis, later often proved right, of someone they've met for only ten minutes."

Some of what Jerre Levy says is entirely speculative, of course. But it might be borne out by the differences recently found by Doreen Kimura, Katie Mateer and others *within* the separate hemispheres of the male and female brain. In the male left hemisphere, as we have seen, language seems to be deployed in brain space rather differently from the pattern in the female. And it is possible that this is reflective of the fact that the female evolved language as a tool for communication, while the male evolved it as a tool to subserve visual-spatial tasks—analytical reasoning. Similarly, it seems that in the *right* hemisphere males have given over a great deal more neural space to their visual-spatial skills than females have. And this may mean that females have been able to deploy in their right hemisphere *other* types of nonverbal, communicational skill—such as emotional sensitivity—that the male right hemisphere cannot accommodate as well.

"If this is so," says Jerre Levy, "then males may be at a double disadvantage in their emotional life. They may be emotionally less sophisticated. And because of the difficulty they may have in communicating between their two hemispheres, they may have restricted *verbal* access to their emotional world."

Evolution. Female intuition. Men's difficulty with emotions. "You know," Jerre Levy says, "I believe in the economy of nature. I have this almost mystical confidence that true things are simple and elegant, and untrue things are complicated and dirty. We are just at the beginning. But I firmly believe that the differences between the males and females of our species will ultimately be found in the cell arrangements and anatomy of the human brain."

5
MAKING CONNECTIONS

UNTIL VERY RECENTLY, virtually no anatomical differences, as we have said, had been found in the brains of males and females. Few anatomists had even bothered to look; they had other uses for the limited supply of available dead human brains. In fact, there were only two references in the scientific literature that seemed even relevant. In 1880, an English scientist named J. Crichton-Browne observed that the hemispheres of women tended to weigh more or less the same, while the weight difference between male hemispheres was much more marked. And in 1963, an American, J.D. Conel, showed that in the brains of four-year-old children cell growth was more advanced in certain areas of the *left* hemisphere in girls, and certain areas of the *right* hemisphere in boys. To these suggestive shreds all that could be added in the 1970s was the observation that men were more likely than women to show left-right asymmetries in regions that were responsible for language in the left hemisphere. Interesting, but hardly conclusive—"We have absolutely no idea what it means," says George Ojemann.

But then, on June 25, 1982, more than nine months after it had been submitted and six months after our visit with Jerre Levy, a short paper appeared in the American journal *Science*. It was discreetly buried, without fanfare or special announcement, among a host of other papers on every sort of subject. But it soon set the telephones of the neuropsychologists ringing. The paper was the result of work done at the University of Texas by Christine de Lacoste-Utamsing and Ralph Holloway of Columbia University. And it was drably titled, as these things are, "Sexual Dimorphism in the Human Corpus Callosum."

The corpus callosum is the elongated bundle of fibers that carries information between the two halves of the brain, precisely the fibers that had been cut in Roger Sperry's split-brain patients. And what de Lacoste-Utamsing and Holloway had found, almost by accident, was that at the back of the brain, at the so-called caudal—or posterior—end of the fiber bundle, it was much wider and larger in women than it was in men. So big and clear was the difference that "impartial observers" could immediately assign to the right sex—"with one hundred percent accuracy"—drawings made from photographs of cross sections. Five months later, at the annual meeting of the American Society for Neuroscience in Minneapolis, de Lacoste-Utamsing and a colleague from the University of Texas, D.J. Woodward, announced that the difference could not *only* be found in the brains of adult males and females. It could also be found in the brains of *fetuses,* between the twenty-sixth and the forty-first week of gestation. It was there, in other words, in the developing brain from the beginning, *long before it ever saw the world.*

For the neuropsychologists, this was enormously exciting news. It was a major piece of what Jerre Levy calls "the puzzle," and it was a piece of the puzzle that *fitted.* For from work on animals, and to a lesser extent from work on humans, scientists are fairly certain that the back part of the corpus callosum is involved in the transference between the hemispheres of visual and perhaps spatial information. "And if one considers," says

Sandra Witelson, "from work that has been done that visual-spatial functions are lateralized in the *male* and more bilaterally organized in the *female,* then it is in this area of the corpus callosum that one might expect to find evidence for it. That a difference has *actually* been found—and been found to be inborn—is *amazing!"*

Sandra Witelson is an enthusiastic, far-ranging neuropsychologist with considerable skills as an anatomist. In the mid-1970s, as a member of the Department of Psychiatry at McMaster University in Canada, she invented something called the dichhaptic stimulation test, a test by which the lateralization of different perceptual functions can be determined in neurologically normal individuals. One test involves feeling with each hand two differently shaped objects placed out of sight and then attempting to identify them in a group of six shapes displayed visually. And it was given by Sandra Witelson, in an often-quoted study, to two hundred right-handed children between the ages of six and thirteen. The results were extraordinarily consistent. The girls showed no hand bias at all on the task; they recognized objects felt by the right hand as often as they recognized objects felt by the left. But at every age from six to thirteen, the boys were considerably better at identifying objects felt by their *left* hand, even though they were right-handed. Sandra Witelson hypothesized that from a very early stage in life boys mainly used their right hemisphere as far as their visual-spatial skills were concerned, while females did not. They were capable of using either hemisphere.

"And that, of course, is why de Lacoste's report is so fascinating," Sandra Witelson says. "Because it supports the idea that human females may indeed have greater communication between the hemispheres than men do. They may not be wired up to have such right-hemisphere dominance. And this raises all sorts of other possibilities which may now be found to have some basis in anatomy. I have suggested, for example, that men appear better at doing two cognitive jobs at the same time, if the jobs depend mainly on different hemispheres, like talking and route-finding while driving, and that women appear better at *single* cognitive jobs which require cooperation and communication *between* the two hemispheres, like reading or assessing a person on the basis of both verbal and visual cues: tones of voice, facial expressions, body language and so on. The wider interhemispheric pathway in women than in men might be related to both. The sex difference might have something to do with the different distribution of left-hemisphere language in women that Dr. Doreen Kimura and colleagues have suggested. And these factors might indeed give women better *verbal* access to the emotional world of their right hemisphere, as Jerre Levy suggests."

The de Lacoste report points to something else. From work that Jerre Levy has done with children and from Conel's observation of the brains of four-year-olds, it is reasonable to conclude that the right hemisphere and its abilities develop faster in boys than in girls, while the *left* hemisphere and its abilities develop faster in girls than in boys. Girls have better linguistic skills earlier. And this gives girls an early advantage in school. Some studies have shown that by age six they're about twelve months ahead of boys, and by nine about eighteen months. Boys catch up, apparently, only after grade school. And much of their catching up seems to be in areas that demand new mathematical and mechanical skills. Now although there is a great deal of controversy about this, males may be better at mathematical and mechanical tasks because these tasks are primarily visual-spatial —they depend heavily on the performance of the right hemisphere. And just as boys have more difficulty with early *reading*, for example—because it depends on communication between the two hemispheres, a communication for which they're undersupplied with connections—so girls now have later difficulty with *mathematics*, precisely because they *do* have these connections between the hemispheres. With larger verbal access to the right hemisphere, in other words, girls are inclined to apply *verbal* strategies to the solution of visual-spatial problems. And that turns out to be more inefficient.

In December 1980, Camilla Persson Benbow and Julian Stanley of Johns Hopkins University in Baltimore published the results of an eight-year body of work. Its subject was mathematical ability and the sources of differences between the sexes. The paper was written with extraordinary delicacy and restraint. And its conclusion was this: "We favor the hypothesis that sex differences in achievement in and attitude towards mathematics result from superior male mathematical ability, which may in turn be related to greater male ability in spatial tasks."

Three months later, with the correspondence columns of scientific journals bristling with objection, they were seen by Diane McGuinness at a scientific conference looking pale and haggard—drained, they said, by the often unreasonable attacks launched against them in the wake of their report. Since then they have been boycotted, vilified and to an extent ignored by the mainstream of psychologists working in their field. And a year later, Camilla Benbow is still clearly surprised by the controversy.

"You have to understand," she says softly, with a distant trace of a Scandinavian accent, "that we didn't start out looking for sex differences in mathematical ability. The Johns Hopkins Study of Mathematically Precocious Youth—SMPY—simply conducted six talent searches in the mid-Atlantic states between 1972 and 1979. We were looking for gifted seventh- and eighth-graders—twelve-year-olds, basically—who, though they hadn't usually been taught any higher mathematics, could still manage a very high score on the math part of the Scholastic Aptitude Test, a test designed for bright, college-bound high school seniors, seventeen- and eighteen-year-olds. What we were looking for, in other words, was a natural aptitude for mathematical reasoning. We found about ten thousand children in these six years."

But they also found something that rather shocked them:

there were many more boys than girls among their subjects. The boys scored a much higher average than the girls. And on no occasion did a girl come first on the test. They were bound to ask why; it was their business, after all, not only to identify but also to *help* mathematically gifted children. So they studied the boys and girls and compared them for every possible variable that might account for the discrepancy between them—preparation in mathematics, a liking for math, the encouragement given them, the number of courses taken and so on. And they could find no significant difference at all except the one in overall ability, mathematical reasoning ability. Since 1979 they have looked at another 24,000 children and have found the same sex difference in ability. And, they have conducted a nationwide talent search for children at the top end of the scale. "We found sixty-three boys—and no girls."

Camilla Benbow, a striking women in her mid-twenties, says she would love to find—or have pointed out to her—an environmental difference that has been overlooked. It could then be corrected. But she quotes a follow-up study completed on a group of girls who were given female role models and were specially taught and specially encouraged. And even *this,* she says, seems to have made no ultimate difference. At the root, still, is the difference in mathematical reasoning ability. When the time comes for girls to use it formally in class—in calculus, differential equations and analytical geometry, for example— they seem to fall even further behind the boys, even though they are gifted and have no anxiety about the subject.

"All this," Camilla Benbow says carefully, "strongly suggests that there's something other than the environment at work. And, if so, then it's likely to be connected to the male's right-hemisphere superiority in visual-spatial tasks. We're just beginning to have evidence that when there are two equally valid approaches to a problem, via words or via images, females tend to choose the approach through words and males the approach through images. Now the approach through images—which are visual-spatial and right-hemisphere—just happens to be much more effective, especially in higher mathematics, than the approach through words. Look at the way mathematicians are forced to talk to one another, through symbols on a blackboard. And so I think that their right-hemisphere approach naturally favors males. From the beginning they're less verbally oriented than females—more oriented to things, to objects in space. They're less dependent on context in their visual-spatial skills—this can be seen cross-culturally from the age of four onwards. And they're more abstract.

"This may help explain, too, I think, why men are overrepresented in certain disciplines in science, something we've also been studying. To be a good physicist or engineer, for example, requires not only mathematical reasoning ability but also skill in three-dimensional visual imagery. And that's probably why few women are found in these fields. To be a good scientist, at all, in fact, seems to require a set of qualities more characteristic of men than of women—spatial ability, a low social interest and an absorption in things. Let's face it, human males like to manipulate *things*—from Tinkertoys to the cosmos." She laughs. "Females are more communicative, more sensitive to context and more interested in people. And perhaps that's why there are so many more women in fields like biology and psychology: like me.

"I'm not saying that the environment plays no role at all in the differences we find between men and women. But I *am* saying that there's something more powerful and fundamental at work here too—something *biological.* We don't know much about the biology of the male's visual-spatial abilities, it's true. But we do know that they appear as early as we can test for them. And we know they're somehow linked to the sex chromosomes and the sex hormones."

6

A SEARCH FOR CLUES

PICTURE TO YOURSELF the minuscule cell which worked and divided to become the person you are today. It is an instant after conception. Your mother's egg has just been penetrated by one of the millions of your father's swimming sperm. The cell being formed now has in it two millionths of a millionth of an ounce of DNA, all the information necessary to produce a trillion-cell creature with your particular brain, heart, nose, eye color and crooked grin. This information is arranged in segments of DNA called genes. And the genes are packed into forty-six separate chromosomes—twenty-three provided by your mother's egg and twenty-three the gift of your father's sperm. They are now in the process of matching up into chromosome-pairs.

Each of the chromosomes is a pack of genetic cards, the result of a more or less random shuffling of genes from each of your *parents'* matched pairs of chromosomes. And so the fifty percent you have inherited from each is organized by chance. There are, however, two exceptions to this rule. And these are two chromosomes that are relatively well protected and passed on *without* shuffling—the sex chromosomes. An X chromosome is automatically passed on to the original cell—and to you—by your mother's egg. And either *another* X or a Y is handed down to you by your father's sperm. If you are XX, as you read this—if you have two X chromosomes in every cell in your body, except your eggs—then you are a woman. If you are XY—with an X and a Y chromosome in every cell in your body, except your sperm—then you are a man. Though there are certain exceptions, as we shall soon see, this is the basic rule.

Now if you are a scientist trying to make connections between the sex chromosomes, the sex hormones and male visual-spatial skill, you cannot just isolate a sex chromosome and expect to find in it a gene coding for some convenient visual-spatial substance that men have and women do not. Nor can you simply inject male sex hormones into women and hope to find in them some immediately enhanced visual-spatial skill. All you can do is to look for indirect evidence wherever you can find it, to look for clues. First, you can see whether particular patterns of visual-spatial skill are inherited. And second, you can test for their skill men and women in whom something has gone *wrong*—either with the expression of the sex chromosomes or with the amounts of sex hormones naturally available to them. Darrell Bock and Donald Kolakowski are the only scientists we know of to have taken the first tack. In the early 1970s they tested members of families and found patterns of skill inheritance consistent with the involvement of a gene on the X chromosome that is recessive—that is expressed more often in males because of the female's second X chromosome. All the *other* bits and pieces of evidence come from the second approach. They come from cases in which something has gone wrong. They come from accidents of nature.

Not long ago, a young Danish girl—we will call her Anna M. —was given a battery of tests. At the time she was a student at a college for kindergarten teachers—a short, sensitive, quiet girl of normal intelligence with a talent for foreign languages. She liked to cook.

Anna M., we are told, had had an ordinary childhood and an uneventful school career. But at the normal time for puberty she had failed to menstruate or to develop either breasts or body hair. And so she had come to the attention of doctors. Her condition was not a difficult one to diagnose. From her failure to develop normally, from the shortness of her stature and her neck, from the wide spacing of her nipples, from her lack of ovaries and from the low level of both female and male hormones circulating in her body, it was plain that she suffered from Turner's syndrome. Whereas all normal men and women have two sex chromosomes, Anna M. had only one, a single X. The second was missing from every cell in her body.

Under ordinary circumstances, as we have said, each man and each woman inherits an X chromosome from his or her mother's egg and an X or a Y chromosome from his or her father's sperm. Sometimes, though, something can go wrong with the way in which chromosomes are divided in each parent before being passed on. A sex chromosome, for example, does not make it across the divide—this is what happened in Anna's case. Or else more than one does. Thus, just as there are women like Anna with only *one* sex chromosome, so there are other individuals, both male and female, with *three.* If one of the chromosomes is a Y, these individuals are recognizably male (XXY and XYY). And they are raised as boys. If there is *no* Y present (XXX and Anna's XO), they are recognizably female. And they are raised as girls.

We will come back to Anna M. in a moment. Let us look first, instead, at the XY males who may be said to have inherited either an extra dose of maleness—an extra Y chromosome—or an extra dose of femaleness—an extra X chromosome. XYY males are usually much taller than average. And they also seem to be more aggressive and more violence-prone than the norm. More important, though, for our purposes here is the fact that *their visual-spatial abilities*—relative to their verbal ones—*are also much more pronounced than is usual in ordinary XY males.* As far as their right-hemisphere skills are concerned, in other words, their extra Y gene has made them exaggeratedly masculine. This makes them different from XXY males, who suffer from what is known as Klinefelter's syndrome. Klinefelter's men—and there may be up to four hundred thousand of them in the United States alone—are usually rather passive and timid. They tend to have small testicles, little body hair and a low level of sexual appetite. For all this, though, their visual-spatial skills seem to be unaffected. Their single Y chromosome seems to be enough to guarantee them visual-spatial skills within the normal male range.

So far, then, we can say that the Y chromosome is implicated in the male's visual-spatial skills. Now how does Anna M. fit into the picture? When she was tested by doctors at the Arhus Psychiatric Hospital in Denmark, it was soon plain that her left hemisphere functioned far better than her right hemisphere. The feeling in her left hand, for instance, was poor. She misidentified objects held in it and she had difficulty mimicking with her left hand a position into which her right hand was moved. *She also had far less visual-spatial than verbal ability—her visual-spatial ability was much poorer than that of the average female.* She scored badly on the so-called performance—as against the verbal—section of an IQ test. She misinterpreted objects and patterns in visual tasks. She misplaced points of the compass. And she made mistakes in a test involving handedness and geometric figures. She also had problems, both in the tests and in daily life, with arithmetic.

The pattern Anna M. showed, in other words—the pattern that virtually *all* Turner's women show—was what scientists call "exaggeratedly feminine." Turner's women, like Anna, are usually shy and retiring. They like to be around children, and they are often drawn both to traditionally female pursuits, like cooking, and to jobs that involve the use of language. Their brains, as we have seen in Anna, are *also* "exaggeratedly feminine," with extreme dependence on the left hemisphere and a marked diminution of abilities in the right. The question is: Why? It is true that Turner's women do not have a Y chromosome and should not be expected, on the basis of our tentative hypothesis, to have as much visual-spatial ability as *males*. But why don't they have exactly the same degree of visual-spatial ability as normal *females*? The answer cannot lie in the environment—Turner's women are brought up, treated, raised and educated as ordinary girls from the beginning. The answer must lie somewhere else, in something that the *second* X chromosome provides for normal women: their sex hormones.

Turner's women like Anna, remember, don't develop ovaries, which are within the gift of the second X. And this means that from about the sixth week of fetal life they do not have available to them the sex hormones that the ovaries manufacture and push into the circulation. Turner's women, therefore, have *much* lower levels than normal women of both estrogen *and* the main male hormone, testosterone, which the ovaries produce in small quantities. And this suggests a *further* possibility that can now be added to our hypothesis about the connection between the Y chromosome and visual-spatial abilities. Could it be that it is testosterone—in males under the control of their Y chromosome—that in women too is responsible for the development of *their* visual-spatial skills? Could testosterone be at the root of it all?

Luckily for the clue-hunting scientist, there are two other accidents of nature that can now be brought to the marshaling of the evidence. First, there are genetic XY males who, because of a defect, are from the beginning of fetal life completely insensitive to the testosterone their testes produce. As a result, they are born, to all outward appearance, as girls. And as a result too, perhaps, as adults, *they have diminished and impaired visual-spatial abilities*.

This could be put down to the environment. Genetic males with this syndrome—and we will be coming back to it later—are raised as girls and face the same educational and cultural biases *normal* girls do. But the same cannot be said of a *second* group who have experienced an accident of nature—men suffering from what is known as idiopathic hypogonadotropic hypogonadism. These men suffer from what is presumed to be a deficiency in particular a messenger hormone, a hormone that in normal men calls up the production of testosterone in the testes. But since it is a condition that does not manifest itself until puberty, men with this mouthful of a deficiency are raised as ordinary boys, with all the cultural and educational biases to which they are supposed to be exposed.

In 1982, Daniel Hier of the Michael Reese Hospital in Chicago and William Crowley of the Massachusetts General Hospital in Boston published the results of tests they had given nineteen men with this disorder, men who had failed to develop normally at puberty and had, as a result, extremely small testes and levels of testosterone similar to those found in women. And they showed that, though their verbal skills were no different, their visual-spatial skills were way below those both of normal men *and* of men who had contracted the same illness—as a result of brain damage or disease—*after* puberty. What is more, they found what seemed to be a direct correlation between the severity of their disorder and the damage done to their visual-spatial abilities. The smaller the testes, the lower the level of testosterone; the lower the level of testosterone, the poorer the abilities. Giving the men testosterone *now*, after the event, Hier and Crowley demonstrated, made no difference to their proficiency at visual and spatial tests. Their visual-spatial competency had been fixed "at, or before puberty."

Visual-spatial abilities, then—our clue-hunting scientist can now say—seem to depend on a minimum level of testosterone. And in males they seem to rely on the presence of the Y chromosome and the higher amount of testosterone produced by the male's testes. By this means the brain of an individual is shaped in a more or less male direction, to produce its speed of development and its characteristic skills. Certain of these skills are more likely to appear in men than in women. And they are likely to be enhanced at puberty, when a fresh rush of testosterone invades the body and males coincidentally—as Sandra Witelson says—begin their catch-up in mathematical and mechanical, if not verbal areas. The result may be what Camilla Benbow finds:

a preponderance of males in professions like higher mathematics, physics and engineering, and perhaps, too, painting, architecture and town planning: all of it derived from man's history as a hunter-gatherer and the male need for visual-spatial skills. Pierre Flor-Henry, another Canadian scientist, is inclined to go even further back in evolutionary time for its origins.

"At its most fundamental biological level," he says, "the brain evolved to facilitate mate attraction and mate selection. And it's to be expected that anything that improved visual-spatial efficiency would be preferentially selected for in the male, which is the sex-*seeking*—and ultimately, of course, grafted on top, the food-hunting—gender. Well, one way of making the brain more efficient is to make it asymmetrical—it makes spatial analysis easier. And another way, of course, is to have refined visual-spatial systems within one hemisphere. Both can be found in the evolved human male, but not to anything like such a marked degree in the female. Why not? Because, as in other species, male and female are *complementary* sexual systems. And to be able to come together successfully to mate and reproduce, they require different behaviors, different abilities and different strategies. How are these differences maintained in other species? By the sex hormones. How are these differences maintained in *our* species? Equally—obviously—by the sex hormones."

PART THREE

THE SEXING
OF THE BRAIN

7

THE SEX CHEMICALS: THE VIEW FROM OUTSIDE

THE SEX HORMONES are among the most subtle and powerful chemicals in nature. And it is only in the past ten years that scientists have begun to get a handle on how profoundly, throughout life, they affect the human brain-body system. One problem is that they play different roles at different times. Another is that they simultaneously operate in different ways in different parts of the system. If you want, however, to understand something about the enormous range of *effects* they can have, then the best place to start looking is at human puberty.

Puberty in the west seems to take place about four years earlier than it did four hundred years ago, probably because of better nutrition and constant exposure to artificial light. But there is not the slightest reason to believe that its processes are any different. Somewhere between the ages of nine and fifteen (though it can happen as early as two, another accident of nature) the body somehow senses that enough growth has been achieved to sustain the exigencies of reproductive life. Then a series of extraordinary developments occurs. The testes and ovaries are instructed to increase rapidly the production of their characteristic sex hormones. And where before there were two genders very similar in shape and body size, now they speedily diverge. Girls become locked into their menstrual cycle. They develop breasts, grow a particular pattern of pubic hair, expand their pelvises and put on weight at their hips, so gaining a low center of gravity and the beginnings of the hip-swiveling walk of a mature woman. Boys, at a somewhat later age—they seem to require more body growth for the exertions to come—develop a deep voice, a receding hairline, new muscles and sweat glands and larger bones. They grow facial hair and a larger penis and they set up continuous sperm production. They *also* become strongly attracted to girls. Where before the two sexes had been often positively indifferent to one another, now—during and after puberty—they respond to the directing grip of their sex hormones with an intense awareness.

Some of these features, though much less marked, can be induced in males and females simply by giving them the appropriate hormones. Give a male-to-female transsexual estrogens (the family of sex hormones related to estradiol) and he will often grow breasts and add fat at hips and thigh; give a female-to-male transsexual androgens (the family of hormones related to testosterone) and she will often grow an enlarged clitoris and gain facial hair, a deeper voice and a masculine musculature. This sometimes happens in women athletes taking so-called anabolic steroids. And it brings us to the next major difference between men and women that the sex hormones produce.

Testosterone is an anabolic steroid; that is to say, it promotes the synthesis of proteins from the fats and amino acids in food. It facilitates retention of nitrogen, potassium and phosphorus. It promotes tissue growth and repair in muscle and bone and, perhaps, in liver, kidney and brain. Estrogen, by contrast, is catabolic; it works to break proteins down. And it makes more likely, therefore, the metabolism of fat and the storage of fat in particular locations in the body: hip, buttocks, breasts and thigh. (Estrogen is routinely used to produce weight gain in cattle.) It also decreases the amount of fatty substances in the blood, so that women tend to have lower cholesterol levels than men. And it slows down growth. Estrogen is now being used to treat boys whose growth, and thus increasing height, is out of control.

The result is what we see. Women are generally smaller than men. And because men and women process protein differently and distribute it differently to different organs and storage sites under the influence of their sex hormones, their bodies are rather differently constituted. Men are likely to be forty percent muscle and fifteen percent fat; women tend to be twenty-three percent muscle and twenty-five percent fat. Men's arms are longer and their shoulders wider. They have larger hearts and lungs and more hemoglobin in their blood. Thus they can pump oxygen to their muscles more efficiently. Their upper body is two or three times more powerful than women's, pound for pound, which gives men an enormous advantage in any activity or sport that requires power, muscle strength (and, we should add, visual-spatial coordination). Women, if they have an edge, should have it in sports or activities that require *endurance*. They are good at long-distance swimming, for example, because their bodies offer less resistance to water and their fat insulates them better against the cold than men. And they are better built for endurance running, because their stocks of fat give them deeper energy reserves.

Bob Goy of the Regional Primate Research Center at the University of Wisconsin in Madison takes us the next step. "Now the changes we see at human puberty don't tell us very much about the effect the sex hormones have on the *brain,* though it's plain they *do* have an effect in controlling attraction and the onset of sexual behavior. But they do tell us two basic things. First, the sex hormones *effect* all these changes by interacting directly with the genetic material at the heart of their target cells. Their target cells are provided with specialized receptors designed to accept them and carry them into the nucleus, where they somehow change the number and nature of the genes being *expressed* in the cells. The blueprint for the job each cell is doing is changed, altered in a masculine or a feminine direction, either temporarily or permanently.

"The second thing that changes at puberty tell us is that the sex hormones are important evolutionary agents, the agents of a very ancient evolutionary program. For all the highly articulated differences they produce at puberty make perfect evolutionary sense. The female has puberty earlier, for example, and her growth is slowed, because it's not to her reproductive advantage to invest too heavily in growth. She develops breasts and pubic hair to demonstrate that she has now reached sexual maturity. And she's given large fat deposits as a protection against the coming of lean times, so that she and any future breast-feeding offspring will survive when there's no food available. She *also* fails to grow facial hair, which makes her face more childlike than the male's, with the eyes taking up more face area. And it's been suggested that this may be designed to evoke a protective response from the male. The male, of course, *does* grow facial hair—it's an indicator of how much testosterone he has in his body. And he invests much more heavily in growth and muscular strength than the female does. This is likely to be part of his *separate* evolutionary legacy—of male-male competition and hunting.

"Now put these two things together—the sex hormones' mode of operation and their evolutionary responsibilities—and you can begin to see, even from the *outside,* some of the ways and areas in which the sex hormones *must* operate on the chemistry and neural circuitry of the human brain, and on their expression in behavior."

When scientists have looked from the outside at the effects of the sex hormones on the brain and behavior—which is hard to do—these are some of the disputed bits and pieces of evidence they have found: Basses have more testosterone and less estradiol than tenors, and they also have more active sex lives. Rapists and exhibitionists have higher testosterone levels than is normal; alcoholics have lower. Old men produce more estradiol and less active testosterone than young ones. Male hair growth seems to increase in anticipation of sex, as an anonymous scientist with a passion for measurement pointed out in 1970. And testosterone levels, too, seem to go up both before *and* after sex. In one part of the northern hemisphere, in Germany, levels of testosterone are highest around September, when most children are conceived. So, in this one part of the world at least, a young man's fancy turns to thoughts of love not in spring, but in late summer.

Scientists have found the beginnings of a connection, in other words, between sexual drive and testosterone not only in men, but also in women. If a female-to-male transsexual is given large doses of testosterone, then her libido increases. And so does the libido of women who for one reason or another—because of disease, medical treatment or persistent and grueling exercise, perhaps—are exposed to higher levels of testosterone than usual. In *normal* women, the period in the menstrual cycle during which testosterone production is at its highest—the days before and during ovulation—*seems* to coincide with the period during which the sexual drive is at its strongest. It *also* seems to coincide with a period when a woman is most sensitive to smell; when she is most *visually* sensitive; and, most fascinatingly, when she is at her most arithmetically able. These fluctuations in ability, if they exist, do not seem to occur in women on the pill.

If there is a connection between testosterone and sexual drive —especially in males—then there is also a connection between testosterone, the Y chromosome and *another* brain behavior found characteristically in males—aggression. Just as Japanese fighting fish can be made more aggressive by the experimental addition of an extra Y chromosome, so *men* born with an extra Y chromosome (XYY) seem also to be more impulsive, more antisocial and, perhaps, more aggressive than normal males. This is likely to be mediated by their testosterone. Juvenile boys treated with testosterone become more aggressive. And there seems to be a good correlation in juvenile delinquents between levels of testosterone and the early date of their first arrest for crime. Prisoners with long, florid histories of violent crime also seem to have higher levels than the normal prison population. And even in hockey players there is a relationship between testosterone and aggression. One study has shown that hockey players who respond aggressively to threat have higher levels of testosterone than normal.

A scattering of other studies has implicated testosterone in a number of other behaviors. It increases behavioral reactivity, they suggest. It enhances persistence and attention. It alleviates fatigue. And it is intimately bound up with the chemistry of the so-called "fight-flight response," the way the body reacts to suddenly perceived danger. Its involvement in these things— from Bob Goy's point of view—makes sense. It makes sense that the sex drive, aggression and testosterone should come together in men, along with intensity, quick reaction and visual-spatial skill, in one evolutionary package. For males in nature often have to fight to mate. And the hominid males from whom we are descended had, above all, to hunt, if they were to guarantee the success of their genetic investment—their offspring. For this they needed precisely the qualities that testosterone (and the Y chromosome) seems to bring together in one bundle.

Having said that, it should be added, however, that the bundle, if it is one, is not particularly *well protected.* And it can easily take on a distorted and antisocial shape. It is young males, after all, whose levels of testosterone are highest, who commit almost all the violent crimes. In 1977, in Norway, ninety-four and six-tenths percent of all criminal acts were committed by men. And much of the crime is, of course, sex-related; a leading cause of the murder of men and women in both Africa and the United States is the suspected infidelity of a woman. Crime, one should bear in mind, is committed by the brain. And there are other distortions, apart from violent crime, that connect the brain, sex, aggression, testosterone and so on. There are, for instance, many more cases of men combining sexual deviance and aggression than there are of women. Aside from their tendencies toward rape and exhibitionism, men commonly practice things virtually unknown in women: homosexual incest, pedophilia (sex with children) and homosexual sadism and masochism. And one of the few ways these things *and* the fantasies they give rise to can be treated, short of brain surgery or castration, is with drugs that *block* the action of testosterone.

So much for men. The picture for women is much less clear, partly because they are hormonally more complicated, partly because they suffer fewer genetic defects than men, and partly because, being less deviant, science is less often called on to treat them. Women's troubles, if any, seem to have to do with *mood* rather than anything else. The premenstrual "blues," for example, are probably caused by an altered balance of their two main hormones, estradiol and progesterone, versions of which are given in the various forms of the birth control pill. And these two hormones are almost certainly somewhere behind women's proneness to depression. They are likely, too, to be at the root of the lack of aggression in the so-called weaker sex. Given externally, progesterone and its relatives induce calmness. And estradiol and its relatives seem to promote a sense of well-being. This may be somehow connected to the woman's essential role as mother. There are a few tantalizing clues that suggest that a changed balance of the two sex hormones before the birth of an infant is directly responsible for the early stages of mothering behavior.

In women, then—although there is much less evidence than for men—the evolutionary package that comes with the sex hormones and the X chromosomes also comes perhaps with some maternal ability but more surely with a sensitivity to mood, an evenness of temperament and a general lack of volatility. Women born with one X chromosome—Turner's women like Anna M.—are attracted to children, but they are also shy, inactive and withdrawn, as we have seen. Klinefelter's men—who have two X chromosomes and high levels of estrogen—are unusually passive. And male-to-female transsexuals given large doses of estrogen *also* become less arousable and less sexually aggressive. This packaging, if such it is, would again make sense. For individual females are the main investors in the continuation of their species; they have more to risk and lose in the reproductive stakes. And so one would expect them to be hormonally protected against impulse, hostility and a misplaced or overeager sexual drive. Males, by contrast, are gamblers. And their patterns of inheritance and the play of the sex hormones within them are under much less firm control.

ACCIDENTS OF NATURE

"MOOD. AGGRESSION. BODY size. Body shape. Use of energy. Behavior," says Günter Dörner in a borrowed student's room at Cambridge University in England. "We have all these differences that appear in human males and females, almost all of them during and after puberty. And that's what most people automatically think of when they think about the sex hormones. They are aware of *some*—at any rate—of what Bob Goy, for example, has called in his scientific writing the *activational* effects of these hormones—the way they set up the reproductive cycle in women and at puberty influence hair, breast and muscle growth and attraction to the opposite sex. What they *don't* know about, however, is what Goy calls the *organizational* effects of these hormones. The sex hormones, you see, don't just suddenly appear out of nowhere at puberty. Nor do they just meander about the body. *They know where to go.* The cells that are their targets have already been primed, in the womb, to respond to the hormones that are now being produced. They've already—long before—been *organized*—by the early production of the sex hormones *themselves,* in a masculine or feminine way. This is true

99

of the body, of the reproductive organs, heart, lungs, liver and kidney. But it is also true of the *brain*. The tissues, neural circuitry and chemistry of the brain have already been stamped during fetal life by the sex hormones. The foundations have already been laid, before birth, for the range of behaviors that will characterize the organism as male or female in adult life."

Günter Dörner is director of the Institute for Experimental Endocrinology at Humboldt University in East Berlin. He has recently flown from the German Democratic Republic to attend a high-level conference of hormone and brain specialists in the old English university city. It is one of the rare occasions he has left his laboratory for the west. And we fly to Cambridge to meet him, aware of the bristle of controversy that surrounds his shock-haired, forthright, twinkling figure.

Since the early 1960s, Dörner, like other scientists, has been working to find a way into the connections between motivation, brain and behavior. And, like other scientists, he has concentrated on the most basic motivation of all—the drive to reproduce—and on the different sexual behavior of male and female. When the scientific community began to understand that it is the hypothalamus that controls the output of the hormones and the different patterns of male and female reproduction, Dörner was quick to find in the hypothalamus of rats what he took to be different male and female sex centers. These centers, formed under the influence of the sex hormones at an early stage of development, were responsible, he believed, for male and female sexual behavior. And he showed that if the rats did not get enough of their appropriate sex hormones during development, then something would go wrong with the formation of the centers and with later sexual behavior. Adult rats would behave in certain ways like members of the opposite sex. They would become, in a sense, "homosexual."

From this Dörner argued that sexual behavior is also stamped by the hormones into the *human* brain while it is still developing in the womb, and that primary human homosexuality is the result of a sexual stamping that has given the brain the wrong gender. He quotes from a study in which male homosexuals obsessively attracted to children were "cured" by an operation on their brain's presumed *female* sex center. And he himself has performed a series of experiments that show, he firmly believes, that both male and female homosexuality are caused by the prenatal effect on the brain of either too little or too much of the main male sex hormone—testosterone.

"There's no doubt," Günter Dörner says in his fluent, accented English, "that this theory is controversial. And it's true we don't know everything we'd like to know about these hormones. We don't know much about the prenatal sex hormones produced by the ovaries. We don't know much about how the *mother's* hormones are involved. But my theory is consistent with what we *do* know from both animals and humans. In humans, monkeys, rats, guinea pigs, birds—practically everywhere we look in nature—the quantities of sex hormones available to the fetus during critical periods of early development stamp into the developing brain a variety of masculine and feminine sexual and social behaviors—usually, *but not always,* in accordance with the genetic sex. The whole story of male and female, you see—and your search for the effects of the sex hormones, if I may call it that—begins not outside, at puberty, but in the womb."

Male and female created He them. And that, of course, is what we see around us—men with testes, a penis and prominent body- and facial-hair display; women, relatively hairless, with ovaries, a vagina and the advertisements of breasts. Men are the male gender of the human species, and women are the female gender. And that is all there is to it.

Not quite—as we have seen. Take the case of Mrs. Went, for example. Mrs. Went is an ordinary, well-adjusted English housewife, married and with adopted children. In England she is, of course, legally a woman. But if she lived in Scotland, no more than a few hundred miles to the north, she would be treated by the state as a man. She is in fact genetically male; all her cells contain both the female X and the male Y chromosome. But she suffers from the rare genetic disorder that we talked about in the context of visual-spatial skills: a disorder called the testicular feminization syndrome. This causes a complete insensitivity to the main male hormone, testosterone. And, because of it, Mrs. Went was born with testes hidden in her abdomen and the external appearance of being a girl. She was raised as a girl, and she remained a girl, impervious to the rush of hormones produced by her testes at puberty. She only discovered her condition at age twenty-three when, anxious about her failure to menstruate or grow pubic hair, she consulted a gynecologist.

In Mrs. Went's case, gender identity—what sex she *feels* she is—has come unglued from her genetic sex. And there are other examples of this phenomenon. There are transsexuals. There is a subgroup of homosexuals and transvestites who identify strongly with the sex opposite their own, like the New York transvestite we tracked down who first fathered and then mothered—breast-fed—his own child. And then there are hermaphrodites. Hermaphrodites are true bisexuals, both male and female, born with one active ovary and one active testis and the ability, under certain circumstances, to impregnate themselves. Usually, however, they are raised as either boys or girls, in one gender identity or the other. And this is the gender identity they choose to keep, even when they have not been surgically altered in infancy, to reflect it.

In the late 1970s, for example, a shy eighteen-year-old Malawian who had been raised as a boy, but who was in fact the three hundred and third true hermaphrodite known to medicine, entered Stellenbosch University Hospital in South Africa, where Willem van Niekerk had been conducting a special study of Bantu hermaphrodites. The young Malawian, named Blackwell, had both a penis and a small vaginal opening. But the main reason he sought medical help was the fact that, during puberty, he had developed two large and finely shaped female breasts. Certain that he was a man, and wishing to continue his career as one, Mr. Blackwell asked doctors to stitch up his vagina and remove his breasts. And they did so.

Mrs. Went, Mr. Blackwell, transvestites, homosexuals and transsexuals like Renee Richards, the doctor and tennis player: it is cases like these that have kept in place the conventional wisdoms that science delivered up to us in the 1960s and 1970s about sexual orientation and gender identity. First, say the axioms of these wisdoms, sexual orientation is not innate but *learned*. It can be learned in such a way that it is concordant with genetic sex (XX or XY) *or* with gender identity or with both, as it is in most of us. Where it is discordant—as it is in homosexuals and transsexuals, for example—it is the result of formative or disordering psychological experience during childhood and adolescence. Second, according to these wisdoms, gender identity is *also* learned. A child can learn to be either male or female quite comfortably, whatever its genetic sex. But after a certain age, after it has learned to be one or the other, it cannot then change its gender assignment without some sort of psychological upheaval. The work of learning, once done—once etched into the brain—cannot be easily undone.

The most famous case of the period underwrote these contentions; it seemed to give them the force of natural law. This case was not an accident of nature, like Mrs. Went and Mr. Blackwell, but an accident of man. In the early 1960s, in the United States, a male child, one of a pair of identical twins, had his penis severed, at seven months, in a circumcision accident. After a good deal of heart-searching, it was decided by the boy's parents and by a group of doctors that included John Money of Johns Hopkins University that he should be raised as a girl, his brother's sister. At seventeen months, then, his testes were removed and a vagina was given preliminary shape. Later he was put on an extensive program of female sex hormones to mimic the developmental events leading to female puberty.

The case was everywhere hailed as a triumph for science. "This dramatic case," *Time* magazine announced in 1973, "provides strong support for a major contention of women's liberationists: that conventional patterns of masculine and feminine behavior can be altered. It also casts doubt on the theory that major sex differences, psychological as well as anatomical, are immutably set by the genes at conception." Masters and Johnson called it "dramatic documentation of the importance of learning in the process of gender formation." And John Money, who originally reported the case, wrote: "The girl's subsequent history proves how well all three of them (the parents and child) succeeded in adjusting to (the) decision."

That seemed to be that. But then, in the early 1970s, away from public attention, the descendants of Amaranta Ternera were discovered. And the controversy in science began.

Amaranta Ternera—we have changed, by request, her name and the names of her relatives—was born 130 years ago in the southwest corner of the Dominican Republic. There was nothing wrong with Amaranta, so far as we know; she seems to have led a normal and ordinary life. But there *was* something wrong with the genes she left behind her in her children. And there *is* something wrong with a number of her descendants. Seven generations later, Amaranta's genes have been located in twenty-three families in three separate villages. And in thirty-eight different individuals in these families the strange inheritance that Amaranta passed down to them has been expressed. These thirty-eight were born, to all appearances, as girls. They grew up as girls. And they became boys at puberty.

Take the ten children of Gerineldo and Pilar Babilonia, for example. Four of them have been through this extraordinary transformation. The eldest, Prudencio, was born with an apparent vagina and female body-shape, just like his next sister-brother, Matilda. Prudencio was christened Prudencia. And he grew up, Pilar says, tied to his mother's apron strings, kept apart from the village boys and helping with women's work. But then something strange began to happen to his body. His voice began to deepen. At around the age of twelve, his "clitoris" grew into a penis and two hidden testicles descended into a scrotum formed by the lips of his "vagina." He became a male. "He changed his clothes," says his father Gerineldo, "which the neighbors just had to get used to. And he fell in love with a girl almost immediately." Today Prudencio is in his early thirties. Like his brother Matilda, now Mateo, he is a brawny, elaborately muscled man. He is sexually potent and he lives with his wife in the United States. Like seventeen of the eighteen children studied by a group headed by Cornell University's Julianne Imperato-McGinley—all of whom, she says, were raised unambiguously as girls—Prudencio seems to have had no problem adjusting to male gender, male sexual orientation and male roles.

It is this which makes Prudencio and the other Dominican children important. *They seem to have had no problem adjusting to male gender, male sexual orientation and male roles.* Like Mrs. Went, Prudencio and the others are genetically male. But what they have inherited from Amaranta is not a general insensitivity to testosterone, like hers, but an inability to process it on to *another* hormone, dihydrotestosterone, which is responsible, in the male fetus, for shaping the male genitalia. In the absence of these, the Dominican children were born looking like girls and they were raised as girls. At puberty, though, their bodies were pervaded by a new rush of male hormones to which they, unlike Mrs. Went, were sensitive. Their male parts—which had been waiting in the wings, so to speak—finally established themselves. And nature finished the job it had earlier botched.

The children, though, did not have the psychological breakdown that the conventional wisdoms predict they should have had. This is crucial, for it *must* mean one of three things. *Either* the children were really raised as boys from the beginning. *Or* they were raised, at least, with a great deal of confusion about what gender they were, in which case one might expect them to have a disturbed sexuality as adults. *Or* they were born with a masculinized brain already established before birth in their "female" bodies, a male brain that slipped comfortably into male expressions when their bodies changed at puberty. By this argument, not only the body is sexed at birth but *also* the brain. And by this argument, nature, in gender behavior, is every bit as important as nurture. Learning, in fact, may have little to do with it.

The parents, as we have said—and Julianne Imperato-McGinley—insist that the Dominican children were raised unambiguously as girls. This means that the third hypothesis—that their brains were masculinized before birth by the main male hormone testosterone—must be taken very seriously. For the fetal effects of testosterone can not only explain the ease with which Prudencio, Mateo and the others passed into manhood, they can also provide a new sort of explanation for the gender identities of Mrs. Went and Mr. Blackwell. Mrs. Went, remember, has been from the moment of conception insensitive to testosterone and to its derivatives like dihydrotestosterone. Her body and brain were unable to respond in the womb to male hormones. The result was that she was born looking like a girl. She happily assumed a female identity, a female sexual orientation and female roles—genetic males with testicular feminization are usually very feminine, fully capable of orgasm and drawn to children and careers as housewives. Mr. Blackwell, meanwhile, *was* sensitive, as a fetus, to the testosterone his one testis was producing. And so, for all the external anomalies of his body, he took to the masculine upbringing he was offered without difficulty, and in adulthood settled for male gender identity and sexual orientation, despite the unsettling arrival of his female breasts.

This idea of the priming of the brain by testosterone can be extended, as Günter Dörner believes it should be, to what Kinsey called "primary" homosexuals—those who have had no heterosexual experience and do not respond to aversive therapy; and to transsexuals, who believe that they are imprisoned in a body of the wrong gender. For it may well be that in their case too, the brain, as it developed, was exposed in the womb to either too little or too much testosterone for the normal expression, in later life, of their genetic sex. They are not, then, in some sense "made" by the environment of their upbringing. Nor are they the product of a sexual choice, freely taken. Rather, they were *born* homosexual, in the body of one sex, but with the brain, to one degree or another, of the other sex. Dörner believes this to be true, especially of males. And he believes that society should now face the question of whether or not it wants to "cure" homosexuality in the womb by giving fetuses at risk male hormones.

Nature versus nurture: the question of free will in sex and behavior. This is one of the more intense theaters of conflict in the general war between the entrenched orthodoxies of psychology and sociology and scientists like Diane McGuinness, Camilla Benbow and Jeannette McGlone. And it is no wonder that the constant scientific debate, especially about the curious fate of the Dominican children, is often so politically charged. For it threatens, in its spreading implications, the liberationist assumptions of feminists and homosexuals. And it undercuts the idea of absolute sexual equality for all.

The case for the prenatal effects of testosterone, and other sex hormones, on gender identity and sexual behavior, however, no longer rests simply on the Dominican children. It is supported, as we shall see, by work done on both animals and humans in clinics and laboratories all over the world. And it is supported, too, by other reports of bizarre human experiences that are just beginning to creep into the scientific literature. There is the patient, seen by Richard Green of the State University of New York, who was born with ambiguous genitals and raised as a girl, but insisted throughout childhood that she was a boy—she threw away her dolls and took up trucks; she formed a male peer group; and she was extremely tomboyish. There is the patient, seen by Bob Stoller at the University of California, who looked like a girl and was raised as a girl, but who, after a decade of demanding to be treated as a boy, was told at puberty that she was right—she had undescended testicles. And there is, too, an odd corollary to the Dominican children's story. In the past five or six years, Julianne Imperato-McGinley, from her base at the Cornell University Medical School in New York, has tracked down other instances of the rare Dominican syndrome. She has found that of the children born outside the United States, all seem to have made the transition from female to male relatively comfortably. In New Guinea, in a tribe where the sexes are segregated at birth and raised separately, two "girls" had suddenly to be rushed through puberty rites and initiated as men. But in the United States such children were recognized as anomalous soon after birth, and all traces of masculinity, including a relatively enlarged clitoris, were surgically removed. These eight children were *made* into girls. They are now in their late teens and consider themselves female. But five of them, says Julianne Imperato-McGinley, may have acute psychological problems. "It is not clear that they can make it as women."

If they cannot, then the reason, quite simply, may be that their brain is the wrong sex for their body. Primed to be male, it finds itself in a female environment, encouraged in female behaviors and exposed to female hormones. And it cannot cope.

Set against all this, of course, is still the one case of the American male identical twin, surgically altered soon after birth and raised successfully, by all accounts, as his brother's sister. "You have to understand," says Milton Diamond of the University of Hawaii, "that this one case was seen, and is still seen, as being of absolutely crucial theoretical importance. Throughout the 1970s, it was written up in an enormous number of textbooks in psychology and sociology. It was included in virtually *every* book on sex differences, every book that addressed itself to the roles, in this society, of men and women. And I must say I doubted its validity from the beginning. Because of my own animal research—and that of my colleagues—not to mention everything I'd seen as a medical faculty member and as a director of the Hawaii Sexual Identity Center—*led* me to doubt it. As early as 1965 in fact I'd taken the view—based on my experience and on what was available in the scientific literature—that nature is very important in establishing an individual's gender identity. An individual's biological inheritance biases his or her future behavior. It sets limits in the womb to the degree of sexual variation any person can comfortably display."

In 1965, Milton Diamond wrote one of the first scientific papers that attempted to gather together all the existing evidence that might support the idea of the prenatal sexual differentiation of the human brain. And in following years, in a series of other papers, he went on to buttress his case. In 1979, then, he was approached by the British Broadcasting Corporation for his help in a film the producers wanted to make about the American twin. They had already talked with John Money and had secured his assistance—he was to be the leading voice in the program. And Milton Diamond, because of the views he was known for, was to be a sort of foil.

"Well, the producers went off to do their filming," he says. "And they talked to a number of psychiatrists who'd been first introduced to the child when she was about thirteen, some three years before. It was plain that the child had *not* made the successful gender switch that has been claimed for her. She was having major problems. She'd refused to talk about any difficulties she'd had in the past, and had been reluctant to talk about sexual matters at all. She had shown considerable ambivalence about her position as a female. One psychiatrist talked about 'significant psychological problems.' And others, who were familiar with the case at the time the film was being made, amplified the point. At that time, she was refusing to draw female figures, saying it was easier to draw men. She was feeling that boys had a better and easier life and wanted to be a mechanic. She looked quite masculine. And she was described as unhappy and ambivalent about her status. One psychiatrist said: 'She is having considerable difficulty in adjusting as a female. At the present time she does display certain features which make me suspicious that she will ever make the adjustment as a woman.' "

When the BBC told John Money what they had found, he simply withdrew his support and refused to be interviewed. The program, however, was aired in Britain at the beginning of 1980 without him. And since then Money has failed to address the issue in print, though his version of the case's outcome is still everywhere quoted.

This one case, Milton Diamond says, does not necessarily prove beyond a reasonable doubt his own view. To do that, he calls in evidence, as other scientists do, all the experimental research, the accidents of nature, like the Dominican children, Mrs. Went and Mr. Blackwell, that are in the scientific literature. "But it *certainly* doesn't support," he says, "the idea that gender identity and sexual orientation are dependent entirely on social *learning*—which is the one and only idea being persistently peddled in the sort of books I was talking about. This is something that everyone—scientists included—ought to face, and face squarely. All the evidence so far gathered points to the fact that the foundation—the fundamental directionality—of a man or a woman's future sexual identity is laid down in the masculine or feminine brain *before* birth. Their future behaviors are not predetermined, of course. But they are *biased*. Just as the basic elements of their social behavior, their skills and abilities."

9

THE MECHANISMS OF GENDER: THE VIEW FROM INSIDE

PICTURE TO YOURSELF again the minuscule cell that will one day be who you are. The egg has just been penetrated by one of your father's sperm. And all the other struggling, swimming sperm—still desperate for the resources of the egg—are now chemically and electrically excluded, condemned to death. The reproductive die has been cast. Inside the egg now the victorious sperm is stripped of its protein coat, and its precious freightage of a millionth of a millionth of an ounce of DNA is freed to line up with the DNA the egg carries—one on one—to form twenty-three pairs of chromosomes. When that has been done, something extraordinary happens in the chemical factory of the cell. After they have found their partners, the genes unwind and replicate themselves, making identical copies of all forty-six chromosomes. And the cell divides. Where once there was one cell, there are first two, then four, then eight, then sixteen.

With each series of divisions, the cloned cells' options are progressively cut off. They begin, as they divide, to take different paths, different directions. And so somewhere along the line there emerges one daughter cell, whose destiny it is to carve out with all its future progeny the human brain, your brain. Within it still are just forty-six chromosomes, forty-four so-called auto-somes and the two sex chromosomes—XX if you are a woman, XY if you are a man. And yet this is enough information to direct the futures of ten billion brain cells and enable you to do every-thing that you can—to walk, to talk, to play Chopin, to do sums and to appreciate the beauty of a September morning. The only thing that makes this progenitor cell—this ancestor or ances-tress of your brain—male or female is just *one* chromosome out of the forty-six, the ambivalent gift of your father's sperm, a relatively large X chromosome or the lowly Y, the smallest chro-mosome of them all.

This can hardly make for much difference, you might think. And you would be right, genetically speaking. What, after all, is *one* chromosome—the X or Y inherited from your father—against *forty-five* others, forty-four of which have been provided in equal ratio by both a male and a female, by both mother and father? Given that who we are—the way we behave and think and dream and have sex—is a complicated business, then it must be scattered over these other forty-five chromosomes as well. And surely this means that the brain of each one of us *must* have inherited bisexual potential, whatever our genetic sex. How can only one chromosome make any difference to *that*?

This is the line taken, quite understandably, by a good many people. One chromosome may be responsible, they say, for the way our bodies look and the way they function. But how on earth can it be responsible for any *other* claimed differences between men and women? In the toys they are supposed to want to play with? In the different abilities they are supposed to have? In the sexual roles they are called on to fill and the sexual tastes it is thought right for them to display? Our brains, they say, must be more *alike* at birth than *un*alike—more bisexual. It must be only *after* birth that sex differences are forced upon them.

This is a perfectly reasonable point of view, on the face of it. And, in a sense, it is a grave evolutionary problem. For if you shuffle traits from both parents, then you are indeed bound to end up with potentially bisexual creatures. What, then, can be done to preserve the great advantage sex confers—the highly various offspring it makes possible—while at the same time ensuring that the two sexes remain physically and behaviorally distinct from one another *and*—very important—interested in playing their separate parts in the business of reproduction?

There are, theoretically, two possibilities. Either gene shuffling for a larger number of the chromosomes can be abandoned. *Or* a more economical solution can be found. The X and Y chromosomes can be put in charge of an *auxiliary* system that will intervene *after conception* in the way the forty-four other chromosomes are expressed. The second option was the evolutionary path taken. From an early point in the history of organisms, substances had been developed that were capable of carrying messages to cell groups specializing in sex-cell production and switching them in either a masculine or a feminine direction. They were capable, in other words, of reaching into cells and altering the way their genes were to be expressed.

Early in the history of the life of this planet, a substance called cholesterol—now our enemy—had become involved in the preservation of separateness, the beginnings of self. It is still, for all its poor reputation, one of the most important ingredients in the building of the walls of our cells. And hormones derived from or related to it had become responsible for all primitive male and female characteristics, all the signaling necessary for the making of seeds or pollen, eggs or sperm. As evolution progressed, building new programs on old ones, three of their number—testosterone, estrogen and progesterone—came to be more and more central to the sexual and reproductive life of animals. They were elected to first and full responsibility for *all* the increasingly complex expressions of sex and sexual behavior and all the energy expenditures that had anything to do with reproduction. Controlled, ultimately, in mammals by the X and Y chromosomes, they stamped the body and the developing brain with its sexual identity and took charge of all the manifestations of maleness and femaleness.

Picture again to yourself the fertilized egg that became who you are. It is somewhere in the second month of pregnancy, and you are about fifteen millimeters from top to bottom. Up to this point, there is no difference between a male and female embryo —all the male and female parts exist in both in primitive form. At about this stage, though, the male and the female begin to take separate paths. If you are to be a female, the gonads—the two collections of germ cells—now begin to develop into ovaries. The male ducts disintegrate, while the female ducts thicken and become the womb, the Fallopian tubes and the upper two-thirds of the vagina.

If you are to be a male, however, your Y chromosome interferes with this process. It forces development in another direction. It causes, scientists believe, production of a substance called H-Y antigen, which sticks to the surface of the potentially ovarian cells and forms them into testicles. And the testicles then put out two sex hormones in sequence. One absorbs the female parts that would have become the womb and so on. And the other, testosterone, protects the male ducts, thickens the spermatic cord and, through a third hormone, dihydrotestosterone, promotes the formation of the male external genitals.

What is interesting, though, about this male sequence is that a number of things can go wrong with it—things that *always* push the development of the male back in a female direction. Strip the H-Y antigen from the cells of a developing testicle in a test tube, and the testicle will reform itself into an ovary. Remove the testicles from the fetus of an experimental animal, and it will return to the path towards femaleness. This refeminizing can be found in humans, too. A number of genetic human males who make it through to life are born apparently female,

like Mrs. Went, either internally or externally or both. The reason is either that they could not produce H-Y antigen or one of
the three hormones it sets in motion or that they were *insensitive*
to one or more of them. In other words, the target cells for these
substances were not equipped with the receptors—or special
receiving stations—that are necessary for them to be effective.
The sex hormones could not enter the cells and start the machinery that switches the expression of their genes in the required masculine direction. Sometimes this receptor deficit or
the failure in hormone production is not total, but a matter of
degree. And the result is males who are feminized to one degree
or another in later life. They have more or less enlarged breasts
or a smaller than normal penis. They are protected from acne
—there is a close association between testosterone and acne.
And they may be infertile. Jean Wilson of the University of
Texas in Dallas claims that from four to eight males out of a
thousand are born with a sexual abnormality of some sort, virtually all of them as a result of genetic defects affecting the production and recognition of testosterone.

What happens to the fetal body of humans, scientists like
Günter Dörner claim, happens at a later stage of development
to its brain. In the absence of high levels of testosterone, and
perhaps under the influence of ovarian estrogens, the brain, as
it develops, follows a female pattern. When testosterone is available to it, however, to any marked degree, then it becomes more
or less masculinized, depending—simply—on the *amount* it can
get access to. To support their case, they point, as Dörner does,
to the work done on animals.

You may not like rats, but rats are essential to science. And
in order to investigate just what effect the sex hormones have
on the brain and on sex-typical activities, drives and behaviors
in humans, science has to start with the rat. Rats are cheap. They
reproduce quickly. They are easy to manipulate. And, in a number of recently discovered ways, they are eerily like humans.
Young male rats, for example, like human male infants, are

more playful, more rough-and-tumble than young female rats. Adult males, too, have different abilities from adult females. Females are better at certain kinds of learning and they are more adventurous in the open. But males are better at figuring out mazes, just as human males are. This requires visual and spatial skills that are likely to be located in the rat's right hemisphere —as it is, again, in humans. Male rats show a tendency to favor their right hemisphere. And Marian Diamond of the University of California at Berkeley has recently found that the back of the male's right hemisphere is significantly thicker than the female's, while the surface of the female's *left* hemisphere is slightly thicker than the male's. This is exactly what one might expect to find in humans, though no one yet has. For in humans, as we have seen, females have greater language skills, predominantly in the *left* hemisphere. And males have greater visual and spatial skills—at the back of the right hemisphere.

This may not seem much to *soi-disant* lords of creation like ourselves. But it actually means a great deal. For all of these abilities and attributes in rats can be altered, in a masculine or feminine direction, by the presence or absence of hormones during the rat's so-called critical period of development. This critical period in rats is a short one and it occupies a period both before and after birth. In humans, of course, it is much longer, and it is probably *all* before birth.

The work on rats that gave rise to these discoveries began with something more simple: the effect of early exposure to hormones on adult sexual behavior. A pioneer was Roger Gorski of the University of California at Los Angeles. "We've known for a long time," he says when we visit his laboratory at UCLA, "that if we give male hormones to female rats during their critical period, they will neither ovulate nor behave sexually like normal adult females. If, as adults, they are later given testosterone, they will behave sexually as males. The reverse is also true. Deprive a male rat of male hormones and later give it estrogen, and it will behave sexually like a female. It will proffer itself and arch its back in the female posture we call lordosis.

"These changes, I originally thought, were probably due to some altered responsiveness of the system to hormones. I thought it unlikely that any *structural* differences would be found in the brain of male and female rats that might account for them. But then various things happened. First, Günter Dörner found sex differences in the nuclear size of nerve cells in the hypothalamus. Then Geoffrey Raisman and Pat Field in England—in a wonderfully elegant and painstaking study—found sex-hormone-dependent differences in the way the nerve cells were *wired*—work that was subsequently confirmed for the hypothalamus and another area of the brain by William Greenough of the University of Illinois. And then Fernando Nottebohm of the Rockefeller University found *major* differences in the brains of songbirds. That *really* set us looking."

In 1976, Fernando Nottebohm and Arthur Arnold—now a colleague of Gorski's at UCLA—announced that they had found two gaggles of nerve cells in the brains of canaries that were three and four times larger in the male than in the female. In canaries, it is the male—not the female—which sings. And they showed that these centers were responsible for the organization of the male's song, *which is both learned and left-hemisphere dominant, just as human language is.* They also showed that the sex hormones were dramatically involved in the formation of these centers and in song itself. For when adult female canaries were given testosterone, not only did their two centers grow but they also started, falteringly, to sing.

Here was the first real connection between the sex hormones, brain structure and behavior. And it led Nottebohm, a courtly, soft-spoken man, to predict two things: first, that whenever the male and female of a species differ in the development of a skill, a correspondingly greater or smaller amount of brain space will be given over to the neural organization of that skill; and second, that the skill and the brain space allotted to it will be dictated by the sex hormones.

This was enough for Roger Gorski and his coworkers. They quickly went hunting for a similar gaggle of cells, or nucleus, in an area of the rat hypothalamus that they knew to be involved in the regulation of reproduction. They soon found what they were after. "We too discovered," says Roger Gorski, "a nucleus —we call it the sexually dimorphic nucleus—which is larger, five to seven times larger, in the male than it is in the female. We couldn't alter this difference by manipulating hormone levels in adulthood, as Fernando Nottebohm could in canaries. But we *could* do so by manipulating them during the rat's critical period, at around the time of birth. Females that we masculinized during this time had a much larger nucleus than normal females. And castrated males had a much *smaller* nucleus than normal males. The size of the nucleus, in other words—just like adult sexual behavior—depends on the hormonal environment to which the brain is exposed during the critical period. And this seems to be true even when it's taken *out* of the brain. Dominique Toran-Allerand, working with tissue from fetal mice at Columbia University, has put the general region that contains this center into culture in the lab. And she's found that it develops differently. The nerve cells *grow* differently, depending on whether masculinizing hormones are present or not. The genetic sex of the tissue, like the genetic sex of our animals," he concludes, "is *immaterial.* It's the sex hormones that are important."

In late 1981, Gorski announced that he and his group had succeeded in transplanting the sexually dimorphic nucleus from male to female rat brains shortly after birth. And they had succeeded in transferring *with* it a later increase in the expression of male sexual behavior. Here again, then, is another strong connection between sex hormones, brain development, brain structure and behavior. And the connections go on. Bruce McEwen, a remarkable neurobiologist at the Rockefeller University, has discovered sex hormone receptors during the critical period in precisely those areas of rat brain which might be thought to organize differences in behavior *other* than sexual— maze running, avoidance learning and so on. And what Gorski has found in rats and Nottebohm and Arnold have found in birds, a scientist we have met before—Bob Goy—has begun to find in a species much closer to us: rhesus monkeys.

When you walk down the corridors of the Regional Primate Research Center at the University of Wisconsin in Madison, the first thing that strikes you is that rhesus monkeys are indeed a lot like ourselves. Their features are in the right place. They are outgoing and energetic. And they are socially complex: playing with each other, grooming each other, dominating one another and all too ready to demote or ostracize a member of the troop who doesn't meet collective expectations. The infants, housed on the fifth floor in groups of five or six mothers, are especially attractive. They careen around their cages noisily, leaping from foothold to handhold, stopping only to romp briefly together and mount both each other and their mother in a sociable panto-mime of sex.

It took Bob Goy five years, when he first came to Madison, to find a way of housing his rhesus monkeys in socially unstressful conditions like these—conditions more or less like the wild, in which their behavior would be natural. And even then he found it virtually impossible to study the effects of sex hormones on adult sexual behavior, as Gorski was doing in rats and he himself had earlier done in guinea pigs. "In long-living, group-dwelling, seasonally breeding animals like rhesus monkeys," he says, "there are just too many social variables that you'd have to take into account, variables we know little about."

What Goy *has* been able to study, though, is the effects of sex hormones on various sorts of sex-*typical* behavior. "We've done some work on dominance, for example," he says, arched over a cup of coffee in his director's office. "Males usually occupy the dominant position in a troop. But we've shown that females whose mothers were given testosterone during pregnancy are much more likely to be the dominant members in a mixed troop, as adults, than are other, untreated females. This effect of prena-tal testosterone—I'm just now beginning to work on estrogen effects—can *also* be seen in the way infant and juvenile rhesus monkeys interact. And that's what I've mainly been working on."

There are four main ways in which male rhesuses at young ages differ in their behavior from females. They initiate play more often. They roughhouse more often. They mount their peers—of both sexes—more often. And they mount their mothers much more often than females do. Bob Goy and his coworkers, however, can produce a male-typical frequency of *all* these behaviors in young females by giving their pregnant mothers thigh injections of testosterone or dihydrotestosterone for various periods of time during the critical period of development which, in rhesus monkeys, is before birth, as it is in us. These females will play rough and so on.

"Now many of these females," Bob Goy says, "are born with genitals that have been masculinized to one degree or another —there's clearly a critical prenatal period for the formation of the genitals. But there's *also* a critical period—much longer and much harder to pinpoint—for every one of these sex-specific behaviors: a period in which the sex hormones affect every single one of them. What's so fascinating, you see, is that they don't all come in one bundle. We can actually separate them out. We can give androgen injections for quite a *short* period of time, for example, and females will mount their mothers more often—but not their peers. Or we can change the period over which we give the injections and get females who mount their peers more often or initiate play more often or roughhouse more often, but don't do all three at the same time. We can even separate out—and I think this is *amazing*—the mounting of male and female peers. You have to understand that, under ordinary circumstances, young male rhesuses mount their peers at random. If there are equal numbers of males and females in a group, then they'll mount equal numbers. What we've recently found, though, is that if we expose male fetuses to additional male hormones for a really short period of time in early pregnancy, then they'll only mount female peers. No other male behavior is affected.

"Now what might this mean? Well, it suggests—in these pri-

mates, at any rate—that the individual traits that make up masculinity are separately controlled by the sex hormones over
time. The masculinization of the brain, which takes place before
birth, in other words, is a slow, complicated, more-or-less process. You get sexist, tooth-and-claw males; you get less 'masculine' ones. This doesn't seem to be true of feminization. Feminization is not a matter of *degree* in the same way. In fact, there are
no feminine traits that we can identify and then suppress by
exposing the fetus to hormones. And furthermore, there are no
feminine traits that are not common to both sexes. Our altered
females, you see, can be masculinized, *but they cannot defeminized.*
They are simply females who've had a male pattern hormonally
superimposed on them. The same rule applies to ordinary
males. The essential femaleness of the species remains at their
core—much, much better protected and guaranteed than their
maleness. And I think there's a reason. In males, nature can
afford a wide variation. But females bear children, and nature
needs every one of them she can get. So the result is what we
see, I think, in both rhesus monkeys and humans. The basic
natural form of both is the female."

This may not be quite the whole story. For some evidence
suggests that femaleness—and the feminization of the brain—
may *also* be a matter of degree, though to a far smaller extent
than maleness. Scientists point to the difference between "exaggeratedly feminine" Turner's women and women who have had
normal levels of ovarian hormones during fetal life. The brain,
they say, may take *positive* steps towards femaleness, even
though the steps taken are smaller and much better secured than
the steps the male has to take towards maleness.

This, however, is some of the evidence Günter Dörner refers
to when he talks about "the work done on animals." Masculinizing hormones, he says, have been shown to affect the size,
growth and interconnections of nerve cells in different parts of
the developing brain of animals. They have also been shown to
organize during the critical period various sorts of skill and

sex-related behavior. Some of these behaviors appear early in life, before puberty. But others require the new rush of hormones at puberty for their full and final expression, just as the musculature, energy distribution, skeletal structure and secondary sexual characteristics of human males and females do. Part of this subset of behaviors in animals is the way they approach sex, the sort of sexual behavior they show. And in both males and females it is entirely dependent on the influence of hormones in early life. The same must be true of humans, he says. Certain skills, abilities and behaviors are organized in the human fetus before it is born, including the directionality of his or her future sex life. "This is demonstrably true in animals," he says one night in Cambridge. "And I think it's becoming clearer and clearer from clinical work done on human patients. The evidence, which is now beginning to come in from clinics all over the world," he says before disappearing into the darkness, "supports me."

10
COMING FULL CIRCLE

HOW CAN ONE argue from rats, birds and monkeys to humans? "One can't," say some scientists. "One can," other scientists say cautiously, believing, above all, in the economy of nature. They point to what we know about humans from the accidents of nature and the sometimes tragic mistakes of man. They point, inevitably, to CAH women.

With CAH women we come full circle, to take the results of work done with animals back into the human brain, as Günter Dörner has done. CAH is congenital adrenal hyperplasia, a disorder of the adrenal glands, which sit just above the kidneys and are responsible for our reactions to stress, among other things. One of their most important products is the hormone cortisol. And in individuals with CAH something goes wrong, starting in the womb, with the chemical pathway by which it is synthesized. Because of a genetic defect, cortisol is no longer the end product. Instead, during the critical period, as the fetus is developing, large quantities of testosterone are made.

In boys this has little obvious effect. But in girls it has the effect of masculinizing, to one degree or another, their external genitals, as is the case in Bob Goy's monkeys. Nowadays, the condition is usually recognized at birth and the female babies are surgically altered, if necessary, and are given cortisone-replacement treatment for the rest of their lives.

Their behavior, though, science is finding out, has already been pushed in a masculine direction. And this is not alterable by surgery or cortisone treatment, however soon after birth these are applied. The male hormone, in other words, has had its effect on their behavior *before birth,* as in Bob Goy's monkeys. And *after* birth this effect can be measured. According to a series of studies begun in the late 1960s by John Money of Johns Hopkins University and Anke A. Ehrhardt, now at Columbia University and the New York State Psychiatric Institute, CAH girls are more "tomboyish" than their female peers. They are athletic and highly energetic. They prefer boys as playmates, and they are quick to involve themselves in organized, competitive group sports. In John Money's words: "They join in boys' neighborhood football, baseball and/or basketball games, often as the only girl."

Some of this behavior has been explained by saying that CAH girls expend energy in a way that has been masculinized: males, and maybe CAH females, have bigger lungs and hearts and a higher oxygen consumption than normal females. But there are *other* differences that cannot be explained this way. For CAH girls *also* prefer toy guns and cars to dolls. They prefer functional to traditionally feminine clothing. And they prefer playing cowboys and Indians to playing house, career-rehearsal games to fantasizing about marriage and infant care. They show little enthusiasm for babies and baby-sitting and little interest in stereotypical girls' activities. Their puberty is often later than other girls', though it is normal because of the cortisone treatment. And they do not become as quickly attracted to the idea of romance and dating with the opposite sex. Later in life, CAH women seem to be attracted, in some degree, to other women. As a group they may show a higher incidence than is statistically usual of bisexuality and even homosexuality—if not in practice, then, at any rate, in erotic fancy.

All of this is vividly reminiscent not only of Bob Goy's monkeys but also of Roger Gorski's rats. "But," says Anke A. Ehrhardt of the New York State Psychiatric Institute, "we have to be *extremely* cautious about this. I find the jump that Günter Dörner makes from animals to humans absolutely unacceptable. These things, after all, are just trends. They're not found in every individual. And in the case of bisexuality, and what may be bisexual and homosexual impulses, we don't even know if these are any more common in CAH women than in the rest of the population. We don't know enough. This is so hard for most people to understand. They think in terms of a hard and fast distinction between what is biologically determined and what is socially determined—nature versus nurture. And all these things must interact with each other. How one behaves, after all, depends a great deal on whether one's behavior is frowned on or not. Homosexuality and bisexuality are not as frowned on as they once were. And so we find these inclinations in CAH women, just as we *might* find them in any sampling of women as a whole. As for tomboyism—well, yes, it's true that CAH girls are *significantly* more tomboyish than a population of girls matched for age, background and so on. But one, tomboyism is perfectly socially acceptable in this society. And two, not every CAH girl is a tomboy. It's not biologically guaranteed."

Anke A. Ehrhardt is a professor of clinical psychology in the Department of Psychiatry at Columbia University, and a very careful scientist. A precise, smiling woman in her forties, she is well aware of the controversy that surrounds her field. She is quick to maintain the importance of learning in the human species. And she discountenances any idea that our sexual and social behavior can be *dictated* by the hormonal environment in the womb.

Nevertheless, for more than a decade now, she has been investigating, more recently with Heino Meyer-Bahlburg, just *what* effect this environment may have. As well as looking at CAH individuals, she has also studied an entirely different population —children whose mothers were given hormones to maintain their pregnancies. This was a habit that began in the 1950s with science's increasing ability to manipulate natural hormones and synthesize new ones. And over a period of thirty years various versions of these hormones were routinely dispensed, not only to women who risked, for one reason or another, the spontaneous abortion of miscarriage, but also to women who had no reason to need science's help at all. It has been estimated that during a thirty-year period ten million women in the United States alone were prescribed hormones during pregnancy.

The most infamous of these hormones was diethylstilbestrol (DES), which in 1971 was linked to genital cancer in the young women who were exposed to it in the womb. It has since been shown to have caused in a number of men decreased penis size, undescended testicles and low sperm count. But DES was only one of the hormones used. Some were estrogens—hormones related to estradiol—given either in a natural form or in a synthetic version like DES. But others belonged to a group of hormones called progestogens. These hormones were, again, either natural (plant- or animal-derived) or synthetic (laboratory-made), and fell into two main categories: some were progesterone-based, and some were androgen-based—they were closely related to testosterone.

The children born after their mothers were treated with these substances differ from controls, as far as can be seen, *only* in the circulating sex hormones they were exposed to in the womb. And Ehrhardt and Meyer-Bahlburg—and groups headed by June Reinisch, now director of the Kinsey Institute, and Richard Green of the State University of New York at Stony Brook, among others—have tried to tease out their effects. The case is clearest for the progestogens. Girls exposed to androgen-based progestogens seem very similar to CAH girls—more tomboyish and energetic than usual and often born with subtly masculinized genitals. Boys *also* seem more energetic and aggressive than their peers, as CAH boys do. ("In my original study," says June

Reinisch, "the results were so striking that I was almost afraid to publish them.") The reverse, however, seems to be true of progesterone-based progestogens, whether given alone or in combination with estrogens. These hormones seem to have had a *demasculinizing* effect. Boys exposed to them appear as a group to be *less* aggressive and assertive than their peers. They show poorer athletic coordination and what one study calls "lowered masculine interests." The picture is similar in girls. They are also less active, less verbally aggressive and less given to energetic play. They express a preference for female—rather than male—friends. And they show an increased interest in feminine clothing, hairdo, cosmetics and children. Whether this will hold true for males and females exposed to estrogens like DES is not yet clear—the work hasn't been done. But preliminary research suggests that they are, as a group, less independent and self-assertive than normal. DES males have been described as less aggressive and more nurturant. And DES females, according to one study, seem to be more left-hemisphere dependent than the sisters they were tested with.

All of the evidence that is in to date clearly shows that in humans as well as monkeys the sex hormones—operating in the womb on the developing brain—are responsible for what Ehrhardt cautiously calls "a sort of pretuning of the personality." Bob Goy is more forthright. "The sex hormones organize the social demeanor of the sexes, their orientation to social problems and the way they go about solving them," he says. One question, however, remains. To what extent do they *also* organize gender identity and the sexual and reproductive behavior the two human genders show after puberty?

The accidents of man—the children exposed to sex hormones in the womb—offer no very clear evidence either way, though there is some connection between progesterone-based progestogens and a low sex drive and erection failure in men, and another possible correlation between DES, low fertility and menstruation failure in women. For better evidence we have to go back to the accidents of nature, as Günter Dörner does. He points to the cases of the American identical twin, the genetic males with the testicular feminization syndrome and the girl-boys with the Dominican syndrome. And he points to another group, human homosexuals and transsexuals—the result, he believes, of *another* sort of accident, an accident of culture: stress. The day after our first Cambridge meeting with Dörner, we meet him at the conference proper to talk with him about his presumption that homosexuals are born rather than made by the environment and by free choice.

"Well," he says, "I saw in rats, as others had, that they could be made homosexual if deprived of testosterone during the critical period of brain differentiation. And I had the idea of giving such homosexual male rats in adulthood an injection of estrogen, arguing that if their brain was indeed feminized, then it would respond as if to a signal from a nonexistent ovary, with a surge of ovulation-inducing hormone, the so-called luteinizing hormone, LH. And they did so. Their brains were indeed feminized, and this was a good way of measuring it. We then applied this technique to human male homosexuals and we found the same thing. Their brains responded with this delayed hormone surge while the brains of heterosexual males did not. It looked as if their brains too had been, at least in part, feminized.

"During this time, Ingeborg Ward at Villanova University in Pennsylvania had been showing that if you subjected pregnant female rats to stress, then their male offspring would have extremely low levels of testosterone at birth and would exhibit this feminized and demasculinized sexual behavior in adulthood— they would become bisexual or homosexual. Well, we repeated her experiments. And then we looked at the human population to see if there was a connection between prenatal stress and male homosexuality. First we looked at the records, to see whether more homosexuals had been born during the stressful period of World War II than had been born either before or after it. And we found that this was correct. There was a very high peak in 1944 and 1945, for example. And then we interviewed a hundred bi- or homosexual men, matched with a hundred heterosexual men, and as many of their mothers as was feasible. What we wanted to know about was the level of stress experienced during pregnancy and prenatal life. Well, we found a *significantly* increased incidence of maternal stress in the bisexual and, in particular, the homosexual population. About a third of the homosexual men and their mothers reported having been exposed to severe maternal stress—such as bereavement, rape or severe anxiety. And about another third reported moderate stress. This wasn't true of the heterosexual men. None of them reported severe stress. And only ten percent reported even moderate stress.

"As a result of this," he says patiently, aware of the people who do not agree with him, "and as a result of studies done in my laboratory going back to 1964, I am forced to conclude that male homosexuality is the result of permanent neurochemical changes in the hypothalamus effected by reduced levels of testosterone during fetal life. This produces a feminization of the brain which is activated, as far as sexual behavior is concerned, at puberty. One risk factor—clearly, I think—is stress, which causes the production of substances in the adrenal gland that depress testosterone levels in the male fetus. And there may be other factors. Whatever they are, though, they permanently alter the neural circuitry of the brain, the nerve pathways that are controlled by the *local* hormones, the neurotransmitters— particularly serotonin, dopamine and norepinephrine. These are three of the substances by which individual nerve cells in different parts of the brain communicate with one another across the tiny gap between them called the synapse. And this particular threesome seem to be the local mediators of the effects the sex hormones have on brain cells, and on behavior, throughout life.

"Now it's possible to show that the levels of these neurotransmitters are altered quite dramatically in different areas of the brain as a result of prenatal stress, in both male and female rats. Lorraine Herrenkohl at Temple University in Philadelphia, for example, has recently demonstrated that not only the male but also the *female* offspring of prenatally stressed mothers have both altered levels of some of these neurotransmitters as adults *and* a poor reproductive capability. Their estrus cycle is irregular. Their sexual receptivity is diminished. They have difficulty becoming pregnant. They spontaneously abort more often than normal females. And they often fail to produce enough milk for their offspring."

We ask Dörner whether he thinks prenatal stress might *also* be involved in human lesbianism. "There's no evidence so far that *stress* is involved," he says. "But there's some evidence that altered levels of testosterone are, although the evidence is indirect. Lesbians and female-to-male transsexuals seem to have abnormal levels, at least in part, of testosterone and estradiol. And if we give them estrogen, their luteinizing-hormone response is lower than that of heterosexual women, suggesting that their brains have been masculinized in some way. The cognitive patterns of their brain, too, may be somewhere intermediate between heterosexual men and heterosexual women. And their body build, on the basis of certain measurements, may be closer to that of a man's. It is also possible," he says slowly, "that they age rather faster than normal women do—rather like men."

In late 1981, three scientists associated with the Alfred C. Kinsey Institute for Sex Research at Indiana University published a report that goes some way to support Günter Dörner's conviction. The report, based on long interviews with 979 homosexuals and 477 heterosexuals, announced that no psychological or environmental variables could be found to account for either male or female homosexuality. Instead, said the researchers: *"Homosexuality may arise from a biological precursor that parents cannot control."*

Anke A. Ehrhardt is still not impressed. "I think Dörner has too much riding on his theory," she says. "Some of the studies he refers to are inadequate. And," she continues briskly, "until there are a series of well-designed, well-controlled studies on humans, I will remain intensely skeptical of the view that learning and the environment play only a small role in who people are and how they behave." She herself, as well as conducting the first major study of DES men and women, is also investigating what she sees as the real story of hormone levels in lesbians.

Roger Gorski, however, is not so sure. "I think," he says carefully, "in the work Dörner is doing, he's taking a great step forward. And he could give us a solid answer as to whether or not there's a dependence on hormones in human sexual behavior. I think the verdict's not in yet. But what he's saying is extraordinarily provocative at every level. You know, for example, that women in our society live longer than men, though it's still not clear why. Dörner says that female rats *also* live longer and that male rats deprived of male hormones during their critical period of development live the same length of time as females. Well . . ."

PART FOUR

THE BRAIN AND THE BODY: A SEPARATE INHERITANCE

A DIFFERENT CHEMISTRY

IF YOU WANT to live a long time, there are a number of things you can do. You can surround yourself with young virgins and breathe in their emanations. Or you can inject yourself with the glandular extracts of young animals. You can subsist on yogurt and kelp and yeast. Or—as the statistics buried in a comprehensive 1964 report suggest—you can get a college degree, get married, sleep no more and no less than seven hours a night and eat fried foods at least fifteen times a week. All of these things you can try. But if you want a guarantee that any of them are going to work, then there's something else you ought to have arranged already. You ought to have made sure that you were born a woman. Or, if born a man, you ought to have had your testicles removed as early as possible. In 1969, James Hamilton and Gordon Mestler of the Downstate Medical Center in New York showed that only castrated men, on average, lived as long as women. But for every year after birth that castration was delayed, there was a corresponding shrinkage in life span of about three months and eleven days.

What does all this have to do with? The sex hormones. If you

135

are a man, after all, there is no essential *genetic* difference between you and a castrate—you are both XY males. And there is only one small genetic difference between you and the woman who is probably going to outlive you: instead of a Y, her second chromosome is an X. There *is,* however, a big difference between the three of you in the sex hormones you can make from cholesterol. And there *is* a big difference between the three of you in the disorders and diseases to which you are likely to be prey. If you are a man and your production of testosterone is intact, then your immune system, first of all, is comparatively poor. You are less well protected against the sea of viruses and bacteria in which we swim. And you are much more likely to be subject to heart disease and heart attack. But if you are a woman producing estrogens and only a small amount of testosterone *or* a man who has lost his testosterone's main sites of production, then you will have few heart attacks. You will be protected against a whole array of diseases from infantile diarrhea and childhood leukemia to Legionnaire's disease and the attacks of the so-called slow-acting viruses. And you will live longer.

If you assumed that a shorter life was simply the product of the tolls taken by the environment, then you were wrong. It is the result of fundamental differences between men and women —and castrates. And this is just the beginning . . .

In the back pages of the newspapers these days, there is almost always something amazing. GENE FOUND FOR DEPRESSION. CRIMINAL BEHAVIOR THOUGHT TO BE INHERITED. MURDERESS ACQUITTED: PSYCHIATRIST POINTS TO PREMENSTRUAL TENSION. BRAIN CHEMICAL TIED TO SCHIZOPHRENIA. And: IS THERE A GENE FOR MATH?

We read these things, but they come separately. We do not see how they hang together. And so we fail to see, buried in these small headlines, a revolution going on—a revolution that will soon change, once and for all, the way we think about human behavior. This revolution involves everything we have discussed: evolution, genes, sex hormones, abilities—the separate inheritances of men and women—and something more, the immune system and the chemistry of the brain. And it takes us far out, to the leading edge of the science of men and women. Right at the edge there are few landmarks, few things known for sure. But such landmarks as there are have already prompted one scientist to say, with some glee: "This research has probably set back psychiatry a hundred years." And they have encouraged another to suggest: "Culture, personality and brain chemistry are really the same. They are just different ways of viewing the same thing."

What does this mean for men and women? It means that at precisely the time we are most avidly rushing to psychother-apists and other doctors of the spirit, science is quietly announc-ing that the game is off, a new die is cast, the rules have changed. We are not the purely "psychological" creatures we thought we were, fraught with "psychological" problems which, if they are to be cured, demand "psychological" understanding. Instead, we are the creatures, to an extent hitherto unimagined, of *biologi-cal* forces. Our responses to stress, our mood disorders, our madness and, perhaps, even our crime are biological in origin and biological in expression—in the brain. And this goes not only for the *major* problems that bedevil society: the one percent of people who suffer from schizophrenia; the five percent who are crippled by illnesses of mood; the two percent who commit almost all the crime and the billions and billions of dollars these cost each year. It *also* goes for the minor problems that bedevil our families and our relationships: the mood swings of parents; the hyperactivity and aggressiveness of children; the come-and-go depressions of women and the irritability and instability of men. At the mysterious heart of all these things lies biology, set up by the genes, mediated by the sex hormones and expressed in a different chemistry in the ultimate home of our personality, our brain.

"A different chemistry." This is the subject of the latest chap-ter in the story of men and women, the "different chemistry" that circumscribes our personality and predisposes us, from the beginning, to different disabilities, disorders and illnesses. For the moment, then, forget psychology—all the assumptions you have acquired about a mind that you inhabit and that you alone can control. Ignore, for a moment, the effects of the environment on who you are and the way you behave. Fix your gaze, instead, on the biological and genetic core of yourself, as a member of one sex of the human species—differently made, differently programmed, differently wired and with a different chemical design—differently "juiced," as one scientist has put it. For if you do, you will begin to see why the small headlines of the newspapers combine into a radically new view of men and women. You will begin to see the causes of many of the misunderstandings and tensions between men and women. And you will begin to see—as science is just beginning to see—why the bewildering strengths and weaknesses of each one of us, man and woman, seem to come packaged together. Why a woman's immune system is superior to a man's, but more likely to attack the body it is supposed to protect. Why men, in general, are superior in math reasoning and visual-spatial skills but are much more likely to be sexual deviants and psychopaths. Why women are strong in areas of communication but are preferentially attacked by phobias and depression. And why there are more males at both ends of the intellectual spectrum, more retardates but also more geniuses.

If you think that psychiatrists, psychologists and all those who have made a professional commitment to the effects of the environment will be horrified by this altered gaze of yours, you are right. But if you think that their spiritual father, Sigmund Freud, would be equally horrified, then you are wrong. Freud treated all sorts of personalities and disorders, among them psychosomatic illnesses, schizophrenia, hysteria and depression. He said many times that one day, for all his theories, a "constitutional predisposition" would be found to be responsible for them. "A special chemism," he predicted, would be discovered at their heart. And so it has been. By inference and indirection, a "special chemism"—of brain, hormones and immune system—has been found at the core of our nature as men and women. And we are at the beginning of a road through this "chemism" that will lead us to a more detailed explanation of why we are differently gifted, differently protected and differently at risk. For the complete story you will have to wait twenty years or so; twenty years marked—if the present signs are anything to go by—by controversy, battle, arguments about free will and radical new approaches to education, health and the treatment of violence, mood and madness. In the meantime, here are the landmarks and the paths that science is tracing between them.

Let us start with heart disease and heart attacks. Forty million Americans have some form of heart disease, and this year about one and a half million will have a heart attack. The majority in both categories are men. The usual, and usually male, explanation for this is: "That's the environment. That's stress. Wait until the same number of women go out into the world and start having to pull the same weight that men do. They'll start suffering the effects of stress soon enough, and with the same results."

This is a common assumption. And it is almost certainly untrue. The connections between the stresses of the brain and the problems of the heart are not at all well understood—this is something that has to be continuously borne in mind, that science knows not a lot, but very little. From what science *does* know, however, three things stand out. First, working women are healthier, in general, than their nonworking sisters. Second, they are protected against the most common form of heart disease by their primary sex hormones, the estrogens. And third, they seem to respond to stress—both chemically and behaviorally—quite differently from men.

Human responses to stress are mediated by a group of brain structures, gathered around and including the hypothalamus, called the limbic system. The limbic system is known to control emotion and what, as we've said scientists fondly call "the four Fs"—feeding, fleeing, fighting and sex. And it directs the body's immediate responses to challenge and danger. When a source of danger is recognized in the environment—a speeding truck, a squealing of brakes, a gunshot—the body is immediately put into overdrive in two main ways. Reacting to incoming information, the hypothalamus bids up from the pituitary—the gland slung just beneath it—a hormone which speeds through the circulation to the adrenal glands with a message to produce cortisol and adrenalin (now usually called epinephrine). These two substances in turn travel through the circulation to the brain and various organs. They arouse the brain and prepare it for fight or flight. They mobilize energy in the form of sugar. And they divert blood from the viscera to the muscles. At the same time, there is a storm of activity in the sympathetic nervous system. Impulses, carried by the same messenger, epinephrine, and by its close relative, norepinephrine, race between the nerve cells towards the heart and other major organs. Heart rate and respiration are instantly increased; there is a greater intake of oxygen and a faster clearance of wastes. Blood pressure goes up. Digestion decreases. The palms sweat; the hair stands on end. And the body is prepared for a massive burst of energy, should it be needed. If it is, the brain has already been alerted, the body primed. And if it is not, then the adrenal glands can be signaled to stop production and the parasympathetic nervous system can come into its own and reestablish the body's normal state. Operating through its own neurotransmitter, acetylcholine, it dampens the system down, depressing the heartbeat and promoting digestion and secretion. The parasympathetic nervous system must be in good working order if the organs are to be protected from strain.

Now in human stress the hormonal mechanisms by which the body and brain communicate with one another to coordinate the fight-flight response seem to be more or less continuously activated. A little stress isn't bad for you—it is a necessary part of life and it may, indeed, be pleasurable. In the long term, though, it can have several unpleasant effects. It can make the body less resistant to infections and, conceivably, to certain forms of cancer. (Stress in rats reduces their resistance to viruses and parasites; in humans a high level of cortisol has been associated with a deficiency of the branch of the immune system that defends against foreign cells and tumors.) It can also, of course, cause heart problems, because the heart muscle, among other things, is forced to work too hard. And it can so excite a center high in the brain that the heart is sent by it into a *fatal* overdrive—a fibrillation, a full-blown attack. Whether these things happen or not seems to depend on the individual's genetic makeup.

But it also depends on gender. So-called Type A people, who have a chronic urgency about time and are hard-driving, competitive, extroverted and aggressive, are known to be particularly at risk from the damaging effects of stress. But it is now beginning to appear that this is true only of Type A *males.* Studies in Sweden and America have recently shown that Type A females, when solving work-related problems, simply do not show the increase in heart rate, blood pressure and cortisol- and norepinephrine-flow that Type A males do. They also do not produce as much epinephrine (adrenalin). Since epinephrine is known to cause coagulation of the blood, Type A women may be better protected against blood clotting, one element in heart failure. (Aspirin—and this may be related—acts as an anticoagulant in men, but not in women.) But even if they do not have this sort of protection, they still do not have as many heart problems as Type A males, even when their overall health picture is the same.

This does not mean, of course, that Type A women—and women in general—are not *responsive* to stress. It simply means that their chemistry is different in some way. Women in general seem to find different things stressful. And they seem to react in a different way to the stress in their environment. If there is one word that can sum up this difference in their makeup, it is emotion. Women tend to be put into stress by the emotional coloration of their lives—not paper problems, but people and communication problems. And when they experience setback, failure and emotional pressure, they do not go into overdrive in the way that men do. They respond emotionally or fall back into depression—which, though sometimes crippling, causes less wear and tear on the body.

The next question, naturally, is: *Why* should there be this overall difference? And the answer, again, almost certainly lies in the evolutionary pressures that affected the development of men and women. Men, the hunters and competitors for sex—the gamblers—were more likely to have benefited from elaborate and fast-acting stress mechanisms in the presence of danger. And women, the nurturers and centers of social groups, were more likely to have benefited from an *emotional* responsiveness to their environment. Depression and the effects of continuous stress may be the different prices they pay for these legacies: an integral part of our maleness and femaleness.

That this is true—at any rate for males—is suggested, finally, by a few pieces of evidence. Scientists working with male laboratory animals have shown that dominance—sexual success and the successful defense and maintenance of a defined territory—is associated with high blood pressure and hardening of the arteries, telltale signs, in humans at least, of the effects of stress. But they have also found that the animals at the top of the heap have high levels of testosterone, just as Type A human males have when they confront the tests scientists give them. The plot thickens. For it is testosterone that makes hardening of the arteries such a problem in human males. It causes the production of a liver protein that ties up cholesterol in the arteries' linings. (A woman's estrogen orders up a protein that disperses cholesterol much more efficiently.) And deposits of fat called plaques are formed. The bigger these plaques, the narrower the arteries, and that much harder the job the heart has in pumping. The heart may fail, stripped of its epinephrine and norepinephrine receptors because of overexertion. Or a blood clot may cause a major obstruction, leading to embolism or stroke.

Findings of this sort are, again, only landmarks in an otherwise empty landscape. But they make it plain that, in stress, behavior, emotion, genes, sex hormones, neurotransmitters, the body and brain are all interlinked. And they point the way toward the discovery of a more general connection between emotion and disease, the brain and the immune system. For the moment, there are only a few curious straws in the wind in this area. Laboratory animals, for example, do not get the hardening of the arteries that scientists try to inflict on them if they are handled a lot—if they are loved. And married people, especially men, are generally happier and healthier than unmarried ones. They have less heart disease. A study recently done at Mount Sinai Hospital in New York showed that husbands who had lost their wives to cancer suffered major changes for the worse in the cells of their immune system.

Having left the men among you deeply worried about an area in which you seem to be at a disadvantage, it is time for us to turn the tables and look at a disorder that is the flip side of the male response to stress—depression. Every year forty million Americans suffer from depression and related illnesses of mood. Two-thirds of them are women. The usual, and usually female, explanation for this is: "Girls are taught from the beginning not to express their anger. So they turn their anger inward on themselves. When they become adults, they find themselves in a male-ordered and male-dominated society. Men fail to give them what they want. And they further stifle and ignore women's capability and emotional subtlety. It's no wonder, then, that women, as adults in this society, are self-destructive and depressed."

This explanation sounds rational enough. And it is probably, in part, true; much of the depression seen in women is what is called *reactive* depression, a response to life events, a response to the stress of a situation. But it still does not explain why women respond in *this* particular way to stress rather than responding the way men do. Why are women protected against the *overdrive* of stress but not against a group of disorders that disastrously affect mood, movement, appetite, sleep and sex drive? The argument from the environment cannot fully explain this. Nor can it explain why, though nothing on the surface of a woman's life is wrong, she can suddenly be sent into an incapacitating, spiraling tailspin downward that requires hospitalization. Psychological explanations of this sort of depression—*vital* depression, which afflicts women five or six times more often than men—are useless. Psychological treatment of it is at best a waste of money and a waste of time; women are likely to become even more entrenched in their despair. No, the only way to understand vital depression and other disorders that seem to be related—premenstrual tension, post-partum depression, phobias, obesity, anorexia and reactive depression—is through women's chemistry: the interaction of genes, body, brain, sex hormones and neurotransmitters.

Let us start again with vital depression, which has many of the features of reactive depression: a disturbance in the sleep cycle and in patterns of dreaming and nondreaming sleep; an inability to experience pleasure; a disruption of appetite; lethargy; and a loss of libido and, often, menstruation. The first evidence that this is not environmentally caused comes from genetic studies. In identical twins, for example, when one twin suffers from vital depression, there is a fifty to eighty percent chance of the other twin *also* contracting it. People with vital depression are fourteen times more likely to have relatives with mood disorders of a similar kind than the general population. And work done in Belgium has shown that adopted children with vital depression are more likely to have that depression in common with their *real* parents rather than their adoptive parents.

This immediately suggests, of course, a *biochemical* abnormality of some sort in depressive patients. And indeed there is now plenty of evidence that in vital depression—almost certainly because of a genetic predisposition—something has gone *chemically* wrong with the same pathways and structures in females that mediate the male's reaction to stress. First of all, patients with depression produce large amounts of cortisol in their adrenal glands. This seems to interfere with a center in the brain stem, governed by the neurotransmitter serotonin, that controls sleep. They also produce less norepinephrine than is normal.

And their comparative lack of norepinephrine has considerable consequences. For it affects on a *continuous* basis various areas deep in the brain where norepinephrine is active. It affects active, dreaming sleep (brain stem), the experience of pleasure and reward (locus ceruleus) and appetite (hypothalamus). And it also seems to affect the way the hypothalamus—by way of the pituitary beneath it—controls from long distance the production of the adrenal stress hormones, especially cortisol.

In depressed people, in other words, the stress loop that interconnects the adrenal glands, brain, hypothalamus, pituitary and back to the adrenal glands has been biochemically pushed out of kilter. And the result is an inappropriate and continuous chemical stress response. The evidence that this is so—and it has to be remembered again that science knows very little about mental disorders like depression—comes from the usual three main sources: other human diseases, animals and drugs. First, people, usually women, with a disease called Cushing's disease have a hypothalamic ailment which *also* results in high production of cortisol in the adrenal glands, and they *too* suffer from depression. Second, any action taken in the brain of monkeys to deplete the supply of *their* norepinephrine subsequently causes in them too all the symptoms of depression—the same is true in rats. And third, the only two classes of drugs found, by accident, to be useful in the treatment of *human* depression both affect systems in which norepinephrine and serotonin are operative. These drugs—the monoamine oxidase inhibitors and the tricyclic antidepressants—are not at all like the widely prescribed Valium and Librium. They have *no* effect, except maybe an unpleasant one, on normal people. They *do,* however, relieve the symptoms of truly depressed patients. And one class of them, the tricyclics, is beginning to emerge as the one treatment science has for the phobias. The phobias—fear of heights, open and closed spaces, water and so on—are obviously stress-related. They involve misplaced and exaggerated stress reactions. And like vital depression, to which they are close kin, they afflict women much more often than men (anywhere from three to ten to one).

The genetic studies, the high incidence in women of depressive disorders of all kinds and the chemistry of stress that underlies the phobias and vital depression: all of these things suggest that a woman's moods and responses to stress are differently organized from a man's. And if so, one would expect, of course, to find at the heart of them—just as we found at the heart of the male's reaction to challenge and danger—the sex hormones. Some evidence for this is just beginning to emerge from laboratories. Walter Stumpf and his colleagues at the University of North Carolina at Chapel Hill, for example, have shown that cells carrying norepinephrine in particular areas of the brain are targets for, or communicate directly with *other* cells that are targets for the sex hormones. The sex hormones, Stumpf and others believe, differentially affect brain circuits in which norepinephrine and its relative dopamine are the neurotransmitters, and differentially affect the functions they control. These include "regulation of reproduction, thermo-regulation, blood pressure regulation, vomiting, feeding, drinking and emotional behavior such as aggression and depression."

Stumpf's work is a dramatic confirmation of Günter Dörner's belief that the sex hormones organize the development of the male and female brain by helping to shape the nerve-cell neurotransmission–pathways they will influence in later life. And it also shows that these pathways, governing all sorts of active and reactive behavior, will be sensitive to any major changes in the amount of the sex hormones they have available to them. This can be seen at the level of individual nerve cells, as the Chapel Hill laboratory has shown. But it can also be seen, in women, in the routine events of ordinary life—in puberty, childbirth, the menstrual cycle, menopause and the taking of the pill. All of these things produce subtle and not so subtle changes in body heat, eating behavior, blood pressure and emotional tone—all the things that Stumpf ascribes to the working of norepinephrine and dopamine. And the upshot of them all is this: Alter the level of a woman's sex hormones in large or even small ways and you will find often quite profound alterations in her mood and personality. Sometimes she will not be in control of her own personality—her hormones will be.

About seven percent of new mothers, for example, suffer for weeks, even months, from severe depression, complete with loss of sexual interest, at precisely the time when their hormone levels have been abruptly altered by the births of their children. And an unknown percentage of women on the pill report a bewildering variety of side effects, including lowered sex drive, altered appetite, irritability and depression. These things are all too often looked on—by lover, husband, doctor, even the woman herself—as psychological in origin, her responsibility, her fault. And they can lead to the breakup of relationships and marriages. An alarming number of separations occur within fifteen months of a baby's birth.

And then, of course, there is premenstrual tension. British psychiatrist Katharina Dalton believes that premenstrual tension affects four out of ten women to some extent, and for eight days—before and during menstruation—it *seriously* affects the life of one of those four. Being on the pill, she says, actually makes the condition worse. Not only do the symptoms include elements of depression—brooding, lethargy, loss of memory and emotional control—they also include an increased incidence of quarrels, accidents, suicides, baby battering and crime, all of it caused by an altered balance of estrogen and progesterone in the late luteal phase of the menstrual cycle, just before menstruation. Premenstrual tension, in other words, is *not* the cultural phenomenon some feminists have announced it to be, a phenomenon caused by socially imposed anxiety about menstruation. It is a *biological* phenomenon. Anke A. Ehrhardt has recorded the case of a year-and-a-half-old girl with both precocious puberty *and* severe premenstrual tension.

(Should this news make men smug about their supposedly uncyclical personality and their ability to control the processes of emotional change, then they should know that they, too, may have a "time of the month." A study done by Alice Rossi at the University of Massachusetts at Amherst showed that a group of men had a period of a few days each month in which they were unusually irritable and tense. The period, however, was not cyclical; it did not occur at predictable and regular intervals. "Under these circumstances," says Alice Rossi, "if this phenomenon is widespread, who would you want doing skilled and responsible jobs—flying a plane, performing brain surgery and so on? Someone whose switches in mood are predictable or someone whose switches in mood are *un*predictable?)

This brings us to one last disorder that affects a woman's mood and personality, sexual and reproductive functions and appetite, a disorder that will help us see, finally, why these functions are so interdependent and vulnerable in women: anorexia nervosa. Anorexia nervosa, which afflicts women—usually during or after puberty—between ten and twenty times more often than it does men, is often thought of as a purely psychological illness, the result of constant pressure on young middle-class girls to remain as thin as possible, despite the new shapes their bodies are taking on. The pressure produces a morbid preoccupation with food and body image. And people with anorexia nervosa often starve themselves to death or else die after immoderate, out-of-control eating binges. The disease, however, is not as new as it is usually thought to be. It was first described, as far as we know, in 1694 in England. *And* it can be genetically and otherwise tied to depression. Anorectics have unusually high numbers of first-order relatives with depression and other disorders of mood, according to Elliott Gershon of the American National Institutes of Health. And they have several chemical abnormalities which are similar to those of depressives. They have the same hypothalamic dysfunction which results in high levels of cortisol. They produce the same low levels of norepinephrine. And they *also* produce, if a recent study is correct, a substance in their urine which promotes pronounced food aversion in laboratory rats.

Why so many women should be struck by such a devastating

and deadly disease—one in two hundred and fifty English schoolgirls and seven percent of Canadian ballet dancers, by recent report—is a mystery. But it is a mystery only so long as it is regarded as a *psychological disorder*—a disorder of eating, a food-and-fat phobia. Anorexia, in fact, is much, much more than this. It is a developmental disease of sexual and reproductive function. Anorectics, like many women with vital depression, cease menstruation if they have begun it at puberty, or else they never start menstruating at all. They have little or no sexual interest. And if the disease is not cured in time they often permanently fail to develop to any great extent secondary sexual characteristics. Instead, their pattern of sex hormone production reverts to the pattern ordinarily found in prepubertal girls. They produce low levels of luteinizing hormone—one of the messenger hormones by which the pituitary communicates with the ovaries—and low levels of active estrogen. *All of these things can be directly related to their weight loss.* And this suggests that anorectics, like depressives, suffer from a disruption of *particular* mechanisms that have been brought together by evolution in women, but not in men.

In humans and other animals, puberty and the maintenance of reproductive function—both controlled by the hypothalamus—are dependent on the availability of food and on food intake, which is also monitored and regulated by the hypothalamus. This is *especially* true of females; it is more critical for them, evolutionarily speaking, since for reproductive purposes they have to commit themselves to a huge investment of stored resources and energy. Puberty, then, *especially in females,* is delayed until a certain body weight has been achieved. And it is *also* delayed if the brain-body system experiences stress in the environment. This is true of animals under a number of conditions—overcrowding in rats, for example, and a low position in the female dominance hierarchy in some monkeys and in chimpanzees. And it is also true of humans. Puberty is often delayed in young girls submitted to the stress of extensive ballet or athletic training. And it sometimes does not occur at all in anorectics under the influence of what seems to be a continuous, purely internal and biochemically induced stress.

The same scenario holds good for the *maintenance* of reproductive function after puberty. If a woman's weight—her fat-to-muscle ratio—drops below a certain level, then her reproductive cycle and the delivery of her eggs are likely to come to a halt. This is true of malnourished women and, in our society, of some athletes and some overenthusiastic dieters and joggers. And if she is exposed to something that her brain-body system experiences as stressful, then the same effect is likely to be found. Such a response would be adaptive. It is not in a woman's interests, evolutionarily speaking, to commit herself to conception, childbirth and child-rearing *either* when resources are scarce *or* when the environment is less than congenial.

The result is what we see in women, but not usually in men: diseases of two related systems differently organized and mediated by their sex hormones—the so-called hypothalamic-pituitary-adrenal axis and the hypothalamic-pituitary-gonadal axis: diseases that combine changes in reproductive and in eating behavior. It also explains why *obesity* is more common in women than in men, and why they are better protected against the damaging effects of it. Overeating can be adaptive for women, since it stores up large amounts of resources against possible famine, enough energy to provide for future offspring. But it is *not* adaptive for men who are not so protected, since *their* evolution required short-term energy expenditure in competition and hunting. Deep in women, in other words, but not in men, are buried the gene-hormone-norepinephrine pathways of the Stone-Age Venuses of Menton and Willendorf, figurines of paleolithic women who were grotesquely fat by our standards, but who were highly valued, it seems, as reproducers.

What it *doesn't* explain yet, of course, is why depression and phobia should be part and parcel of the female reaction to stress, but not the male. But for this too an evolutionary explanation can be found. Take the phobias, for example, which have recently been found to be highly correlated with psychosexual dysfunction and depression. The phobias usually appear in women *only* in the child-bearing years. And they involve fears, interestingly enough, of precisely those things that would have been dangerous in the environment in which we evolved—heights, water, animals, open and unprotected spaces and enclosed spaces with no exit or escape. A tendency to be afraid of such things would be favored as a genetic inheritance, to be expressed in women but not in men, since women with the inheritance would enhance the survival both of themselves and their offspring.

The same sort of argument, finally, can be made for depression. For most of our evolutionary history, isolated women could not survive—women are not well adapted to hunting, as we have said. To maximize the food supply, then, for themselves and their dependent infants, they *had* to be interdependent members of social groups. Indeed, they were the necessary glue that held these groups together. A woman's tendency to depression in the face of stress, then, may have been an adaptive mechanism that reinforced her interdependence and accelerated her back into the group by producing a cry for help. In today's society there are few if any close-knit social groups. There is a cry for help, but no help comes. Depression has been called, in at least one study, a disease of growing epidemic proportions in the countries of the west.

OF HEMISPHERES, MOODS AND MADNESS

PIERRE FLOR-HENRY is a slight, dapper, pipe-smoking Franco-Hungarian in his forties. He is clinical professor at the University of Alberta in Canada and director of admission services at the Alberta Hospital. And he is a scientist who spends much of his research time trying to pull together into one overall picture all that is now being discovered about the two brain hemispheres, the chemistry and the disorders of men and women. He first became interested in the subject when studying temporal lobe epilepsies—electrical seizures that spread out from damaged focuses in a particular area of the left or right hemisphere.

"What's interesting about these epilepsies, you see," he says during a visit to New York, "is that when they begin early in life in the *left* hemisphere, they're sometimes associated with sexual deviation—fetishism, for example—and with driven, aggressive, psychopathic behavior. Later in life, they're associated with a set of symptoms that look a lot like schizophrenia. This is not at all true of *right*-sided temporal epilepsies. When *they* start early in

152

life, they have an association with orgasm—an attack can produce orgasm. Later in life, they can produce the symptoms of depression.

"Now this distinction between left- and right-epilepsies is *exactly* the distinction between the adult behavioral disorders that differentially strike men and women. It's *men* who are the sexual deviants and the psychopaths. They commit almost all the violent crime. And it's *men* who suffer from schizophrenia—or at any rate from a form of schizophrenia that's earlier, more chronic and more deadly than it is in women. *Left*-sided. Women, by contrast, don't have these problems. Fetishism, violent sexual behavior, violent crime and early-onset schizophrenia are either comparatively rare or virtually never found in women. No, what women suffer from is depression, mood disorders and the orgasmic and sexual problems that often accompany them. *Right*-sided, according to the evidence of the temporal-lobe epilepsies. What these epilepsies immediately suggested to me, in other words, was that men and women are vulnerable in the hemisphere in which they are less effectively organized for the characteristic skills and abilities they show— men in the *left* hemisphere, where their verbal skills are comparatively poor, and women in the *right* hemisphere, where their visual-spatial skills are less secure than a man's."

Over the past five or six years, in a series of influential papers, Pierre Flor-Henry has been slowly solidifying a theory which draws on behavioral studies, electrical recordings of brain activity, the effects and side-effects of drugs and brain damage, the observation of mental patients, genetics, neurochemistry, anthropology and evolutionary theory. And there is no doubt in his mind that in his theory lies a reasonable explanation for the often elaborate differences between men and women. The human right hemisphere, he believes, developed in such a way that visual-spatial skills were linked in it to mood, movement and sexual fulfillment. This organization became particularly pronounced in males—the sex-seeking gender. And it made the controls later exercised by the verbal left hemisphere relatively precarious in males. Psychopaths and sociopaths, he believes, are exaggerated right-hemisphere males—with diminished verbal capacity and understanding and an exaggerated visual and spatial skill—aggression. Male sexual deviants, he thinks, suffer from a different failure—a failure of left-hemisphere inhibition—and from some damage by which the right-hemisphere sexual response can only be reached through one fragment of behavior.

"This doesn't happen in females," he says. "Their disorders are primarily right-hemisphere disorders. Phobias, for instance—phobias are obviously disruptions of visual and spatial perception, movement and mood. And the same association can be seen in depression. Depression is a dysfunction of movement—depressed people don't jump about. It's a disturbance, obviously of mood and, this time, of sexuality. And it *also* involves an impairment of visual-spatial skills—this is very common in depressed patients. It's interesting, too, I think, that in cases of hysterical paralysis and psychosomatic pain—both of which are more common in women—the symptoms most often appear on the *left* side of the body, which argues the involvement of the right hemisphere.

"Now why should these differences appear? Well, we're beginning to find out that the sex hormones differently activate, during development, the two sides of the brain. And we know that dopamine and norepinephrine pathways are *also* differently distributed between the two hemispheres—put *very* crudely, dopamine seems to be left-hemisphere, norepinephrine right. The basic male and female pattern, then, is laid down before birth by the interaction of the sex hormones and these neurotransmitter systems. But there can be defects in the process by which this occurs, genetic defects. We know from genetic studies, for example, that schizophrenia tends to run in families, just as depression and heart problems do—there's a very high concordance for schizophrenia in identical twins, and children who are adopted and later develop schizophrenia are much more likely to share their schizophrenia with their *biological* parents rather than their adoptive ones. The same is true for criminal behavior, alcoholism, hyperactivity and even shyness. What's fascinating too, I think, is that the defect can have a *different* effect on behavior depending on whether the person affected is a man or a woman. There's considerable evidence now that alcoholism, antisocial personality, hysteria and hyperactivity cluster in families. But hyperactivity and alcoholism are expressed almost always in the males. And hysteria is expressed *only* in the females."

These diseases and disorders, Flor-Henry is quick to point out, are not *always* or automatically inherited. Rather there is a genetic—and therefore chemical—predisposition, a predisposition in the way the brain's pathways and hemispheres are organized. And this predisposition can be triggered into expression by cues of various sorts: by damage of some kind, by dramatic alterations in hormone levels or by stressful events in the world. In females, more often than not, this results in depressive disorders in which a *decrease* in norepinephrine and a decrease in right-hemisphere functioning can be seen. And in males, more often than not, it results in disordered *aggression,* in which there is an *increase* in norepinephrine and an increase in right-hemisphere functioning, with a corresponding decrease in the left. Males are also more vulnerable, by the same token, to a variety of disorders in which the restraining influence of the left hemisphere is interfered with. Schizophrenia, hyperactivity, Tourette's syndrome and the Lesch-Nylan syndrome—in which patients obsessively tear at their own flesh—all seem to be left-hemisphere disorders. They all seem to be dopamine-related; the only effective drugs available for their treatment are ones that alter the levels of dopamine in the brain. And they are all, if you count *early-onset* schizophrenia, predominantly male.

All of this suggests that it is a woman's *estrogen* that protects her against these disorders. Just as it protects her against heart problems and the damaging effects of stress, so it helps to protect her against *either* an exaggerated right-hemisphere response or these debilitating left-hemisphere diseases. A man's testosterone does neither of these things. Instead, it *predisposes* him towards them.

"You know," Pierre Flor-Henry says, echoing Bob Goy, "Nature, in the organization of the female brain, seems to have taken out much more insurance. Male brains don't seem to have received this kind of insurance. They are less protected, less stable, more various, more out on a limb. And I think that's because, in the large scale of things, individual males don't matter very much. For the purposes of reproduction, they're interchangeable—throwaways. And that has left nature free to experiment with them. That's why there are more sexual deviants and psychopaths among men. That's why there is more retardation and brain disorder among men. And that's why there are also more *geniuses* among men. The line that divides them is a small one, I think."

It is said that there have been three major revolutions in science, revolutions which changed forever the way men and women thought about their place in the world. The first, as we said at the beginning of this book, was Copernicus's, which established that our earth was not the center of the universe. The second was Darwin's, which showed that we were not directly made by the shaping hand of God. And the third was Freud's, which demonstrated that we were something less than rational, independent creatures, in *conscious* command of our own individual destinies. A fourth is the revolution of the new science of men and women, an important part of which is the emergence of a new *biological* psychiatry. For it makes plain, as scientists Paul Wender and Donald Klein wrote in their recent book *Mind, Mood and Medicine*, that we often cannot *by ourselves* control, even with psychological help, our moods and behavior —"which is contrary to many theological and philosophical positions." Instead, as men and women, we are locked into the unfolding of a biological inheritance which can sometimes, willy-nilly, result in states and disorders that may once have been adaptive, but now threaten the stability of individuals and the stability of the society we have built for ourselves.

This has far-reaching implications, first of all, for the way in which we deal with intent, motivation and rehabilitation in crime. Take premenstrual tension. In November 1981, British psychiatrist Katharina Dalton appeared in court as a witness for the defense of one of her patients, a twenty-nine-year-old barmaid named Sandy Smith. Sandy Smith had had thirty previous convictions, for arson and assault among other things, and she was already on probation for stabbing to death, in 1980, another barmaid. This time she was charged with threatening to kill a policeman. Katharina Dalton, however, was able to demonstrate that all of Sandy Smith's crimes were connected by a twenty-nine-day cycle, and by premenstrual tension. And Sandy Smith was given three years' probation. The very next day, November 10, the same defense—premenstrual tension—was brought up by the very same defense witness, Katharina Dalton, in the case of another woman, Christine English. Christine English had had an argument with her lover and had run him over in a car. After evidence was heard, she was discharged—conditional for a year —after pleading guilty to manslaughter. The court ruled that at the time of her crime she had "diminished responsibility." Instead of being imprisoned, both women are now receiving treatment with progesterone.

If this seems as unreasonable and worrisome to you as it did to many British lawyers, doctors and feminists, then consider this third case. In July 1974, in southern Massachusetts, a young man called Charles Decker picked up two teenage girls who were hitchhiking to an amusement park. They got on well together and spent some hours driving around, drinking beer and smoking marijuana. Then quite suddenly, without provocation, Charles Decker attacked the two girls with a stonemason's hammer, fracturing their skulls. Virtually immediately afterwards he came to his senses, dropped the girls off at a place from which they could be quickly taken to a hospital, telephoned his father and gave himself up to the police.

At the trial Charles Decker's lawyer presented an original defense. Decker, he argued, was innocent by reason of insanity. But he was not insane for any of the usual psychological reasons. Instead, he suffered from a chemical abnormality of the limbic system that resulted in an unusual reaction to alcohol and in an inability to control his own violence.

Charles Decker did not go unpunished. But his defense was probably accurate. He probably *did* have a limbic disorder which is often induced in more obvious ways. Charles Whitman, for example, who in the 1960s climbed University Tower in Austin, Texas, and from his vantage shot seventeen people, was found after death to have had a brain tumor. And Vernon Mark, a Harvard neurosurgeon, talks of a patient he once had who tried to decapitate his wife and daughter with a meat cleaver. The patient had gone through a change of personality in the months preceding the incident, just as Charles Whitman had. And by the time Mark saw him, he was so violent that police had to bring him wrapped in a fishnet. It subsequently turned out that the attemptive murderer had a brain tumor too, underneath his right frontal lobe and pressing directly on his limbic system. The tumor was removed, and the man's violence disappeared.

Cases, and defenses, like these are to date rare. But they raise important questions that we ought to face now, that we will *have* to face sooner or later, as science comes to know more and more about the genes, hormones and neurotransmitters involved in violence, mood and madness. Is a woman responsible for the effects of her moods? Is a man responsible for his aggressiveness or his reaction to stress? Is a male criminal responsible for his crimes or does the responsibility lie with his testosterone levels and his lopsided brain organization? If the responsibility is not *personal,* then how do we begin to deal with it? Do we monitor the entire population for hormone levels and neurotransmitter ratios, for example, to see who is likely to threaten us with violence and sexual deviation, or else threaten themselves with depression, schizophrenia and suicide? Do we give neurological tests to prisoners or blockade them with drugs that will bring

their testosterone and neurotransmitter levels back into balance? And how early do we start with these protective measures
if the hormones and genes have done much of their work before
birth? Do we begin to submit *fetuses* to hormonal and genetic
examination?

These are no longer academic questions. Scientists at Johns
Hopkins University are examining the brains of people with
"conventional and unconventional sexual preferences," looking
for hormonal, chromosomal and structural differences. They
are also successfully treating persistent male sex offenders with
a drug that blocks the action of testosterone. A few miles away,
at the National Institutes of Health in Bethesda, Maryland, psychiatrist Markku Linnoila has found what seems to be a low level
of serotonin in psychopathic killers and schizophrenics who
have attempted suicide. Low serotonin levels have already been
linked to aggression and violent suicide in other studies. And
Linnoila believes that they are to do with a general impulsivity
that can lead to violence towards oneself or others. Psychopaths,
he says, tend to have histories of childhood behavioral problems
and adult alcoholism. And this means that measurements of
serotonin might be made early in life for their predictive value
—they can be used to predict the children and young adults at
risk. Serotonin levels can then be increased in them, with drugs
that already exist, to prevent violent killing. At the same time,
British scientists are measuring the levels of *other* neurotransmitters and hormones in an attempt to predict future behavior.
In two separate studies, testosterone levels and norepinephrine-
epinephrine ratios have been suggested as predictors of a pris-
oner's ability to adjust and conform outside the prison walls.

This may not seem much. But it must be placed against the
background of *other* advances being made in science. In 1979,
for example, scientists at the National Institutes of Health and
at the Rockefeller University reported a major advance in the
repairing of defective genes. In experiments with mice they were
able to inject a single gene into a defective living cell, curing that
cell's otherwise fatal genetic flaw. And the *rewriting* of genetic

scripts in humans to eliminate potential risks came that much nearer. Then, consider this: In 1981, using a new technique for tracing the passage of genes between *human* generations, Lowell Weitkamp and colleagues at the Universities of Rochester and Toronto announced the location of a gene they believe to be involved in human depression. And it is in a very odd and suggestive place. It seems to be on chromosome 6, close to genes involved in schizophrenia and CAH, the disorder that masculinizes female fetuses in the womb. And it is either among or very close to genes that regulate the development of the human immune system.

This should give us some pause, as science rushes toward an age in which the genetic manipulation of humans becomes possible. For the human organism is extraordinarily complex. And it may well be that to intervene in it at the level of a single gene may have profound effects in other, unknown parts of the system —effects we cannot know until our knowledge of its intertwining, overlapping processes is far greater than it is today. It is in this sense, again, that science is the cutting edge of our future. One future it already prefigures is a future littered with the accidents of ignorance—a blithe irruption, made possible by sophisticated technologies, into genetic processes that are still imperfectly understood. And another is a future in which our hand has been stayed until the genetic connections between disorders like schizophrenia, depression, CAH and the immune system have become better known. Again, we can outrace our humanity. Or, at the edge of a knowledge on the brink of being gained, we can wonder at it. The choice of a future—as we shall see once more in the next chapters, in the connections between the brain, disorders, diseases and the immune systems—is up to us.

13

THE NEWEST FRONTIER

IN LATE NOVEMBER 1982, two men met late at night in the bar of a Boston hotel. One of them, a short, fast-talking man in his early fifties, carried a briefcase. The other, a younger, sunnier man, wore in his buttonhole a red carnation, so that he would be recognized. They had never met before. And, on the face of it, there was no reason for them to be enthusiastic about each other's company.

If this sounds like the beginning of a detective story, then it is. It is a detective story even now being written, a detective story that is sifting clues, gathering information and trying to bring together into a coherent theory all the further differences between human males and females that remain. Science, as Sir Peter Medawar said at the beginning of this book, "begins as a story about a Possible World—a story which we invent and criticize and modify as we go along, so that it ends by being, as nearly as possible, a story about real life." Both men, that night in the Boston bar, had a piece of the story to tell.

The older man was Norman Geschwind, the James Jackson Putnam Professor of Neurology at Harvard University, described simply by scientists as "the best neurologist in America." One of this remarkable, protean man's many interests lies in the so-called developmental disorders, disorders which affect the left hemisphere and language ability and strike human males far more often than females. These include the severe emotional and communicational disorder of autism (four to one); hyperactivity, which is marked by an inability to concentrate and a short attention span (five to one); stuttering (five to one); and two other disorders—developmental aphasia, or extreme difficulty in learning to talk (five to one), and dyslexia—"word blindness" or extreme difficulty with reading and writing (up to six to one).

The reason why the meeting in the Boston bar might have been thought to be unlikely—why scientists, up to as little as a year or two ago, might have thought the bar discussion that took place unfruitful—is that the second, younger man that night was not a neurologist at all. He was an immunologist. Robert Lahita is, in fact, assistant professor of immunology at the Rockefeller University in New York. And his special interest is in auto-immune diseases. These are diseases in which the immune system, instead of protecting what is self and attacking what is other —viruses, bacteria and so on—turns on the body it is supposed to protect and mounts an assault on tissue in a variety of areas. Auto-immune reactions may in fact be responsible for a large number of human diseases. But of the ones identified for a particular disease—multiple sclerosis, rheumatoid arthritis, systemic lupus erythematosus and myasthenia gravis, for example —almost *all* affect women more often than men. And they affect them, by and large, *after* puberty, while the developmental disorders which affect males appear *before* it.

Males, females; before puberty, after puberty; neurological problems and immunological problems. Why on earth were the two men so enthusiastic about meeting so late at night? What on earth did they have to talk about? *Handedness.* They talked about left-handers and right-handers and the common ground that the differences between them might be opening up. Geschwind, before they separated, took a questionnaire from his briefcase that he wanted Lahita to give to his auto-immune-disease patients. He wanted to know how many of them were left-handed or had left-handers among their immediate relatives.

This is a brand new frontier-in-the-making in the emerging science of men and women. And it brings into new and mysterious connection all that we have so far learned about the sex hormones, the genes and the two hemispheres. It also brings in a new ingredient: the male and female immune system.

The particular piece of Sir Peter Medawar's story that it represents may take years before it comes into sharp focus. But in order to understand its beginnings—the enthusiasm with which Geschwind and Lahita met that night and the way science is moving forward, through such meetings, towards the the secrets locked within the male and female body and brain—we once again have to go backward and unravel all the clues that led to their appointment. We once again have to go backward to the beginning of all human development—the meeting of egg and sperm.

Sperm carrying the male sex chromosome are more stream-lined, and they seem to swim faster and have more staying power than sperm carrying the female sex chromosome—even at this level they seem to be gamblers. And between one hundred twenty and one hundred forty males are conceived for every hundred females. From there on in, however, it is downhill all the way for males. More males are spontaneously aborted during pregnancy. And though they retain a slight edge at the time of birth—one hundred six to one hundred—the decline continues. More males than females are born dead, blind or ambiguously sexed, either internally or externally. Seventy percent of all *other* birth defects are associated mainly with males. Thirty percent more males than females die in the first few months of life, and they suffer more from every disease of childhood except whooping cough. The result of all this mayhem is that by the time of puberty the head start achieved by the male sperm has been lost. And the population of men and women has become about equal, at a considerable cost in males.

What all this means is, as science says about a great many things, "imperfectly understood." But the excess and special vulnerability of males in the womb is used by the armchair theorists of sociobiology to argue that in a polygamous species, which they think humans are, there is a genetic advantage to the production of males. Males, however, require a bigger parental investment than females—they mature more slowly—and to be a genetic success they must be totally fit for the sexual competition to come. This being so, it is in the interests of the mother—other things, like the food supply, being equal—both to opt for the male over the female sperm *and* to somehow cut her losses if the developing male is less than perfect. She would not be inclined to take such drastic measures with a female embryo, since a female embryo represents a smaller investment and, whatever her defects, a continuing good chance of reproductive success.

There may be some truth in this. Certainly there is much more genetic experimentation and rejection going on in the woman's womb and reproductive tract than used to be thought. First, in some cases of infertility, the woman makes antibodies that lock onto and cause the destruction of her husband's sperm—apparently because they share many of the same immune genes. So she has the *potential,* at any rate, of discriminating with her immune system between male and female sperm, which carry different cell-surface markers. Second, it is beginning to emerge from studies done in England that nearly fifty percent of all pregnancies are spontaneously aborted, often without the mother knowing it and usually because of some chromosomal abnormality. So she *also* has some way of recognizing, and rejecting with her immune defenses, an embryo's genetic makeup.

These mechanisms, then, may be at work in conception and the maintenance of pregnancy. But they are not the *immediate* cause of the male's difficulties both before and after birth. This has little, except perhaps indirectly, to do with the mother's investment. Instead, it is almost certainly connected to the elaborate transformations he has to go through in the womb. More can go wrong with the processes of development through which the male has to pass, as we have seen. So more males are compromised and rejected. And, as a result of all the hormonal changes to which they are exposed, they are born less sturdy and less ready for the world than girls. They are five percent heavier at birth than girls, it is true—about as heavy as the woman's pelvic structure permits. But they are four to six weeks behind them in physical maturity. Their fontanelle, the sheet of skull bone that protects their brain, closes later than girls'; they are more fractious and irritable as babies; they are more at risk from the effects of lack of stimulation. And for a long time they lag behind their sisters. Bone ossification and dental maturity are achieved earlier in girls. Girls sit up, crawl and walk, as well as talk, earlier.

Boys, in effect, are born prematurely. And it used to be argued that it was this prematurity of theirs, together with the slower development of their left hemispheres, that was responsible for the prevalence in them of the learning disorders. All of these disorders, the argument ran—with the possible exception of hyperactivity—are *language* disorders, left-hemisphere disorders. And they are the result of minimal brain damage, sustained either in birth—through the cutting off of the oxygen supply, for example—or at some time *after* birth because of a fever or a convulsion or a bump on the head. These things do not affect girls so much because of their head start in brain organization, their better organized left hemisphere and their faster-closing fontanelle. And they do not affect the boy's better developed and securer *right* hemisphere. But they *do* affect the boy's *left* hemisphere and produce the things we see—dyslexia, autism, stuttering, aphasia and perhaps also hyperactivity and even schizophrenia.

The same argument used to be applied to left-handedness. Left-handedness, the argument ran, appears in about eight percent of the population. And genes seem to play little part in its inheritance: Eighty-four percent of left-handers are born to two right-handed parents. There *must,* therefore, be some environmental factor that comes into play either at or soon after birth, a factor that produces the left-handedness found at a very early age in infants. Even as late as 1975, Paul Bakan, then at Simon Fraser University in Canada, argued that it *too* was the result of a complicated and traumatic birth. The circle, then, was for the moment closed. And Sir Cyril Burt, who pointed out a generation ago that special schools for "mental defectives" contained a high percentage of left-handers, appeared justified. It was all to do with the vulnerability of boys' brains to early traumas. These traumas produced left-handedness—more common in males. And they caused the developmental disorders. Many people with the developmental disorders are indeed left-handed.

The early-damage argument may, in fact, apply to *some* left-handers, just as it may apply to *some* cases of hyperactivity, for example. Nevertheless, it is by no means the whole story. For a strong case can now be made for the idea that both left-handedness and the learning disorders are the end result of the same *developmental* process, a process in which the usual pattern of left-hemisphere dominance for language is altered in the womb. Painfully little is yet known about this—the work, again, has not been done. But there are two asymmetries in areas of the brain that are important for language that appear in fetuses, newborns and in adults. And they seem to be less marked in left-handers —that is their left and right hemispheres seem to be more similar. At the same time, there is another, much *bigger* asymmetry in humans that usually distinguishes between left and right hemisphere—the right hemisphere is wider and projects more at the front, while the left hemisphere is wider and projects more at the back. This too can be found in newborn infants. But it is much less marked in many left-handers, and it is sometimes actually *reversed* in the brains of schizophrenics, autistic children and dyslexics.

This argues not for brain damage but for some skewing developmental pattern that proceeds to a certain point in left-handers but is even more exaggerated—it goes further—in people suffering from these disorders. And there is one more piece of evidence that this is so. In 1979, Albert Galaburda and Thomas Kemper, colleagues of Norman Geschwind's at the Harvard Medical School, examined the brain of a dyslexic man who had died in an accident. The man was left-handed, as were his father and three brothers, also slow readers. And his brain seemed to show why. First, the language areas in the temporal lobes showed little or no asymmetry, unlike the case in the majority of brains. And second, in his left hemisphere, in the same language area, there was an abnormal arrangement of tissues and cells. Cell layers were disorganized, and cells and islands of cortical tissue had somehow *migrated* to the wrong place.

Galaburda has since examined a second dyslexic brain, and he has found a similar pattern of disorganization. Norman Geschwind is quite clear about what this means. "What's happened in these two brains," he says, "and perhaps in the brains of many, if not all, dyslexics is a miswiring of the actual basic structure of the brain. It couldn't have been caused by mechanical injury, internal bleeding or a cutoff in the blood supply during or after birth. It *must* have occurred during the formation of the brain tissue in the womb."

If this is so, then precisely how does it work its effects on behavior? What *other* similarities are there between left-handers and dyslexics and the people, usually male, who suffer from autism, stuttering and so on? How do they differ as a group from right-handers? Well, in right-handers the left hemisphere almost always controls speech-related activities, language abilities. But this isn't true of left-handers. In many, perhaps the majority of left-handers, there is a diminished degree of left-hemisphere ascendency over language. And same applies, to an even *more* marked degree, perhaps, to stutterers, autistic children and dyslexics, *whether they are left-handed or not.* Their problem, in other words, is not simply that they have some brain damage or failure of development in the *left* hemisphere. It is that the whole functional relationship between the two halves of their brains has been altered from normal. Stutterers, for example, have been shown in recent studies to have bilateral representation of speech and to use language areas on both sides of the brain, *except* when affected by a drug that causes them to stop stuttering. Dyslexics, on the basis of tests designed by Sandra Witelson, have bilateral representation of visual-spatial function, at least. And they too may have some language abilities on the "wrong" side of the brain.

In autism the pattern may be similar. Children usually become, or are observed to be, autistic before the age of three. They are socially aloof and indifferent and preoccupied with repetitive routines. They are very resistant to any change in their regimen. And they often fail to develop, or have severe abnormalities in, both verbal and visual-spatial skills. They are extremely difficult to test, then, by comparison with normal children. But, even so, the available evidence all points in the same direction. Some autistic children, as we have mentioned, have the same lack of brain asymmetry, shown on the CAT scan, as some dyslexics. And they also show similar patterns of brain-wave activity over *both* hemispheres, unlike normal children. It looks again, then, as if the usual left-right balance has been fundamentally altered in them in some way. The result may be what it is reasonable to think we see in autism: a complete suppression or chaotic redistribution of left-hemisphere language and the keying-up to a painful pitch of right-hemisphere visual-spatial perception. Ten percent of autistic children show what amounts to genius in some highly circumscribed area of visual-spatial ability. Despite their handicaps, they can be remarkable mathematicians or calendrical calculators. They can build awesomely elaborate mechanical devices. Or they can draw or paint or play music brilliantly—all right-hemisphere skills. There is some evidence, interestingly enough, that their abilities fade when their disorder abates, as it sometimes does.

"Now," Norman Geschwind says in the speakers' room at the November 1982 meeting of the Orton Dyslexia Society, "what principle can we find that will tie together the unusual patterns of cerebral dominance that seem to be found in these conditions

and the fact that it's *males* who are usually affected? Well," he
says, scattering references to scientific papers as he proceeds,
"there's evidence that the cells that are going to form the cerebral cortex take shape in the central core of the fetus's brain
before it's five months old. But there is evidence to suggest that
they mature and migrate at different rates, depending on which
hemisphere they are headed for. The right hemisphere, it appears, develops earlier. And this is probably the result of some
influence which is slowing down the growth of the left. This lag
in the maturation of the left hemisphere will be found, I think,
to be more pronounced in male fetuses."

What Geschwind suggests is that the factor most likely to be
responsible for slowing down for growth of the left hemisphere
is testosterone. For testosterone, as work done in the laboratories of Roger Gorski, Günter Dörner and Marian Diamond, for
example, points up, does affect the development of certain
structures in the brains of rats. And since testosterone may slow
down the rate at which cells migrate and gather in the left hemisphere, Geschwind believes that the left hemisphere delay will
be greater in male fetuses who are typically exposed to much
higher levels of this hormone in the uterus than females. Conse-
quently, it favors the development in them of the *right* hemisphere. "This would account, you see, for the prevalence of
left-handedness in males. And it would also account for Galaburda's findings in dyslexics of an anomalous migration of nerve
cells to the language area of the left hemisphere. Some altered
balance of testosterone during the critical period of the left
hemisphere's development is likely, it seems to me, to be involved—as it is likely to be involved in the other learning disorders that differentially strike males."

None of this, of course, is of much concern to Robert Lahita
—he has a completely different row to hoe. But in 1980, unknown to him, that began to change. For in November of that
year, Norman Geschwind made his annual journey to the meeting of the Orton Dyslexia Society. One of the sessions he at-

tended was on the *genetic* contribution to dyslexia, the incidence of dyslexia in the *relatives* of people with the disorder. After the main speaker had finished his presentation, the session was thrown open for discussion. Geschwind suggested that it might be a good idea to look at not just dyslexia itself, but at *other* disorders that might show up in the families of dyslexics. A genetic susceptibility, he said, might take on a different form in different people. He mentioned the work of British scientist Michael Rutter, who had shown that people with autism were much more likely to have relatives with dyslexia than the general population. "A good scientific rule is: Don't only look at the thing that interests you," he said. "Look elsewhere."

The Orton Society meetings attract each year a large number of dyslexics and their relatives, as well as teachers and scientists from various fields. Immediately after the session, Geschwind was surrounded by people clamoring to tell him their family's medical history. Two main themes emerged from the group. First, dyslexics themselves or their parents or siblings seemed to have suffered from *other* learning and language disabilities, such as hyperactivity or stuttering, for example. And second, they seemed to have suffered much more than Geschwind thought reasonable from allergies, migraine and auto-immune disease.

"It was really quite startling and surprising," Geschwind says, when we catch up with him again at the 1982 Orton Society meeting in Baltimore. "We've known for some time that the developmental learning disorders come in clusters, just as we've known that there's a high correlation in all of them with left-handedness—even when people with these disorders are *right*-handed, they're likely to have left-handers in their families." But here was a very curious set of new associations.

As a result of what people at the Orton Society meeting told him, Geschwind began to look for similar associations both in patients and in people outside the clinical setting. And after several months of observation he decided to test the associations out formally. The dyslexics and their relatives talked about allergies. And that was interesting enough—stutterers also tend to have large numbers of childhood allergies, and food allergies are much more common than usual in hyperactive children. But migraine and auto-immune disease—they kept coming back to these.

So he got in touch with a former student of his, Peter Behan, now at the University of Glasgow, and together they devised a questionnaire which included answers about handedness, learning disabilities and auto-immune disorders. They then gave this out to two different British populations. And they separated out the answers given by people who were *strongly* left-handed or *strongly* right-handed. To date, they have collected 500 strong left-handers and 900 strong right-handers. And this is what they have found. The left-handers have about ten times the rate of learning disabilities (ten percent to one percent). They have about two and a half times the rate of auto-immune disorders, particularly of the thyroid gland and the gut (eight percent to two and eight-tenths percent). And the incidence of these disabilities is much higher in the *relatives* of the left-handers too. They have three times the rate of learning disabilities and twice the rate of auto-immune disorders.

"The people at the Orton Society were right, then," says Norman Geschwind. "And I was very fortunate to be around people who are used to paying attention to themselves and their families. There *is* a connection between left-handedness and migraine—we established that in another study. And there *is* a connection between left-handedness, learning disabilities like dyslexia and auto-immune diseases like ulcerative colitis. There is a strong interrelationship, in other words, between four conditions that differentially affect human males and females: left-handedness and learning disorders in males, appearing before puberty; and migraine—the rate is more than two to one female over men—and auto-immune disease in females, appearing *after* puberty."

Robert Lahita and Norman Geschwind now have something to talk about.

14
THE IMMUNE SYSTEM
AND THE BRAIN

"THE IMMUNE SYSTEM," says Robert Lahita, "is the only system in the body that approaches the brain in the complexity of its organization. And in many ways it's rather *like* the brain. It recognizes and reacts to the outside world. It's capable of an *enormous* range of responses—it learns, remembers and forgets. And, like the brain, its basic elements are shaped in the fetus before birth, while it is still in the womb.

"The system has two main roles, to identify and protect what is self and to identify and destroy what is other. And it can go wrong in two major ways. First, acting through one or other of its different classes of defense cells, it can launch an attack not on the viruses, bacteria and so on for which it was designed, but on essentially harmless proteins like those of goldenrod pollen. The result is an allergy beginning in childhood—and the child-hood allergies predominantly affect males. Second, it can some-how forget the lesson that it learned while the fetus was still in the womb—that anything it comes in contact with during that time must be regarded as self. And it can suddenly begin an

172

assault, at any period of life, on the cells it's supposed to protect. The result is a so-called auto-immune disease, and auto-immune diseases predominantly affect females.

"This is the beginning of immune differences between males and females in our human species. But it is only the beginning . . ."

Males are more likely to be left-handed. And they are more likely to suffer from learning disabilities. But there is another risk that they have to confront as they grow: that a genetic defect, extremely rare in girls, will cut short their survival. Males, remember, have not two X chromosomes but an X and a Y. And this means that if a male has a genetic defect in his single X chromosome—inherited from his mother—he has no backup protection from a second, *normal* X chromosome—inherited, in girls, from their father. He is much more vulnerable, then, to any and all disorders in which a distorted or damaged X chromosome plays a part. These include a form of mental retardation called Fragile X syndrome, in which the X is misshaped and thinned at one end and the testicles grow to several times normal size; hemophilia, the bleeding disease from which the males of the last Czar's family suffered; and seven *immunological* disorders, among them the lymphoproliferative syndrome, which makes a common virus lethal to the boys that have it and causes certain cancers of the immune system; and X-linked agammaglobulinemia, which results in a complete inability to make antibodies—the body's main line of defense against viruses and bacteria and which, until recently, caused inevitable death before the age of one. A young man who lives near us in Connecticut, David Camp, is the first boy with X-linked agammaglobulinemia to have lived beyond that age. He is an energetic, mischievous tribute to the bone-marrow-transplant treatment first used against the disease in Minnesota by immunologist and pediatrician Robert Good.

Already we can see, then, connections between immune problems and maleness. And we do not have to look far to find more.

For even when not suffering from a genetic defect, the male is still less well protected against viruses and bacteria than the female. His body makes lower levels of two blood proteins essential to the making of antibodies—slightly lower levels of immunoglobulin G and significantly lower levels of immunoglobulin M. This means that he is unequally prone to infantile diarrhea, childhood leukemia, cancers of the lymph system, diseases like Legionnaire's disease, respiratory ailments, hepatitis and gastro-intestinal illnesses. At the root of his vulnerability, almost certainly, lies testosterone. Little is known about this yet —there are few landmarks in this particular part of the landscape. But testosterone, when given from the outside, seems to act in all humans as a general depressor of the immune system. Estrogen seems to have the opposite effect. Given externally, it *promotes* the production of the two immunoglobulins, especially immunoglobulin M. It enhances the activity of so-called T-cells, an important arm of the immune system. And it seems to have a generally boosting effect on the whole system. In ordinary life this effect is, of course, cyclical, just as the production of estrogen is in women. It accounts not only for the fact that women are better protected in general—only castrated men have immune systems that approach the efficiency of women's—but also for the fact that they are *best* protected around the time of ovulation.

Ovulation marks the time when a female in nature is most likely to come into direct contact with a stranger who is perhaps infectious. But it also marks the time when the female's body has to do something it is normally fiercely set against doing—to tolerate within it cells whose surface markers identify them as foreign. A woman's body has to tolerate, refrain from attacking and allow sperm to live for some seventy-two hours. "And then," says Robert Lahita, "it has to support within it for nine months—*and not reject*—a fetus, a bundle of tissue that is antigenically foreign to her, because of the father's contribution to its genetic makeup. Why doesn't she reject it, as she would a transplant? The females of several species of mammals, including our own, are actually usually more *efficient* than males at rejecting grafts, tumors and so on.''

Obviously what the female has to do, in accepting sperm and maintaining pregnancy, is to alter and modulate her own immune system; suppressing one arm of the system, perhaps, so that it will tolerate the sperm and then the fetus inside her, while at the same time boosting *another* arm, so that she has extra protection—as she does—against infections. The question is, of course: How is she able to do this? Some people think it begins with the inheritance of the *two* X chromosomes, so that a woman has a double set of immune-regulating genes, genes that allow her a greater and more sophisticated immune capacity than a man. And this may be so. Whatever its source, though, it obviously has to do with the sex hormones. It is progesterone, for instance, which *also* rises at ovulation, that is thought to downregulate the immune system just enough to allow within-species propagation; it suppresses cells that would otherwise kill the sperm. And it is progesterone, too, that is thought to be central to the immune processes by which the fetus, for nine months or so, escapes rejection.

"The problem is, we know very little about these processes,'' says Lahita. "We know very little about the genetics of the immune system and the way it's influenced by the sex hormones. We know very little about the way in which *both* systems interact with *other* hormones and *other* systems in both the body and the brain. All we have to go on, in humans, is evidence from diseases and disorders in which something has gone *wrong* with the immune system. The most obvious of these are diseases in which the immune system turns violently against the body it's supposed to be protecting—the auto-immune diseases.''

The price that women have to pay, it seems, for their natural immunological superiority is that some unusual event—the arrival of a virus, perhaps—can trigger an overreaction by which elements of their own defense begin to attack components of their own cells. It is a price paid much less often by immunologically weaker men. Males are *less* likely in general to suffer from multiple sclerosis, in which an attack is mounted on brain tissue, or myasthenia gravis—the disease from which Aristotle Onassis died—in which the acetylcholine receptors at the junction between nerve and muscle, including heart muscle, are attacked. They are less likely to contract certain forms of juvenile-onset diabetes and rheumatoid arthritis, the latter of which, like migraine, can go into remission during pregnancy or during the taking of the pill. They are less likely, too, to suffer from a whole range of diseases in which the immune system acts to alter radically the balance and effect of the steroid hormones. These diseases are still very mysterious. In some cases, they seem to be brought on by stress. And they have profound effects on the brain and on personality. They include Addison's disease, in which underproduction of hormones by the adrenal glands causes apathy and depression and, in later stages, hallucinations and psychosis; Graves' disease, in which overproduction by the thyroid gland produces tension, overexcitability and disruption of the menstrual cycle; and systemic lupus erythematosus (SLE), which Robert Lahita at the Rockefeller University is now studying.

"SLE, I think, is the absolutely *prototypic* disease of this sort," says Lahita, full of enthusiasm for the general truths the study of SLE may uncover. "These other diseases affect women over men three to one, four to one, five to one. But SLE, after puberty, affects them on the order of *ten* to one and maybe more. Basically, it's an inflammatory disorder. But what actually happens is that the body mounts an attack on the genetic and protein-making machinery inside the cells of its own tissues. And this can affect brain, lungs, muscle, kidney, joints, heart and skin. About half a million Americans suffer from SLE, which is called lupus—the Latin word for wolf—because one visible symptom can be a rash on the cheeks, thought originally to give the face a wolf-like look. This doesn't always appear, though. And it often makes SLE an extremely difficult disease to diagnose.

"Now why is this disease so extraordinarily interesting? First, because it may be brought on by stress, and there's some evidence that it flares up after emotional upsets. So stress and the brain are involved from the beginning. Second, because it produces in a percentage of people many of the symptoms of depression, obsessional neurosis or schizophrenia. So it involves a *profound* connection between the brain, the immune system *and* behavior. Third, because males born with two X chromosomes and a Y seem more likely to get it—as they are other autoimmune diseases—than are normal males. So the two X chromosomes are involved. And fourth, because women who have it are made very much worse when they're on the pill; it usually starts at puberty, with few new cases after menopause; and its symptoms are very often aggravated during menstruation. So the sex hormones obviously lie somewhere at its heart.

"It's the pattern of the sex hormones in SLE that we've been investigating at Rockefeller. And what we've found out is that two things seem to have gone wrong in these SLE patients. Their estrogen is being processed in a very odd way. They're making too many by-products that have strong hormonal effects and too *few* by-products that *don't* have hormonal effects but *do* interact, as neurotransmitters, with the dopamine and norepinephrine networks in the brain. In a sense, they're making too little brain-active estrogen. At the same time, though, they have much less active *testosterone* than normal women. And the approach through testosterone looks promising. At present, there are too few good treatments for this mysterious disease. But there's one animal, the New Zealand black mouse, that can spontaneously develop SLE. And this animal follows the human pattern—more females get SLE than males, except for *castrated* males, interestingly enough. Now work done in France and by Norman Talal's group at the University of Texas in San Antonio has shown that testosterone works to *delay* and dramatically *improve* the symptoms of SLE in the New Zealand black mouse. And it may well be that it will work as an effective treatment in humans as well. Stress, then—emotion, sex chromosomes, sex hormones, neurotransmitters, a deranged immune system *and* mental disorder—who knows what truths about men and women the study of SLE will help uncover? But for the moment the irony is that, to treat it in women, doctors will soon be borrowing from men something that lies at the root of *their* response to stress, their left-hemisphere weakness and their immune inferiority—testosterone."

Response to stress. Left-hemisphere weakness. Immune inferiority. How can we connect these things *back* now to left-handedness, the learning disorders, problems of cerebral dominance and perhaps, to add them to the mix, the disorders of depression and schizophrenia? What, at the mysterious heart of the brain and the immune system, might these things have in common?

To find out, we have to stand back for a moment and survey the evidence, like detectives at the beginning of a difficult case. We have to follow the trail of clues that led to the meeting in Boston between Norman Geschwind and Robert Lahita. We have to look for a pattern.

The first place to look is at the disorders that have been identified as auto-immune. What features do they share? There are several. First, they tend to affect males either early or late in life, before puberty or after the age of about forty, while they tend to attack females between puberty and menopause—myasthenia gravis, for example, is a disease of young women and older men. The rule is not absolutely hard and fast. But in general females are worse affected when their levels of estrogen and progesterone are comparatively high. And males are worse affected when their levels of testosterone are comparatively low. XXY males, who are low in testosterone and high in estrogen compared to normal males, have, as Robert Lahita says, a high incidence of SLE and other auto-immune disorders, as might be expected. And men with hypogonadotropic hypogonadism—who *also* have abnormally low levels of testosterone—often suffer from at least *one* immune disorder, according to a recent report from two groups at Tufts University near Boston and at

St. Bartholomew's Hospital in London: celiac disease, the disease from which many *autistic* children suffer.

The second feature the auto-immune diseases have in common is *genetic.* Where a gene association is known for them, they are *all* associated with genes on the human chromosome 6. Chromosome 6 is the home of what is called the major histocompatibility complex (MHC), a cluster of genes that regulate the various and essential jobs the immune system has. They are responsible for normal cooperation between cells. They are responsible for the many different ways the body has of recognizing and attacking foreign invaders. And they are responsible for the cell-surface markers that give the tissues and cells of each individual their own unique identity.

Here, as detectives, we begin to approach the heart of the mystery. For though it is not quite clear what *other* tasks these genes have, it is beginning to emerge that they are somehow involved in *the way the cells of our male and female bodies and brains grow, recognize one another and migrate towards one another in the womb.* And they *also* seem to control in the developing brain-body system the production of testosterone and the effects it has. They are involved in the weight of the testes, the levels of testosterone in the blood and the sensitivity to testosterone that people like Mrs. Went have somehow lost.

Here at last we have something that can connect the learning disorders, left-handedness and auto-immune diseases that Norman Geschwind and Peter Behan have found in the same populations—testosterone. Testosterone, as we have said, acts to produce the *normal* pattern of cerebral dominance and lateralization in right-handed males. But it *also* acts as a depressor of the immune system; it shrinks the thymus, the gland beneath the breastbone that is responsible for the production of T-cells. *Low* levels of testosterone in the fetus, therefore, might very well have *two* separate effects. It might *alter* the normal patterns of brain organization and cell migration. And it might drastically *increase* the efficiency of the immune system. The result may be what Geschwind and Behan have found—an association between left-handedness, learning disorders and an immune system too highly geared up for the body's own good. These effects may appear independently of each other, or they may appear together. This may depend on the *stage* at which the fetus's brain hemispheres and immune system were exposed to a hormonal imbalance, how *long* they were exposed and how *great* the shortfall of testosterone was. Again, as in Bob Goy's monkeys, it may be a matter of degree.

The proof of all this lies ahead. But already there are a few more clues that suggest it is correct; they fit neatly into what Jerre Levy calls "the puzzle." In late 1982, an Israeli group provided some evidence that autism is not only *linked* to an auto-immune disease, but is *itself* an auto-immune disease. At about the same time, Albert Galaburda and his colleague Gordon Sherman began to find the same sort of abnormal brain-cell migration Galaburda had found in dyslexics in the brains of the New Zealand black mice that are prone to an auto-immune disease linked to chromosome 6 in humans—SLE. These are two small pieces of the puzzle. Another is the possible genetic connection recently found by Shelley Smith, then of the University of Miami, between dyslexia and a gene on chromosone 15 which might, Norman Geschwing suggests, be the same chromosone 15 gene that codes for a protein basic to both testosterone production *and* the setting up of the immune system. A fourth is the responsibility of a gene or genes on chromosome 6 for *another* disorder in which testosterone works to affect brain organization and behavior—CAH.

In CAH, remember, high levels of testosterone are produced by the fetal adrenal glands, because an enzyme is missing that is necessary for the routine production of cortisol, the hormone involved in stress. And stress, of course, is a *third* feature many of the auto-immune diseases, and migraine, share. They are often brought on by stress and exacerbated by stress. It looks as if something has gone profoundly wrong in them, as in CAH, with the basic chemistry of stress. This immediately gives them something in common with depression and schizophrenia, which have *also* been linked with genes on chromosome 6; with anorexia nervosa, perhaps; and with the male homosexuals made in the womb, Günter Dörner believes, as the result of stress on the pregnant mother.

We ask Norman Geschwind whether the same principles might be at work in all these things. "We just don't know," he says, "though I do think Dörner's work is interesting. We *do* know that all of these systems interact: the genes, the sex hormones, the stress hormones, the neurotransmitters of the brain and nervous system and the cells of the immune system. They each have a direct effect on each other at the molecular level. And what Dörner, among others, has shown is that in the womb these interactions are made extremely complex. For the fetus and the mother who carries it are one interacting whole. And they are both responding to the environments they find themselves in. You have, in other words, *two* sets of genes, sex hormones, stress hormones and so on influencing each other—the fetus's and the mother's. You also have the *father's* genes, which are present in the fetus, and the mother's father's and mother's genes which are present in her, to add to the complication.

"It's not just the genes of the fetus, then, that are important; —genes by themselves won't tell us everything we want to know; there's no single gene as such for dyslexia or autism or depression or left-handedness or homosexuality. All there are are interlocking sets of potentials or predispositions which can be forced into expression by the environment, most *importantly,* in the first place, by the hormonal and immune environment of the womb.

"We know very little of the details of this. But we know just enough to be able to make some predictions—and that's the business of science, to make predictions and test them. It could be predicted, for example, that male homosexuals have rather different immune systems from the general, heterosexual population, and there's some evidence that that may be so. It could be predicted that dyslexics and their relatives have a high incidence of early white or gray hair, which is often found alongside auto-immune diseases and which may itself represent an immune-attack on the pigment-forming cells of the hair follicles. We're now looking into this, and I'm fairly sure it's so. And it could be predicted, last, that in women with auto-immune diseases like SLE, and in their families, there is a higher incidence of left-handedness and learning disorders than usual. That too, as you know, I am already studying."

A few days after our meeting with Geschwind—by chance— we met a young woman who suffers from SLE, currently under treatment with prednisone and a cytotoxic drug. We asked her whether there were any left-handers in her family. "My father," she said, "and probably one of my brothers—he was encouraged to change hands." Any learning disorders? "Yes," she said. "I also have dyslexia."

This, in scientific parlance, is an anecdote. And an anecdote and a quarter, the saying goes, will buy you a cup of coffee. The truth of the connection between left-handedness, SLE and the learning disorders will have to wait for what science calls "the numbers"—the same "numbers" Albert Galaburda is waiting for with his New Zealand black mice—and for the results of Norman Geschwind's and Robert Lahita's collaboration.

One last coda for this chapter, for left-handers who may be horrified to learn of a seeming predisposition for learning disabilities and afflictions of the immune system. Nature is evenhanded, both in the abilities and disorders that are parceled out to men and women *and* in the balance of the failings and skills that are handed out to left-handers. In 1979, Marian Annett of the Lanchester Polytechnic in Coventry, England, showed that there was a high proportion of left-handers among artists, musicians, mathematicians and engineers, in people with an advanced degree of the same right-hemisphere visual-spatial skills possessed so narrowly by some autistic children. And in late 1982, Camilla Benbow at Johns Hopkins University looked again at the mathematically gifted children she had located in her previous studies. In them too she found a large number of left-handers, three times the number of the general population. Even when they were right-handed, almost half of them had a parent or a sibling who was a left-hander.

Echoing Pierre Flor-Henry's view about the fine line that separates retardation from genius, Norman Geschwind says: "In principle, you might be able to prevent the learning disorders by altering the hormonal environment in the womb or by using the techniques being made available by genetic engineering. But if you did, you'd certainly want to find a way that would protect the often *superior* talents of left-handers and people with these disabilities. There is something else that ought to be added too. Even if left-handers do have a higher rate of certain diseases, they may well be found in the future to have a lower frequency of others. After all, women get all sorts of diseases that men do not—and yet they live longer because they have far less heart disease and other disorders.

PART FIVE

SEX

15

WHY SEX EXISTS

IN 1965, BEHAVIORAL scientist S.D. Porteus wrote: "If a visitor from outer space, who was familiar only with asexual reproduction, were to survey the human scene, the subject of (her) greatest mystification would be the differentiation of the sexes. The obvious outward, physical, physiological and mental differences would seem to (her) tremendous, but when confronted with observations of temperament, disposition, habits, attitudes, strengths and weaknesses, predispositions of immunities in health and records of . . . achievement, (she) would probably conclude that men and women belong to two different species . . . Only the fact that the two species interbred freely might possibly disturb (her) theory. . . ."

He feels her presence—a stir in the room, a smell, a tone of voice. And he turns. Suddenly his muscles stiffen. There is a faint flush on his face. His heart beats faster. And his pupils dilate as he continues to look across the room.

She notices his quick reaction to her. And her sympathetic nervous system responds as if to danger. Her pulse quickens.

187

Her palms tingle with warmth. A blush suffuses her face. She glances downward to hide the moment, half-conscious of a prickling in her scalp. Her nipples suddenly press disquietingly against the stretched silk of her dress. She feels for a second as if she has been attacked. Her breathing becomes quicker, shallower. She pulls distractedly at a cigarette, dimly irritated. But when she finally looks up at him to meet his stare, her pupils too are subtly wider than they were a few moments before.

Each is now intensely conscious of the other, gradually drawn into a performance with many spectators but a real audience of one. The drama they play from across the room is one of glances, gestures and tones of voice, of coded information given and received. The result is a flurry of small-print news about suitability, status and availability, each item buried in the gathering bustle of the party. He shows his leanness, his success with others, his clothes, his tan, the readiness of his smile. She offers him a softness, a seriousness and an adroit, flirtatious coolness with the man she is talking to. As she moves, she runs her unringed fingers down the long cascade of her throat. A glimpse of breast is proffered, then deferred. The senses of both become heightened. And the drama—uninterrupted—moves into a new phase. Wherever they go, moving still in circles that never quite touch, she hears his voice, arguing, laughing, teasing. And he follows her constantly with his eyes. Finally, she stands apart from the others for a moment, fishing with her tongue for a piece of ice in her glass. Their eyes lock as she looks up again. For a second she feels panicked. But then he is at her side.

The restaurant is well chosen, uncrowded, candlelit. A piano plays softly, sealing off the diners from one another. They sit in a well of separateness, testing each other, gently probing. It is a process as old as man. She watches his quiet authority with the waiters, the way he eats and moves and sips his wine. She measures his real interest in her, sifting the clues of words and eyes and mouth and tongue. He takes in the glow of her skin, the whiteness of her teeth and the smooth promise of her body. And he leans forward to touch her hand where it lies, curved, around the stem of her wineglass. As the evening deepens, their talk becomes more muted and more charged. Amid the spell each has managed to weave around the moment, a decision has now to be made, unvoiced and undiscussed.

To that decision, to their new closeness, comes the hormonal status of their bodies. As they talk, seemingly idly, in the restaurant, it is the balance of estrogen and progesterone in her that helps produce her glow, her self-assurance and her readiness. And it is the level of testosterone in him that induces his confidence and the sort of canny, disguised aggression that he is showing in his pursuit of her. All of these hormones act, as we know, upon the brain. And they interact there with chemically controlled systems governing memory, learning, past associations and expectations of pleasure and reward. From the beginning of their drama, the brains of both have been regulating and following the intricate patterns of their courtship—one step forward, one step back. Sensory receptors have recorded the looks, the movements, the words, the food, the wine, the touch. All that information has been integrated with experience and anticipation at a high level of the brain. From there the good news has traveled to self-reinforcing brain circuits controlling pleasure and reward. Messenger chemicals—in this case dopamine and norepinephrine—have carried it downward to deep brain structures that are responsible for emotion and motivation. All of these interlocking systems, influenced by hormonal messages from the secreting glands of the body, are constantly communicating with each other, totting up the pluses and minuses of the flirtation and initiating behavior that will carry it forward. And each can still respond—to too much food and drink, too bold a move, a false word, a bad impression—by influencing the others to turn off, tune down, withdraw.

Their evening, in other words, is first and always a matter of "the right chemistry." And at the heart of it—as they drink their coffee, still wondering, waiting for the outcome—is the bundle of tissue at the base of each of their brains, the hypothalamus. The hypothalamus is the keeper of the border between brain and body. It receives from and transmits to virtually every area of their brains. But at the same time it is in constant two-way communication with the outlands of their bodies. At the moment it is monitoring and modulating their blood pressure, their temperature and their breathing rate. It is inspecting their appetite. And it is integrating, expressing and pushing forward their separate drives towards sex. Neither, of course, is aware of its influence. But it was the hypothalamus—acting through the long-distances messengers of the pituitary gland—that ordered up from testis and ovary the levels of hormones that began this evening. And it is the hypothalamus now that is bidding up from their adrenal glands the cortisol and epinephrine that are responsible for the heightened charge and warmth of their encounter. It makes her exquisitely sensitive to the hand that reaches out to touch her face, to the leg that is stretched out, gently leaning against hers. And it makes him feel, by calling up more testosterone and an accelerated sperm production, a new tightness in his loins.

Nothing is said. They walk through the night, he with his arm about her, touching the curve of her breast, imagining it, imagining her, without clothes. Nerve impulses race back and upward in her, to spine, to brain, to hypothalamus. And once more her nipples press against the material of her dress. A rise in circulating estrogen makes her moist. She moves closer to him and they stop to kiss, each gravely and slowly exploring the biology of the other's mouth. They stand still for a moment, understanding through smell and the sensation of breath and heartbeat that they are now part of a common arousal. Somewhere in the wash of hormones and the complex brain-talk of the messenger chemicals, a decision has been made. She shivers, though it is not cold. The tiny hairs along her forearms become erect.

Inside the apartment, he gradually strips her of her clothes, whispering, kissing, reassuring. His excitement feeds on hers as he uncovers her. He sees her swelling lips, the rush of blood to her areoles and the blush that spreads across her body. The reservoirs in the erectile tissues of his penis fill up with blood and trap more and more of the blood that the brain orders up in compensation. Fully erect now, he quickly removes his own clothes. He teases at her breasts with his mouth. He runs his hands down her flanks, reaching little by little towards the center of her. He fingers her clitoris, which also engorges with blood to become erect. He explores the wetness being spilled out into her vagina from glands lining the entrance and walls of her vaginal canal.

Both are now creatures of the lower brain and the autonomic nervous system—the control of the reasoning forebrain has been removed. The parasympathetic nervous system is causing moistness and hardness: the drop of moisture at the end of his penis, the discharge of hormones from glands in armpit, breast and pubic skin. And the sympathetic nervous system is washing the muscles of both of them with epinephrine. Their hearts are racing faster. Their breathing has become heavy. Their muscles are taut. Meanwhile, their adrenal glands are pumping out testosterone in a mix of other hormones, making her clitoris more sensitive and giving him an extra urgency, centered on his penis and the reflex arc that now governs his erection from nerve centers at the base of his spine.

Automatic nervous impulses rush to their pelvic muscles. Their excitement mounts—moving, moaning, smell, taste, touch, hearing. She pulls him towards her. He enters her. Now both are working, matching the rhythm of their movements to each other, thrusting, lifting and pushing. Slowly the sympathetic nervous tension builds in each of them to a higher and higher pitch. Pressure changes in her womb. Blood vessels are increasingly constricted. Glands are burdened. Muscles are drum tight. But then, suddenly, release. The right hemisphere of the brain takes complete command, and the parasympathetic system suddenly erupts into action to take over their bodies. The messenger chemical acetylcholine takes the place of epinephrine. And where before there was tension, there is now an explosion into calmness. The muscles of his penis contract involuntarily, to send a stream of sperm arcing into her. Nerve impulses race towards his brain. And "Yes!" he cries in a great exhilaration of air. At the same time contractions begin to ripple along the walls of her vagina as he shudders within her. They reach upwards towards her womb and downward again to her pulsing, disgorging clitoris. A new hormone, oxytocin, is released from her pituitary. Her skin darkens. "Yes!" she cries too as she plummets back to rest.

They are quiet for a moment, as hearts slow, blood pressure drops and their bodies return to normal. He is very quickly asleep. But she lies awake, as substances within the ejaculate now inside her cause the contractions in her womb and vagina to continue, only more slowly, helping in the transport of the sperm. As he begins to breathe more deeply, she continues to feel vaguely aroused.

Porteus's visitor from outer space would be somewhat mystified by all this. Being familiar only with asexual reproduction —cloning—she would have grave problems, as Porteus says, with both sexual reproduction and the gender differences that conspire to make it possible. She would also have a hard time explaining to her distant bosses just how it is that the males and females of one species have come to dominate the planet. Where would she begin? We are not the biggest of all species—the blue whale is a thousand times larger. We are not the longest living —a bristlecone pine can outlast a hundred and fifty human generations. We are not anything like as numerous as birds or insects or plants. And we don't reproduce particularly fast; species of bacteria, for example, can do in twenty minutes what takes us nine months. Only two things, in fact, combine to make us in any way special. The ratio between our brain weight and body mass is among the highest on earth. And we are by far the sexiest creatures—that we know of—in the universe.

This is the backdoor way into the complexities of the human brain—through the processes of sex and reproduction. For the brain, as well as being who we are as men and women, is also, to repeat, the product of the long passage of our shared evolution. It is the expression of genes serially selected by generation after generation of men and women for transmission into the next. And the mechanism through which the successive acts of selection were made is, in the first instance, in our species as in almost all others, sex. Sex requires that, in the making of a new individual or individuals, genes from *two* individuals who have reached sexual maturity should be mixed. One of the individuals is female—in mammals, she carries the X chromosome. The other individual is male—he carries the Y.

Let us suppose that Porteus's baffled intergalactic anthropologist is told of this. And let us suppose that she is told something else important for her understanding: That there is one thing that every individual of every species, both sexual and asexual, has in common. Every individual is merely a protective envelope containing the seeds of propagation, skillfully packaged to maximize the likelihood that it will live long enough to produce more of its kind. In asexual species like her own, the means of production is cloning—the individual requires no outside help. But in species like ourselves, the means of production is different. The attributes of our bodies and brains are transmitted by sexual means. They are designed to meet the requirements of survival and successful reproduction, which in our case includes courtship and the pursuit of sex.

She has at this point, let us imagine, a reasonably good grasp of evolution and the processes by which genes are inherited. "I see," she may very well say, "different creatures are *in brain and in body* the expressions-in-action of their DNA, their genes, designed, with more or less success, to meet the demands of particular environments and particular lifestyles. If an individual inherits a *poor* combination of genes, a combination that results in an inability to survive or to surmount obstacles—or results in inappropriate sexual behavior or unhealthy offspring—then the combination doesn't make it through to the next generation, the next evolutionary round. Only if a combination, or a DNA mutation, supplies an *advantage*—a new feature, a new chemical, a new quirk of behavior—is it likely, then, to survive and prosper and spread through a whole population. And only if enough of these changes *do* occur and accumulate in a population, so that it's no longer able to mix with the group of which it's an off-shoot, do you arrive at a new species."

Armed with this information about the connections between DNA, the brain, the body, the pressures of the environment, sex and reproduction—let us further propose—our visitor then begins to study one of the species closest to us: the chimpanzee. It has always been assumed that the chimpanzee and his relative, the gorilla, are the distant cousins of man—they split off from the path that led to man ten or fifteen million years ago. But recently the DNA and similar proteins in chimpanzee, gorilla and man have been compared by several groups, notably that of Vincent Sarich and Allan Wilson of the University of California at Berkeley. And they have established that, genetically, there is only a one-percent difference between them; *they are ninety-nine-percent identical.* The evolutionary time scale, then, has had to be rewritten. For the gorilla and the chimpanzee are not in fact the distant cousins of man, several times removed. They are virtually our brothers.

The first thing our visitor will notice about chimpanzees is that they have small brains, less than a third the size of modern man. She will also notice that they live at the periphery of the jungle, not on the open grasslands on which man is supposed to have evolved; that their birthrate is very low; that they do not usually cooperate in food-gathering or give each other food; and that their sex life is both communal and rudimentary, by comparison with ours. Chimpanzee males have sex, if possible, with every individual female in their troop who comes into heat. And they have sex several times. They usually, in effect, take turns: queue up for what is, in the end, an unsophisticated and functional sexual performance, without introduction and not face to face, and lasting about seven seconds. This species-specific sexual behavior is organized, our visitor now knows, by the genes, and it is expressed in the chemistry and structure of the brain.

And it means that, in evolution, no selective advantage was conferred on any chimpanzee individual, male or female, who went about things in any different way. It is also, however, expressed in the body. For if our visitor looks closely, she will see that, although male chimpanzees do not compete with each other for access to females, *they do compete with each other in sperm production.* Male chimps have testicles six times larger than humans, when body weight is taken into account, and they produce very large quantities of sperm. Given their breeding system, in other words, natural selection has favored males who can outproduce their peers and so gain a slight edge in the representation of their genes in the next generation. The same correlation between large testicles, group living and a free-for-all breeding system has been found in other primates.

The picture in humans, as we all know—and as our visitor quickly found out on arrival—is quite different. First, as a percentage of body weight, human male testicles are small, as they tend to be in other primate species with a one-to-one breeding system. And second, humans, both male and female, seem to be designed for a much more elaborate and complex sexual performance. We are hairless, for maximum visibility and sensitivity. The male penis and female breasts—indices of sexual maturity and reproductive ability—are carried up front, permanently on display. We tend to copulate face to face, to have as much personal contact as possible. And we have sex much more often than chimps do. Human females show none of the outward signs of estrus that female chimpanzees display. Human beings are not hidebound by breeding seasons or breeding cycles, as they and almost all other primates are. Instead, we have sex not only for reproduction but also—as she has seen—for pleasure.

Possessed, now, of the useful tool of comparison, our visitor will notice, as she scans the species, two things about humans that seem to be related to their sexual behavior, things that further distinguish them from their nearest relatives. First, they have long mateships. They are basically, if shakily, monogamous, unlike almost all other primates except the gibbon and the siamang. And second, they have a division of labor between the sexes; they cooperate, and there seems to be general agreement about who does what. Out of a total of two hundred one societies listed in George Murdock's *Ethnographic Atlas,* cooking is a strictly female activity in one hundred fifty-eight and exclusively male in only five. Hunting is done by males in one hundred sixty-six societies out of one hundred seventy-nine and never exclusively by females. It is the same story for other job assignments. Males are almost always responsible for lumbering, metalworking, house building, fishing and the making of musical instruments. Females, by and large, take over weaving, clothes making and the preparation of drinks and narcotics. This elaborate division of labor is virtually unique in nature, except among birds.

Having understood this much, our visitor from outer space would want to put two and two together for her report. Genes and sex chromosomes; large brains; complex sexual behavior, pleasure, monogamy, cooperation and division of labor. Could these things explain why human beings have come to dominate the planet Earth? But, if so, how could so much be achieved by the only one percent of genetic change from chimpanzees? And, if so, why did this small genetic change produce such large differences between human males and females—much greater than they are between male and female chimps? By now other questions, too, would be crowding in upon her. What is the general connection between sex and the brain? Why is it that large and large-brained creatures have sex, while only small and small-brained creatures reproduce asexually? What is the advantage of sex? And what is at the root of all maleness and femaleness?

To answer these questions, Porteus's visiting explorer will have to go a long way back in history; past our first settlements a mere 15,000 years ago, past our first tools and past our beginnings, backward in evolutionary time and out into nature, to ancestral species that have been around for millions and even billions of years, long before our arrival. There she will have to ask two further questions that are basic to who we are, questions that the population of her galaxy, all female, are also desperate to have answered. Why does sex exist? And why do males exist?

These may seem trivial questions with an easy answer—it is for the good of the species, to speed up their evolution. But it's not as simple as that. As George Williams of the State University of New York at Stony Brook has pointed out, selection takes place not at species level but at the level of the *individual* and of the individual's genes. And sex puts the individual and her genes at a tremendous disadvantage—only *half* of her genes are transmitted to the next generation. The disadvantage, then, in genetic terms, is exactly fifty percent. And to counteract it, there must be found for sex a corresponding fifty percent advantage. This presents an awesome task for evolutionary theorists. For the genes for even a one-percent disadvantage will very quickly disappear from any population, other things being equal.

For some years now evolutionists have been using computers in their search for a solution. And for the past three or four years they have been playing the generation game with a vengeance, using high-speed electronics to trace the success or failure of genes under different circumstances over thousands of millennia. Until very recently, though, they simply could not come up with a scenario in which genes for sex would establish themselves and be continuously selected for. They were of one mind with George Williams, who wrote in the last paragraph of his seminal *Sex and Evolution:* "I really do not understand the role of sex in either organic or biotic evolution. (But) at least I can claim . . . the consolation of abundant company."

In 1980, however, William Hamilton, a tall question mark of an Englishman now at the University of Michigan at Ann Arbor, began quietly publishing a series of extremely elegant papers in which he offered an original solution. And his solution has important implications for the connections between sex, the sex hormones, the development of the brain and the immune system.

"Men and women," Hamilton says carefully in his office at the university's Museum of Zoology, "are descended from the first multicellular organisms. And I've always been puzzled by how these organisms could come together and survive. It's true that there are certain advantages to being multicellular if an organism is competing with smaller forms. With different groups of cells performing different functions, it can form a protective layer against the outside environment and so be able to colonize new habitats. It can make more efficient use of energy, like plants growing towards the light. And it can move. But it is still, for all that, at a distinct *disadvantage* to forms of life that have held on to the one-cell option. First, it grows and reproduces more slowly because it's larger and more complex. And second, it has to find a way of coping with a new problem. It has to find a way of recognizing which cells belong to its little community and which don't, which are friends and which are enemies. It has to have a self-recognition system, a biochemical password or passwords of some sort—the beginnings of a rudimentary immune system. If it doesn't have this, its cells can't be expected to stick together and cooperate. And if it doesn't have this, then it won't be able to identify and defend itself against the one-cell enemies that try to enter, attack and use its cells for their own purposes: viruses, bacteria, parasites.

"Now in the business of self-recognition and defense, these parasites will always have a distinct edge over multicellulars. For they reproduce much faster—look at bacteria, which divide every twenty minutes or so. And in an interaction of this kind, where one organism is constantly trying to figure out a way into another, and the other is constantly having to find a way to keep it out, evolution favors the one that breeds quickest. For natural selection operates in it at a higher rate. Fast-breeding parasites, in other words, can always adapt to master the multicellulars' defense system more quickly than slow-breeding multicellulars can adapt to change it—mutations will provide them with the passwords and they will win. So the multicellular, in the end, will *always* be overwhelmed by forms of unicellular life unless—and only unless—it can come up with a *new* genetic trick to level the odds, to speed up the making of new passwords and new defense chemicals. That trick, I believe, was sex. Sex—the mixing of genes between *two* multicellulars—would make for radically new arrangements, new passwords, new immune defenses, to help keep the parasites out. Sex would now give the multicellulars an edge in the evolutionary game of catch-up, but only a small edge. And so, as it gets larger and larger, all the way down to us, sex would constantly be selected for. Sex would have to continue and parthenogenesis—cloning—would disappear, *except* in small, peripheral populations where there are few or no parasites. This is what we see in nature.

"This brings me to a second point," Hamilton continues. "In evolution, new programs are derived from old ones. Our complicated immune system is derived from the multicellular's need to keep out invaders. Our nervous system is derived from its developing need to monitor the environment and communicate internally between groups of specializing cells. And our sex hormones are derived from its need to regulate and time the manufacture of its sex cells. All three systems, in other words, *coevolved* together out of the basic need to recognize what is *self* and what is *other*. And it's no surprise that they should be so intricately interlinked in us today."

If Hamilton is right, then it was the requirement of an immune system and the existence of parasites that made sex desirable: it gave a fifty percent advantage to the organisms that adopted it. And it was sex in turn that made large growth, and hence the need for a large brain, possible: in a sense the brain, from its beginnings, developed for the purposes of sex. But this still doesn't explain why there are *two* sexes, so different from one another. Exchanging genes, after all, doesn't necessarily mean that there should be any *difference* between the two exchangers. When bacteria, for example, use sex, as they do, there is no difference that can be found between the giver of DNA and the taker. Why two sexes, then?

Here evolutionary science really *does* have an accepted answer. When the evolutionary step towards sex is taken by a multicellular organism, cells specifically designed for mixing and reproduction are produced. But, as Graham Parker of Liverpool University in England has shown, there is an inherent instability that acts against their always being of the same size. The pressures of competition begin—selection pressures. These selection pressures favor slightly *larger* sex cells than usual, a slightly larger investment in the individuals to be made from them. And these, in turn, make for cheats—*smaller* sex cells than usual, produced in greater numbers to compete for the bigger ones.

"From then on," says William Hamilton, "the pattern becomes clearer and clearer. The small sex cells become more and more competitive; they become highly mobile, they learn to swim, while the large sex cells become immobile and fixed. The cheats become sperm and the cells for which they compete become eggs. And that's what we end up with. Sperm and eggs. Small investors and large investors. Egg-seekers and egg-providers. Males and females."

16

UP THE LADDER: THE SEXUAL TWO-STEP

WITH THE ARRIVAL of males and females, sex in nature becomes almost unbelievably various. But it *does* conform to certain rules that stem from the fundamental imbalance between them—the fact that the female is the egg-provider and the male the egg-seeker. And it *does* make use of certain basic mechanisms and a certain basic chemistry—in evolution, new programs have been progressively built on top of old ones. If we are to understand the implications, then, of the differences between the him and her with whom we began this particular story, the differences they have inherited, we have to look at the path that sex in nature took towards ourselves.

The first thing to be said is that every male or female organism in nature has one job only, the only job on which selection operates: to find a source of energy in the environment where it finds itself and to use that energy to grow and reproduce successfully into the next generation. The second thing is that, as we approach the branch of the evolutionary tree on which we sit, the male and female sex hormones have taken over the timing, attraction mechanisms and, above all, energy expenditures that this job requires.

These expenditures of energy are different in males and females because the amount of energy they invest in their *sex cells* is quite different. Sperm is a cheap and easily renewable resource; in humans, males can produce in half a second more sperm, the smallest cells in their body, than the eggs a woman can produce in her whole lifetime. And so males in nature can afford to spend their energy searching out more than one batch of eggs. Their imperative is to develop ways of locating and then persuading as many females as possible to accept their sperm. Whatever ways are successful are selected for in the bodies, brains and behavior of males, under the general control of the male sex hormones. Females, meanwhile, have to make a larger investment of energy in their eggs. And it is in their interests to develop energy-efficient ways of guarding or withholding them and only delivering them up to the best males—the best male genes—available. To do this, they have to develop ways to *discriminate,* to choose between the genes on offer. And whatever qualities contribute to their successful choice are selected for in the bodies, brains and behavior of females, this time under the general control of the female sex hormones.

The imbalance created becomes particularly marked with the emergence of animals onto dry land. For now males and females, instead of simply discharging their sex cells into the environments of sea and air, have instead taken the less wasteful option of coming together to mate; there is internal fertilization; reproduction is less hit or miss. Under this new dispensation, females continue to spend as much energy as they can afford on their valuable sex cells. But they can now *maximize* their investment, for the good of their individual offspring, by investing in a smaller number of them. They can now produce *large* eggs, stocked with nutrients (birds and reptiles); they can provide a long period of internal gestation for growth (mammals); and they can also provide the extended maternal care for which their production of eggs—their already large investment—has preadapted them (birds and mammals). Depending on their species and their environment, then, the brain-body system of females is now committed to the working out of an equation that involves the resources available, the need for growth and the length of the reproductive life.

They now have to come up with an answer to the question: How many eggs and offspring can I afford to produce and rear, if necessary, on the energy budget I have at my disposal? This is the female's prime, and selfish, concern. And, given it, she cannot afford to divert her energies to other activities. Although she needs to achieve a certain size for egg production to be able to start up, she cannot, for example, spend *too* much time and energy on growth, or she will be outproduced by her less energy-wasteful sisters: her genes will be at a disadvantage. And she cannot afford, unless there is a good reason for it, to spend too much energy on other potential departments in her life: movement and competition for a mate. It is in her best interests to let the competition come to her.

Males, by contrast, have quite different limitations on their energy budget, even though their aim is the same: to push as many copies of their genes as they effectively can into the next generation. They do not usually provide care or resources for their offspring—the female does that for them. And their sperm remains cheap. They can afford, then, to spend much more of their energy on the finding and securing of a mate or mates. Where size is of *no* advantage, males can afford to remain small and start their reproductive lives as early as possible, earlier than a female can. And where size *is* an advantage—where there is overt male-male competition, for example—they can afford to spend much more of their energy on growth than females can afford. Males, in other words, have more options than females have, though they too have to work out, in brain and body, the environment-growth-resources equation and answer a question of their own: How do I maximize my own chances of reproductive success and minimize the chances of other males? How much energy can I afford per mating and per breeding season?

Relative size, relative growth, different forms of competition and different ages at the onset of reproductive life, which we call puberty: The males and females of different species have found different answers to their reproductive questions in different environments. But, whatever the answers are, they are under the direction and control of the male and female sex hormones, the language that testis and ovary speak to the male and female body and brain. They are also *complementary* to one another. They are locked in together. For a male who has answered *his* question successfully is by definition a partner in an evolutionary two-step with a female who has answered *hers* successfully. The mating system in any species is the expression-in-action of this evolutionary two-step, passed down through the genes from generation to generation, given direction by the sex hormones and expressed in the male and female body and brain. Males, the sex-seekers, are likely to have inherited superior visual-spatial skills, as Pierre Flor-Henry says, and a capacity for aggression. Females, the sex competed for, are likely to have evolved with a more balanced and discriminatory brain.

The basic sexual strategies of male and female—the pursuer and the pursued—have usually conspired, in internally fertilizing animals like ourselves, to produce a rat-race, dog-eat-dog polygyny. This polygyny, on the face of it, looks as if it works to the disadvantage of the female. But in fact it works hugely to her advantage. For by keeping hold of the manufacturing end of reproduction she has forced males into the service business and they must jump to her tune. They are in the genetic bind of having to do whatever it is that the female requires of them. Irven DeVore, a Harvard anthropologist, is quite certain of this. "Males," he says unequivocally, "are a vast breeding experiment run by females."

One of the things males are usually locked into doing by the female is to compete with one another, thus sorting out for the female's ultimate benefit the toughest, the most ambitious and the most resilient genes from the weaker and less capable. Another, of course, is to court her. Courtship is the elaborate process by which a male and female organism scan, tune and prime one another hormonally for the difficult and perhaps dangerous business of internal fertilization—the male inclined to rush, the female slow and patient. Courtship in nature takes many forms. And sometimes it works to protect males, who can find out in the process whether a female has already been inseminated or not. Usually she hasn't, though; it is not usually in her interests to attempt more than one mating. And so courtship, for the most part, is no more than a job application questionnaire designed and selected for by the female employer. The questions are many and subtle, and they are all interrelated. First, is the male of the right species? Females cannot afford a cross-species mating, a mistake, as males, who risk only a few sperm, can. Since they have much more at stake, their recognition mechanisms are under much firmer hormonal control. Second, is he vigorous? Nature is full of chases, displays, dances, forced marches, obstacle courses and other tests imposed on the male by the female. And it is clear that they are designed to deliver information not only about the male's genes, but also about his hormonal levels and his sperm capability. (If he has recently mated elsewhere, he will have less hormonal drive, less sperm on call and less vigor.) Third, is he resourceful? Can the male find food, build a nest or command a territory, and so pass the genes for these things down to a female's (male, at least) offspring? Precopulatory demonstrations of territory, home building and gifts—of either protein or symbolic value—are equally common. And fourth, is he sociable? Is the male capable of modulating his hormone-driven behavior, so that his aggression is channeled into actions that prime the female for ovulation? It is the quality of the male's inborn or partly learned performance that induces in the female's body the hormonal conditions necessary for a successful mating. If the male shows aggression or less than perfect skill in any part of his performance, the female brain can often shut down production of the messenger hormones that govern the delivery of her eggs.

The media through which these questions are asked and answered are sight and touch; copulation itself, in some mammals, causes the release of the female's valuable eggs. But they are also hormonal; information about both male and female is passed between them via substances under the direct control of the sex hormones—pheromones. Pheromones are the products of specialized scent glands; in humans found in, but not confined to, their armpits. They appear in urine, including human urine. And they carry, for animals at least, important information about a potential partner's hormonal status and readiness for sex. They may also, Hamilton believes, carry information about an animal's identity—his or her immune makeup. And this may explain why there is so little incest in nature. Incest, in Hamilton's terms, is the mating of two individuals whose immune systems are closely related. And it makes sense that a mechanism through which it could be avoided should have evolved. For mating between two related immune systems would produce offspring without the advantages to be derived from fifty-percent gene shuffling. They would fail to stay ahead in the immune race against parasites.

These, then, are the separate legacies of maleness and femaleness. And for every species the rule that governs them is the same: Sex, reproduction and whatever it takes to help the female and her offspring survive are inextricably linked in a genetic program that is ultimately dictated by the female. It is she who takes on most of the physical responsibility for the continuation of the species. And whatever qualities she chooses in the body and behavior of a male—whatever qualities there are in her that encourage her to make a successful choice—are then bred into the future population. They become part of the genetic blueprint that governs the sexual and reproductive behavior of both males and females in the future.

In the vast majority of species, then, the female's choosiness has resulted in an arrangement by which males are forever competing with one another for the limiting resource of her eggs.

But in a number of species, group-living species like chimpanzees, males have been bred into a line of work that directly benefits the female and her offspring and alters the balance of power between male and female—protection. This is a job for which the male has been preadapted; where there is an advantage to being large he can afford to be larger. But it doesn't put an end to male-male competition. And it still only directly favors *some* males, as many as the female group needs for it to be able to exploit efficiently and safely the resources available in its territory. The rest are excluded unless they can fight their way in or otherwise displace the males that control or protect the group.

The imbalance remains, then, and the females ultimately dictate the shape a species' society takes on. Only if a *further* step is taken does the imbalance disappear. Only if the males of a species are bred into a line of work that is even *more* essential to the individual female and her offspring than their collective protection do the beginnings of sexual equality arrive. This step has been taken by ninety percent of birds and by a few primates, including the gibbon, the siamang and Homo sapiens. The step is male parenting.

Male parenting, which humans provide in greater measure than any other species, is a remarkable step forward for the female. And it frees her from having to take sole responsibility for providing for her offspring, and it allows her to have more infants than she otherwise could. It comes, however, with a price tag. For if male parenting is to be established as a pattern, the female has to give up some of her old power. She has to do something to correct the biological imbalance. In polygynous species, it does not matter much whose infants are whose—assurance of paternity is not part of the polygynous package. But if a male is to be expected to provide resources over the long haul of child-rearing, then he has to have some guarantee that the children are actually his. This is the key element in the human sexual trade-off that governs the sexual and reproductive behavior of *our* species. For hundreds of thousands of human generations it has been built into our genetic program: resource-producing males and paternity-guaranteeing, mothering females coming together and remaining together for the sake of their children.

Owen Lovejoy is a bearded, brisk, tough-minded man in his thirties, a professor at Kent State University in Ohio and another of the new generation of scientists who are bucking old assumptions and facing up to old, unanswered questions. At Kent State and elsewhere, Lovejoy holds positions in anthropology, human anatomy and orthopedic surgery. He has worked in close association with Donald Johanson, the discoverer, in Ethiopia, of the now famous Lucy—the skeleton of the earliest known upright-walking hominid. And he believes that male parenting, in our species, was ultimately responsible for human civilization.

"The species which offers the most intense and highest-quality paternal care is man," he says. "And I believe that the emergence of paternal care is absolutely fundamental to our evolution. Anthropologists have always argued that it is the use of tools that separates man from all other primates. Tools, big brain, language and upright posture: they all somehow come together in one evolutionary bundle. And I think that's nonsense. For me, there's only one thing that can explain all the things we want to have explained: walking on two legs, intelligence, culture, dominance. And that's the mating and parent-care pattern that evolved in our species—the division of labor for greater reproductive success. A sort of monogamy. We'll never find it in fossil form, of course. But I believe that it's basic to our emergence as Homo sapiens."

We talk, over several hours, in an off-campus motel restaurant, a favorite haunt of Lovejoy's. "Look," he says, "I'm an early type. And we early types aren't interested in what's gone on in the last four or five hundred thousand years. We're interested in the long haul of human evolution. And that's what makes Lucy so fascinating. Because she presents us with a problem. First, she's three and a half million years old—older than *any* tools or human culture we know of. Second, she's not very smart—she has a primitive skull much like an ape's. But third, despite all this, she had a body that was fully upright and she could walk in exactly the same way we walked in here. Now why would she need to do that? To hunt? To avoid predators? No. She'd be much better off on all fours. Upright humans can only do about forty percent of the speed of the patas monkey; they can only just outrun a fast snake; and their walking speed is about the same as a chicken's. Hardly what you'd want in the dangerous open grasslands hominids are thought to have evolved in after they left the forests. Would she need to do it to feed? No. The teeth of Lucy's species show that they were generalist eaters. And you don't need upright posture in the savanna on *that* diet. *Why,* then?" Lovejoy leans on the question. "The answer is simple, it seems to me. Lucy's species—*Australopithecus afarensis*—our earliest known ancestors, were *food* carriers. And long before they moved out into the open savanna they carried food to one another.

"No big deal, you might think. *Very* big deal. Because, to exist, an adaptation as big as this has *got* to show a reproductive advantage. The enormous anatomical change necessary for this behavior *must* have to do with survival and reproductive success. It's not just early men suddenly deciding to be nice to each other for no reason. Where would be the incentive? Well, there obviously *was* an incentive, and I propose that it was the result of a new deal between males and females and a new way of bringing up offspring, the whole thing cemented by sex.

"The best way to see what I mean is to look at chimpanzees, our nearest living relative. Chimps mature very slowly, just like humans. They have biggish brains for a primate. And they use rudimentary tools and weapons and they walk upright once in a while. They avoid incest. They have quite elaborate kinship networks. And they even sometimes prefer—we're beginning to learn—one sexual partner over a breeding period. But the one thing they *don't* do, as we do, is forage for one another. A mother, carrying and often dropping and damaging her infant, has to feed and fend for herself. This means that a female chimp can only *manage* one infant at a time. Her birth rate is very low. The result is that chimps are barely able to maintain their population—they're becoming extinct. They've never been able to leave the forest where they evolved.

"Early man, you see, faced the same problem. And evolutionarily speaking, there's only *one* way round it. Put up the calorie intake of the female and allow her to spend more time parenting, preferably in a protected spot, so that she can take care of more than one infant at a time. The male, in other words, has *got* to start providing food. How can he do this? He can't carry it in his mouth, as foxes and birds do. He *has* to walk upright and use his hands. And why should he do this? What does he get in return? Reliable sex and reliable care for his genetic investment."

Sexual access and some guarantee of paternity in exchange for more resources than the female can command for herself, all for the good of the children: This is the basic trade-off involved in what Owen Lovejoy calls "a sort of monogamy." And certain things follow from it. Human females don't advertise or announce when they are fertile. Their ovulation, in other words, is concealed. And they are more or less continuously sexually receptive. A woman can and will take on a man more than a few days each month. A number of *other* primates seem to have taken small steps in one or the other of these two directions. But their combination is extremely marked in humans. And Lovejoy believes that they appeared as part of the evolutionary package that included male provisioning and general upright posture.

This would indeed make sense. For if the female of the species can find a way of concealing when she is fertile, she can manage to do two things. She can encourage her male to stay with her throughout her cycle, if high on his agenda is successfully producing children. And at the same time she can discourage strange males from competing for her eggs and undermining his confidence in his paternity. Being willing all the time can now be added to this strategy as a reinforcer. For it further binds the male to the female and further commits him to repeated efforts to reproduce himself. This is, if you like, the beginning of recreational sex. But it has nothing to do, evolutionarily speaking, with any later history of philandering and one-night stands. Quite the contrary. But it is the gilding of the lily, the final setting of the seal, on the male-female unit.

And from it all that we think of as human flows. "This new arrangement," says Lovejoy, "is extremely democratic; with one on one, most males can now find mates. It enlarges the social group, which is a huge advantage. It's highly socializing, rather than antisocial, because you now have double parents, families, more complex kinship systems and an increasing individuality— everyone knows who belongs to whom. It allows for an extended infancy, which allows for a more gradually developing brain. And it frees the hands, encourages the adoption of devices for carrying both food and infants and prepares the ground for later weapons and tools. It's also more fun. Because all those things that make for the *enjoyment* of sex are now selected for—anything that reinforces the long-term pair bond: the prominent penis; female breasts permanently on display; face-to-face copulation; hairlessness; the pleasure of orgasm. All of these would serve to keep the male and female together and help their children to become smart enough to survive."

Owen Lovejoy's theory, since its first launching in full form in 1981, has had to face a number of criticisms from both physical and cultural anthropologists. Lucy's bipedality, it has been claimed, was an adaptation to the need to climb and walk in *trees,* and is therefore likely to long predate her. (There are no fossil bones available to prove this one way or the other.) Those rare species of primates that are *monogamous,* it has also been claimed, show few if any differences between the sexes in size, height and body shape. Humans do. And they must therefore be descended from and remain, a species characterized by polygamy and male-male competition, as other primates are.

Many more questions will have to be asked and answered, and

much more work by both fossil hunters and primatologists will have to be done before the debate can be settled. But as Jerre Levy often says: "We have to ask ourselves what is *reasonable* for us to believe on the basis of the information that we have. Does the new information that arrives fit into the picture that we've *got*?" In Lovejoy's case it does. For recently Robert Martin of University College, London, looked again at the central question that has to be explained by all anthropologists—the size and immaturity at birth of the human brain—from quite a different perspective from Lovejoy's. And yet he arrived at essentially the same answer as Lovejoy—*food.*

Martin compared the brain weight, body weight and metabolic rate of a large number of living mammals and primates, including ourselves. And he found a close correlation in all of them between the mother's metabolic rate and the limit of brain development set while the fetus is still in her womb. He then looked at their diets and the stability or instability of their environments. And he concluded, first of all, that in order to grow a brain and body as large as a human's are at birth—twice as large as would be expected in a primate with the same length of gestation—a species mother would have to have evolved in a stable environment. And she would have had to adopt a high-energy feeding strategy. In terms of energy, the growing of such a brain and body would be extremely costly. And it would demand from the first—from the first split between apes and hominids—a steady and unerratic food supply.

This does not necessarily mean that it was the male who was providing it, though it strongly suggests it. Something else does, however. The human brain at birth is as large as the female's pelvic engineering allows. If it then doubled in size, as it does in the great apes, then our brains would still be the size of our two-million-year-old ancestor's, Homo habilis. Instead it *quadruples* in size. This again, Martin points out, must have required in our evolution an enormous investment of energy, an increase in the amount of food available to both mother and young. Human infants are born fetal and completely helpless, much more helpless than the infants of the other higher primates. To maintain and feed them while their brains are quadrupling in size must have demanded of our ancestors an intensification of parental care and, almost certainly, a new feeding strategy. Meat, Martin thinks, was probably crucial to the development of the human brain; and with it, necessarily, the ability to hunt for meat. Human females are not well adapted for hunting—their pelvis is too wide and low for efficient high-speed running, and their arms are not as effectively geared as males' for throwing. Males, then, became specialists in the hunt. They had already developed the visual-spatial skills necessary for it. Thus they became—by the time hunting became common, at least—the provisioners of concentrated protein to their mates and off-spring.

Cloning to parasites to sex to males; to a nervous and hormonal communication system to different reproductive strategies to polygyny, a division of labor and "a sort of monogamy": By this route we arrive at the large brains and dominance of Homo sapiens. This is the evolutionary basis on which the male and female brain is built. The lesson is plain, we hope, as it must be by now for Porteus's asexual visitor from space. If you think human, think old. If human life is a day, then our movement into settled communities was sixteen and a half minutes ago; the Industrial Revolution, which has unalterably changed the patterns of our lives, was fourteen seconds back; the condom and the computer were invented just as you get to the end of this sentence. And if you think human, think animal, or, rather, two sorts of animal, male and female. For hundreds of thousands of generations these animals have been selecting each other for the differences between them. And the differences are there to be found in the chemistry of the male's and female's body and brain.

17
AN ANCIENT LEGACY

IN EARLY 1971 an undergraduate concentrating in psychology at Harvard College published a paper in the prestigious British journal *Nature*. Her name was Martha McClintock. And she had decided to apply some science to what had been, up until then, a purely anecdotal phenomenon: the fact that female friends and roommates seemed to menstruate in synchrony. For five months she had recorded the periodicities of one hundred and thirty-five women living in a Boston dormitory, and she had found that it was indeed true. Between October and March the gap between friends' and roommates' cycles had narrowed significantly compared to randomly matched controls. It wasn't the moon or the tides or the food or the lighting. It was the result, apparently, simply of the fact that they spent a good deal of time together. Martha McClintock noticed something else, too. Women who rarely dated had longer cycles than the average. Several of her subjects remarked that they became more regular and had shorter cycles when they dated more often. Something was clearly passing between these women and between men and women.

By an odd coincidence Martha McClintock's paper appeared in *Nature* shortly after a paper written by an anonymous male scientist. This scientist lived in isolation on an island for long periods of time. And being what Lewis Thomas calls "quantitatively minded," he took to measuring the dry weight of the hairs left behind in his electric razor after each shaving. He noticed that it went up—his beard grew much more rapidly—when he left for the mainland and encountered women and his "sexual partner."

This, however, was not the end of the McClintock story. Some years later a colleague of Michael Russell's at the Sonoma State Hospital in California told him of her own experience of the synchrony effect Martha McClintock had studied. On several occasions, she said, she had noticed that her own cycle seemed to pull that of other women into line with it. Russell saw a way to test this. He asked "Genevieve" to wear sterile cotton pads under her armpits, to collect her perspiration. Then, three times a week for four months, in another lab, he applied a liquid to the upper lip of sixteen female volunteers. For half of them the liquid was alcohol; for the other half it was alcohol and "essence of Genevieve." The results were extraordinary. The cycles of the first group did not change. But after four months the gap between the cycle-starts of the second group had significantly narrowed. The women had never met "Genevieve." Smelling her, though without being conscious of it, seemed to be enough to shift their periods towards hers.

Michael Russell's study, done in the mid-1970s, has only recently been published. And Martha McClintock's original work on spontaneous synchrony has only recently been replicated by two groups, one at the University of Nebraska, the other at Stirling University in Scotland. Winifred Cotter of the University of Pennsylvania has recently confirmed, too, that McClintock's observations about women who dated are likely to be right. She has shown that women who have a regular sex life with men tend to have shorter and more regular cycles than women who do not—their eggs appear more regularly. This is also true

—and the fact is highly suggestive—of women who work with natural and synthetic musks, substances related to testosterone, the hormone responsible for the anonymous scientist's beard growth.

What does this have to do with? Pheromones—and evidence of old evolutionary programs, buried beneath new ones, still at work within us.

Pheromones, as we have seen, are intimately involved in the courtship of animals, the processes by which a male and female animal orchestrate their coming together for the purposes of mating. And they are best known in the world of insects. But in mammals, too, they carry and convey a wide range of information. Identity, dominance, ownership of territory and sexual status: All these things are communicated through the medium of pheromones—which, in mammals, go into production at puberty, are linked to the sex hormones and are to be found in urine, sexual secretions and the products of specialized scent glands. In rats and mice, male and female pheromones—present in urine alone—can have a bewildering number of effects. They can produce aggression, delay or speed up sexual maturity, suppress or induce estrus, shorten or lengthen the estrus cycle, alter the growth and size of the testes; and otherwise affect maternal behavior and sexual arousal and performance.

In rats and mice pheromones are sensed by and exert their influence through a specialized organ called the vomeronasal organ. And since humans were assumed to possess no such organ, the possibility of their communicating through similar pheromones was brushed aside. Recently, however, it has been found that a percentage of humans do indeed have a more or less vestigial vomeronasal organ. And McClintock's and Russell's work, among others', has forced scientists to think again about the possibility of human pheromones. Humans, after all, they argue, are also urinating, secreting mammals with specialized scent glands that develop at puberty in the armpits and elsewhere. Do we too, then, produce pheromones that still have a subtle, adaptive effect on male and female behavior? And do they too work their effects through the most neglected of all human senses, smell?

Smell is mediated in humans by the cells of the two olfactory bulbs, little pieces of the brain, in effect, which peep out onto the protected surface of our bodies and lock onto the chemicals that permeate the environment. There are about five million of these cells in humans as against, for example, the dog's two hundred and twenty million. Smell, then, is not as important in human, as it is in canine, affairs. But the impulses received by human olfactory cells still travel to higher areas of the brain via the evolutionarily ancient limbic system—the system that controls our emotions, our sexual behavior, our appetites and our responses to stress. And the receptors of the olfactory cells are still geared, it seems, to the particular smells of male and female excretions. Smell itself, indeed, is still in some mysterious way in humans fundamental to sex. The nose, first of all, is made of the same sort of erectile tissue as the clitoris and the penis. And there are a number of tantalizing clues that connect smell with the sexual organs. Turner's women, for example, who have no ovaries, have a relatively poor sense of smell. And a percentage of men with undeveloped testes have no sense of smell at all. Robert Henkin at Georgetown University has shown, furthermore, that menstrual problems are often accompanied by an impaired sense of smell. And Henkin has also studied people who, for one reason or another, have lost the ability to smell. About a quarter of them reported to him a loss of libido and some of the men complained, interestingly enough, of diminished beard growth and shrinking testes.

All of this research is still in its infancy. But it has already made plain that human beings have certain scent skills of which they are completely unaware. Richard Doty of the Veterans Administration Hospital in Philadelphia, for example, has shown that humans can tell people apart by the smell of their hands, their T-shirts or the undershirts they have worn to bed and that they can distinguish the sex of an unseen person whose breath they are smelling. And Gary Beauchamp has shown that humans can be taught to discriminate accurately between male and female urine. Such odor abilities may indeed be used routinely by humans, but unconsciously, below the level of consciousness—Michael Kirk-Smith of the University of Warwick has shown that trace quantities of an odorant, not consciously smelled, can have an effect on mood and emotion. And they may be intimately involved not only in the synchrony of menstruation, but in other processes central to human as well as animal sex and reproduction.

Michael Russell in California and Aidan Macfarlane at Oxford University have separately investigated, for example, the role of scent signals in mother-baby communication, or "imprinting," as it is called in animals. And they have been able to show that human infants do indeed respond to their mothers by scent alone. At six weeks sleeping babies turn their heads and make sucking motions towards their mothers' breast pads, but ignore or cry at pads from strange mothers and pads moistened with cow's milk. At six days, awake babies can discriminate by scent between their mothers and strangers. This communication by scent also seems to work in reverse. In recent work Michael Russell tested mothers at six hours after their babies' births—the earliest time possible, since babies in the United States usually spend their first six hours in isolation. And he showed that mothers could recognize their babies and differentiate them from others by smell alone.

Mother-baby bonding is one scientific point of purchase. Another is the possible involvement of a pheromone in human aggression. A boar's androstenone—a pheromone that produces sexual receptivity in sows—tends to make other boars aggressive. A substance in the urine of male mice has the same effect on other males. Is this true of humans? The work of Ching-tse Lee's group at Brooklyn College suggests that it may be. In the mid-1970s Lee was investigating this aggressive response to urine in mice. Since mouse urine is notoriously difficult to collect, he decided to substitute for it human urine.

Again, the results were highly suggestive. Urine from girls, women and young boys produced no effect. But the urine of adult men had exactly the same effect on the mice as mouse urine. The Brooklyn group has been trying to isolate and identify the compound responsible, which is likely to be a steroid, a relative of testosterone. And it remains to be seen whether it will have an effect on human behavior. But scientists given to speculation are already pointing to a possible role for it in the sexual hostility of men's room graffiti and the aggression of men gathered in large groups.

The third area is, of course, sex. But it wasn't in humans that the first candidate for a human sexual pheromone was found. It was in rhesus monkeys. Richard Michael and Eric Keverne at Emory University in Atlanta, Georgia, isolated from the vaginal secretions of female rhesus monkeys a number of estrogen-dependent fatty acids, which they claimed acted as a sexual attractant to males. They called them "copulins." And they later showed that these were also present in a percentage of human females: In greater quantities at mid-cycle, when the female rhesus monkey is at her most attractive; and in lower quantities in women on the pill, the taking of which makes female rhesus monkeys less attractive to males. They even showed that human vaginal secretions, when smeared on the monkeys' genitals, were as alluring as their own.

Michael and Keverne were careful in their reports; they stressed that human beings were not rhesus monkeys; they argued only by inference and association. But their findings, for all that, caused an enormous public brouhaha. Scientists remained extremely skeptical. Michael Goldfoot at Bob Goy's Primate Research Center in Madison, Wisconsin, was already showing that sex in rhesus monkeys was not as simple as Michael and Keverne seemed to want it to be. Scent might well be an element in it, but learning and motivation were much more important. Later experiments with humans also seemed to pour cold water on the Emory group's theories. For all their testing for copulins before and after orgasm; for all their observations of sexual partners using perfumes containing copulins; and for all their attempts to rate the pleasantness of vaginal odors at various points in the female cycle, scientists were unable to find any uncomplicated correlation between human sex and Michael and Keverne's fatty acids.

Perhaps, though, scientists were looking for altogether too crude an effect. And, as so often occurs in these stories, there is one tantalizing piece of evidence to suggest that this is true. In 1974, an audience of psychology students at Hatfield Polytechnic in England were asked by a group led by John Cowley to assess the leadership abilities of three men and three women who were running for the office of student union secretary. The students were all given surgical masks to wear—to hide their facial expressions from the candidates, they were told. In fact, though, half the masks had been smeared with tiny quantities of either vaginal acids or androstenone, the boar pheromone that is now used to prepare sows for artificial insemination. Their effects on the audience's assessment of the candidates were very strange. The men, as it turned out, seemed unaffected by either substance: They did not differ in their overall judgment from men wearing unmarked masks. But the women showed remarkable differences. Those wearing the female scent tended to give higher ratings to candidates with diffident, retiring personalities, and lower ratings to confident, assertive candidates, than did the control group of other women. And those wearing the male scent preferred an aggressive, positive secretary.

Many inferences could be drawn from this: about the "musky" smell of adult males and the effect, on women who work with them, of musks, which are related to androstenone; about the olfactory ability of women, which is at its most sensitive, as Richard Doty was confirming, at mid-cycle, around the time of ovulation; and about the possibility, then, of male and female scents acting in concert in an informational system to make a woman more "feminine" and more open to an assertive male at precisely the time she is at her most fertile, while at the same time allowing her to read the male's hormonal status. Copulins might be thought to be the female arm of such a buried informational system. But what was the male arm?

In the late 1970s, George Dodd of the University of Warwick identified two compounds in human sweat which he believes to be likely candidates. One of them he has gone on to isolate, purify and synthesize. It is called, in short form, alpha-androstenol. It is found in much greater quantities in men than in women. It is related to musks and to androstenone. And, in pure form, it smells almost exactly like sandalwood.

George Dodd's work is partly financed by the perfume industry, as is much of the work being done on smell in America. And he himself runs a perfume-making company. So his discovery, perhaps inevitably, once more raised a storm, particularly in the British press. The newspapers dwelled lubriciously on the idea of an aftershave incorporating alpha-androstenol or a derivative and pointed to the presence of androstenone in the sex shops. So obsessively did they harry George Dodd that, he told us with some bitterness: "It may simply be impossible to do this kind of work."

Dodd, then, remains tight-lipped, especially about the part alpha-androstenol may play in sexual attraction. All he will talk about is "strong suggestive evidence for a physiological role." From our conversations with English researchers, though, it is plain that alpha-androstenol also has other effects, subtle behavioral effects like those noticed by John Cowley for vaginal acids and androstenone. Tom Clark, for example, of Guy's Hospital in London sprayed it in minute quantities in a number of telephone booths at a London railroad station and saw a marked increase in time of occupancy by both men and women. Michael Kirk-Smith sprayed it in the same minute quantities on a chair in a dentist's waiting room and noticed something slightly different. Women seemed strongly drawn to the chair; they made straight for it, while men were either neutral or averse to it. Kirk-Smith also did two further experiments with alpha-androstenol. In one he asked a group of men and women to react to a series of photographs, both in and out of the presence—in the air—of trace amounts of it. In the other he asked both men and women to evaluate a number of men, some of whom had been unknowingly anointed with it. The results, again, were subtle and strange. In the first experiment the chemical seemed to make nearly everyone, both men and women, rate photographs of women as sexier, warmer and more attractive. In the second it seemed to have a different effect on men and women. The women consistently responded favorably to the wearers of alpha-androstenol while the men, equally consistently, downrated them.

The Monell Chemical Senses Center is the one institution in America devoted wholly to smell and taste, the brain's ways of assessing its chemical environment. And on the day that we visit an article from a Canadian newspaper is pinned to a notice board on the ground floor. Its first sentence is underlined and surrounded by exclamation marks: "At the Monell Chemical Senses Center, scientists behind locked doors are searching for the ultimate aphrodisiac." It is not, as we have seen, as simple as that.

But it *is* potentially revolutionary. In one of the corridors, for example—lined up—are cages of small South American monkeys called marmosets, swinging from their perches, gibbering, moving restlessly. Marmosets have been studied here by a group headed by Gisela Epple from almost the beginning, in the late 1960s, of the center's life. For they are marking animals. Wherever they go glands in their genital region smear into their environment information about the gender, identity and relative dominance of the marking animal. Marmosets, too, have an odd characteristic. In any group only one female, the most dominant, is fertile at any one time. If she loses her position, leaves the group or dies, a newly dominant female becomes fertile in her turn. But she too suppresses the breeding cycle in the others.

There is, in other words, a contraceptive agent in the dominant female's smear which delivers, through the noses of the others, a suppressive message to the hypothalamus and pituitary that control the reproductive cycle. And scientists at the Monell, using gas chromatography and mass spectrometry, are virtually certain what it is. It is an estrogenic steroid, a close relative of substances used in the pill. And it may provide humans with a natural and safe contraceptive, to be used in vanishingly small quantities—it is only a tiny fraction of the dominant female marmoset's glandular output—and to be applied by a new route, through the nose. Scientists in India have already used to good effect a nasal spray containing low levels of two hormones used in the pill. And Sven Nillius at the University of Uppsala in Sweden has been using the nose as a conduit into the bloodstream of a further hormone—luteinizing-hormone-releasing hormone (LHRH)—which is central to the control of reproductive function.

The work with marmosets and its possible future application brings to mind once more Martha McClintock and "Genevieve." For that research, too, contains the elements of dominance and control over the reproductive cycle. We ask George Preti, another of the Monell's senior members, what he thinks, in this atmosphere of quantitative analysis, of the work with humans. Is he a skeptic?

"No, I'm not a skeptic," he says, "though it's true I'd like to see a nice, real, proven effect: taking something from a particular odor source, exposing people to it and seeing a universal effect. Nor do I think it's foolish. For if there are long-distance chemical messengers that affect mood, reproduction and sexual behavior, then we may be able to get our hands on some very powerful and subtle tools—tools that will allow us to intervene, at the hormonal level, to increase libido or inhibit ovulation, for example.

"The truth is, though, that we don't know enough. We don't know enough about the contents of saliva, or vaginal secretions or the products of the apocrine glands to be able to predict what we'll find. But that doesn't mean that we're not making headway. We've been looking at the contents of vaginal secretions, for instance, and seeing how they alter at mid-cycle, at ovulation. And we've been looking at mouth odor, mouth chemistry in women, and we've found that that too changes at particular times, during menstruation and again at mid-cycle. So we may not know all the details yet. But we've already got two good, and rather simple, ways of predicting ovulation across the whole population."

Monell has applied for and received patents for chemical tests that are likely soon to be used in the home by women who wish to become pregnant.

And sex attractants? Few scientists will admit that they are a major focus of their research. But there is no doubt that the perfume industry remains intensely interested, especially, perhaps, as represented by the figure of Henry Walter, the scholarly, affable lawyer who is the chairman of International Flavors and Fragrances. "Of course we're interested in them," he says over lunch in his Manhattan office. "But then we've been using sex attractants in perfumes for thousands of years. Musk, for example, though now largely synthetic, came originally from the male scent gland of a small deer that lives at high levels in the Atlas Mountains and the Himalayas. It uses it to mark territory and attract mates. Civet comes from the scent gland of the civet cat, which is native to two small areas on the coasts of Africa. And castoreum comes from the scent gland of the European beaver. So for thousands of years we've been covering up our *own* sexual smells—which our nasal receptors may be specifically designed to detect, if work done by John Amoore in California is right—with the sexual smells of animals.

"But there's much, much more in all of this than just sex attractants. Odor, for example, may play an important role in human disorders—our olfactory system and the way we smell can be altered in disorders and diseases. Schizophrenics and temporal lobe epileptics often have olfactory hallucinations, and there seem to be disturbances of a similar kind in a number of depressive patients. Schizophrenics *also* have a characteristic odd smell. And the same is true for a number of other human diseases. Well, we don't know how far this goes. But there are Sanskrit texts that seem to refer to diagnosis by smell and treatment by smell for neurological disorders. Musk is still used as a medicine in Tibet and China. And the word in old Persian, I've been told, for druggist is the same as the word for perfumer.

"It's also interesting that the olfactory system is very similar in some ways to the immune system. Both are involved in recognition and fine discrimination. Both have to face an enormously wide range of contingencies—all the organisms and chemicals that an individual will encounter in his or her environment. And the cells of both are important enough to be constantly regenerated and renewed. That's why I spend so much of my time talking to, and doing what I can to help, scientists like Edward Boyse at the Memorial Sloan-Kettering Cancer Center in New York. Boyse believes that the immune system and smell are connected at a fundamental level. He thinks that pheromones, along with all the rest of it, identify the immune status of an animal.

"So I think we're on the brink of something very important here," Henry Walters continues, "something that connects smell, sex, disease, the immune system and the brain. And the nose may provide us with a new experimental avenue into the brain: into the world of the neurotransmitters, into disorders, into the circuitry of pleasure and into the systems that control emotion, and desire and stress. George Dodd is already proposing tranquilizing smells, to aim straight at the old 'smell' brain. And there's just a suggestion, no more than an anecdote, really, that smell might be useful as a treatment for schizophrenia. A nurse in a Michigan schizophrenic ward used a floral spray and found that her patients responded favorably to it."

If the immune system and the sense of smell are interlinked, as William Hamilton believes and Edward Boyse's work has gone some way towards showing, then it is because of our ancestors' coevolved need to keep out invading parasites and at the same time sense in the environment first sex cells, then individuals of the same species but of the opposite sex. Program was built upon program and this linkage was maintained under the moderating control of the sex hormones. And it remains, it seems, in us still today. Estrogen enhances the sense of smell and testosterone diminishes it—precisely the same effect both have on the immune system. During pregnancy a woman's altered balance of hormones affects both her immune system, as we have indicated *and* her sense of smell: her ability to smell decreases and she is often affected by odd taste and smell preferences. Around the time of ovulation, too, the time when she is committing her valuable egg to the possible exploitation of a male, her immune system and her sense of smell are again fundamentally altered. Her immune system is geared up except for the environment of her reproductive tract. And her sense of smell becomes keen. If work done in the 1950s by French researcher J. Le Magnen is right, a woman at mid-cycle is a hundred to a hundred thousand times more sensitive to musk—the basic male smell—than she is at any other time. If this is so, then a woman is *both* attracted to and protected against the intimacy of courtship and coitus at the time when successful reproduction is most likely.

HE AND SHE

NOW WE CAN come back to the story of our twentieth century, "he" and "she," and to the sex that takes place between
them—obviously an enormously complicated transaction. For
it involves the chemistry of two brain-body systems: courtship,
attraction, arousal and what Masters and Johnson have called
EPOR (excitement, plateau, orgasm and resolution). And it
has involved literally millions of variables. For our twentieth-
century hero and heroine, it has depended on chance. It has
been carried through a delicate dance of moves and counter-
moves. And at any point anything could have nipped it in the
bud—a distraction, a missed cue, a twinge of guilt. It has also
been dependent not only on them, but on the culture that happens to surround them: the environment, the fashion. If one of
them, for example, had worn saucer-shaped lips, a large nose
ring or whole-body basket-weave tattooing—signs of considerable beauty elsewhere—the evening would never have begun.
And if he or she had poked the other in the eye or bitten at the
other's eyebrow—the fashion elsewhere—it would never have
continued.

Their attitudes to sex, in other words—and much of what they do during it—are local custom. They're to do with religion and law and upbringing and experience. They're learned. Fellatio, cunnilingus and all the other variations on the theme that we omitted from their story may be enjoyable. But they too are learned (usually only in societies that are maritally stable—which, by that definition, we are). The point is that in all of our sexual jousting there is an enormous amount that is purely cultural. And if we're going to be able to say anything fundamental about it, we're going to have to strip away culture and aim straight at the biological heart of the scene between him and her. We're going to have to look at the biological inheritance they have received from all the sexually successful parents who preceded them—all the evolutionary *programs* that govern how they go about sex and who they are attracted to.

"What we have to do is look across *all* human cultures and see if they fit a central hypothesis," says Donald Symons, associate professor of anthropology at the University of California at Santa Barbara and author of *The Evolution of Human Sexuality*. "The hypothesis is this: Since human females, like those of most animal species, make a relatively large investment in the production and survival of each offspring—and males can get away with a relatively small one—they'll approach sex and reproduction, as animals do, in rather different ways from males. During our evolutionary history, the sexual desires and dispositions that promoted reproductive success for *one* sex probably spelled reproductive disaster for the *other* sex. Therefore, assuming that our brains, like the rest of our bodies, were designed by natural selection, men and women today ought to differ in their sexual psychologies. Women should be more choosy and more hesitant, because they're more at risk from the consequences of a bad choice. And men should be less discriminating, more aggressive and have a greater taste for a variety of partners, because they're *less* at risk. This is, in fact, what we find.

"Furthermore, individual males and females aren't equally valuable as mates. So brain mechanisms ought to have developed that enable them to detect and be attracted to the most reproductively valuable members of the opposite sex, the ones most useful to their genes. Males would look for health, aptness for motherhood and youth—it's in their interests to tie up a woman's whole reproductive career. And females would look for something else: health, certainly, but also strength and long-term resources; whatever was necessary for the survival of *their* genes.

"Now the first part of the hypothesis," Donald Symons continues, "is supported by studies done all over the world on people of different ages, classes and sexual preferences. Men tend to be the sex-seeking gender. And women—if you read *The Hite Report,* for example—are simply not as interested in casual sex, even though they sometimes believe they *should* be and would be happier if they were. What they require from sex in general is some sort of emotional involvement.

"The second part of the hypothesis holds up equally well. Let's start with men. Men in all cultures prize health and cleanliness—good skin, good teeth. They set great store on physical attractiveness. And this attractiveness is always associated with *youth.* Why? Because youth is when a woman is most valuable, reproductively speaking. She can only have and care for a certain number of children in her lifetime, and so the earlier a man acquires her, the better. Detecting and being attracted by signs of female youth are part of the male's genetic program.

"Youth, though, is not a criterion that women apply to men. For a man's reproductive value can actually *increase* with age. And it's not as dependent on his physical appearance—though, as I've said, health is important. It has *much* more to do with reliability, status, prowess, skills and the ability to command and accumulate wealth. During our evolution, then, women who attended to *these* signs of value would have had the reproductive edge over those who paid court primarily to youth and physical attractiveness. And there would have been selective pressures to ensure that such a tendency survived in women today. In fact, that's what we see. While men are sexually drawn to younger women, women routinely marry older men—and not necessarily Adonises. It's more a case of the resources which older and more reliable men have had time to gather.

"The upshot of all this is that men and women have different sexual psychologies. And these psychological differences—expressed in the brain—underlie all heterosexual transactions. Women control what males have always needed—the ability to carry and reproduce their genes for them. And so a man tends to pursue sex aggressively—it's a trivial expenditure of energy with a potentially big payoff. For a woman, though, sex is something else. Women, after all, have always had one of their few, expensive eggs and their bodies on the line. And so sex for a woman remains a valuable *service,* a service that has to be carefully traded."

Back to the restaurant. For now we can see what has been going on in the attraction between him and her. Originally, of course, she noticed him because he so obviously had eyes for her. Then she liked what she noticed. And then, almost unconsciously, she began to absorb all the clues in him that suggested status and resources (and potentially valuable genes): his clothes, his tan, his ease with others, his leanness. All of these things carry shifting social meanings. A tan, for example, once meant outside work, manual labor; now it means money for vacations. Thinness once meant the poverty of undernourishment; now thin is in; it is the poor, by and large, who are fat. He, meanwhile, went through a similar but different process. Status—clothing, jewelry and so on—was clearly important to him, but his appraisal was mainly physical. What he assessed, as he watched her, were her age, her skin, her hips and her breasts, all signs, at bottom, of her fitness for motherhood. And since he thought her beautiful, one can assume something else—that in appearance she was somewhere close to the population average. Standards of beauty vary widely from society to society, but they always represent *an averaging of what the people in the society look like.* And there are genetic reasons for this, reasons that are part, too, of his sex drive. For the average is the mainstream of the genetic pool in any society and, other things being equal, the average—the mainstream—is a better bet, genetically speaking, than something on the fringes.

All this has been considered. And now, as they order their food and eat their dinner, they are at a second stage, a stage at which, if she stops to think about it, she holds all the cards. For if sex is to be had, she has to say yes. She has to be convinced that there is no danger in their intimacy, that he is gentle and reliable. To find out whether this is true or not she requires courtship. She needs evidence. She needs, in evolutionary terms, to make sure that the man can and will stay around long enough to provide resources for her and her offspring. This decision, for a woman, is crucial. And in order to deal with it women have developed mechanisms that make them much more discriminating, guarded and conservative in their sex drive than men are—as have females everywhere else in nature.

She sits opposite him, in other words, possessed of a different evolutionary inheritance, an inheritance expressed in the chemistry and architecture of her brain. She has an enhanced ability to read his character from gesture, posture and tones of voice. Her senses are more finely tuned. And her brain is organized in such a way, as Jerre Levy says, that she has readier access to the emotional content of what she is experiencing. She is quick, therefore, to react to the slightest sign of danger. And she responds sexually not to *instant* cues but to atmosphere, all those collective cues that are signaling warmth, intimacy and *absence* of danger—attentiveness, a soothing voice, whispering, touching.

Something of who she is, as she watches and tests him, can be seen in the huge industry of romantic magazines and fictions aimed at her; she requires a certain *ambience* for sex. When it comes to representations of sex—in books and pictures, for instance—she responds most to those in which the relationships are *believable*. As for her own sex life, her sexual willingness requires a psychological go-ahead, a green light in the mind. John Wincze of Brown University Medical School and Patricia Schreiner-Engel of Mount Sinai School of Medicine in New York have found, in separate studies, that a woman often shows *physiological,* vaginal arousal when watching sex films or listening to erotic tapes. But she does not by any means always *feel* aroused at the same time, as men always do. There is a potential cut-off, it seems, a gap, between the responses of her body and the conscious part of her brain.

She is protected, then, by nature from making the wrong snap decision about him. And she has been provided by evolution with a *further* protective mechanism, the effects of which are all around us in western society. She is, quite simply, less visually arousable than he is, and her brain does not respond in the same way to visually arousable material. In a recent study, both men and women were asked to watch an erotic film. Afterwards their norepinephrine levels were measured. Norepinephrine, as we have seen, is testosterone-influenced; it rises in aggression, self-assertion, euphoria and hyperactivity. And its levels were much higher after the erotic film in men than they were in women.

Being less visually excitable would, of course, make sense for our imaginary woman. It would be counterproductive to her reproductive purposes to be instantly aroused by the sight of any male body. He is not so restrained; he has different evolutionary aims. So he eats her up with his eyes, undressing her in his mind, constantly drawn to her mouth and lips and the rift valley between her breasts. It is no wonder that the pornography industry is raking in millions of dollars from his visually oriented male libido, but not from hers. There is no woman's magazine that can find a market solely on the basis of male nudes; they sell, rather, to male homosexuals. And it would be hard to imagine male masseurs in a massage parlor servicing female clients abstractedly and without arousal—as females can, as she can, with males.

What does this all add up to in the attraction between him and her? Well, if he is much too aggressive, he may not be successful with her; there is more ultimate compatibility, studies show, between two people when the man is not sexually overassertive. What he has to remember is that her approach to sex is less of what poet W.H. Auden once called an "intolerable neural itch." This does not mean that she cannot be instantly attracted to a man. And it doesn't mean that she cannot pursue a large number of sexual partners. But it *does* mean that the attraction she feels is unlikely to be a purely physical one. And it *does* mean that, in being promiscuous, she may have some difficulty overriding the evolutionary programs within her. For she is doing something that in evolution worked not to her advantage, but to men's. She is not a man. She has not inherited the male pattern of sexual behavior. And, like it or not, as a number of studies have shown, she is *less* likely to experience orgasm during a one-night stand than she is in the context of a stable, long-term relationship.

The idea of evolutionary constraints on sexual behavior is inimical, especially to women. We are prepared to accept the role of an evolutionary timetable in the scheduling of the dramatic events of puberty. But we imagine that from that point on we are on our own, in some sense. What we fail to understand is that the hormones, through whose agency the events of puberty unfold, continue to affect, in subtle ways, our sexual behavior throughout life.

At puberty—when male and female first become attracted to each other—the hypothalamus-pituitary-gonadal axis takes on its adult configuration. The hypothalamus transmits to the pituitary the messenger hormone, LHRH. And LHRH causes the pituitary to release into the bloodstream two further hormones, FSH (follicle-stimulating hormone) and LH (luteinizing hormone), which then home in on particular targets. FSH in men starts up sperm production. LH instructs the testes to produce testosterone, which then travels to various tissues in the body and back to the pituitary and hypothalamus in a feedback loop.

All three hormones are more or less continuously produced in men, and their testosterone levels go up and down several times a day. So it is very hard to tell how this system affects their sex lives except, perhaps, by helping to maintain a persistent sex drive.

It is a different story in women, though. For the three hormones are intimately involved *both* with the rigorous timing of events during their menstrual cycle *and* with the ebb and flow of their sexual appetite. The way they do this is complicated. FSH is basically responsible for the production of estrogen, and LH for the production of progesterone. And the rise and fall of these two further hormones during the twenty-nine-day cycle of ovulation and menstruation are accompanied by changes in sexual readiness and desire. In 1978, a group at Wesleyan University in Connecticut published in *The New England Journal of Medicine* a study which showed that interest in sex and the level of sexual behavior in women increased about twenty-five percent during the three-day period of ovulation, but *not* in women who were on the pill. The study was thought worthy of an accompanying editorial by Robert Rose, a pioneer researcher of sexual behavior at the University of Texas. "The rather extreme assertion that sexuality in human females has become independent of biologic influences," he wrote, "ignores our evolutionary heritage, a large number of animal studies and the crucial role of reproductive biology in general. And yet this belief . . . is also difficult to challenge with relevant and reliable data collected on human subjects."

Five years later the science of all this is still in its infancy. For science is still strictly limited in the number of ways it can look at human sex, just as it is limited in the ways it can look at the human brain. It can show men and women erotic films while their penises and vaginas are fitted with strain gauges and measurers of blood-vessel constriction. It can measure the level of their hormones in blood plasma and urine. It can wire up the heads and bodies of men and women making love and masturbating. It can look at men and women who suffer from sexual disorders and dysfunctions because their supply of estrogen and testosterone, for example, or the workings of their hypothalamus or pituitary or adrenal glands or brain hemispheres have been interfered with. And it can then try out various drugs on them, including the hormones and chemical messengers it has found to be involved in the sex lives of animals. All this is very crude. But despite its crudeness, science is nevertheless, little by little, telling us that even in a behavior which seems so utterly controlled by the free choice of the individual, an integrative, constraining chemistry is at work.

Back to the restaurant. One of the things we can imagine about *her* presence here is that at some point she has painted her mouth, put on eye makeup and dabbed a drop or two of perfume behind her ears and between her breasts. That is something that women have been doing on such occasions for thousands of years. They are ancient sexual signals. More important, though, for our purposes, is that they actually *mimic* hormonal events that take place in a woman's body. Lip paint stands for the swelling and reddening of the lips during sexual arousal. Eye makeup is part of an old knowledge that our pupils automatically dilate when we see something we think is attractive, and we become more attractive as a result. (Belladonna, which used to be part of a woman's cosmetic repertoire, produced the pupil-dilation effect directly.) And perfume—well, perfumes, as we have seen, have traditionally used the sexual scents of animals to augment the grace notes of our own hormonal communication system.

She does all this dabbing and daubing because she is feeling good about herself, confident, subtly sexy. And the reason, let us assume, is that she is somewhere near the point of ovulation, in the middle of her cycle. Estrogen, roughly speaking, is the hormone of the first part of the cycle. It prepares her body for the egg, and for sex. It builds up the lining of her womb and vagina, and it also makes her feel and look good. It subtly raises her temperature and gives her body tone and color. She glows. Around the time of ovulation, there is then a rise in progesterone levels, the first impact of which is to make her receptive. And this is accompanied by a peak in adrenal-produced testosterone, which makes her clitoris more sensitive and increases her sex drive. At *no* other time in her cycle do these three hormones coincide in her in the same way. Only at ovulation do they conspire to give her this unique readiness for sex, as well as an enhancement of her immune system and three of her senses: sight, taste and smell.

There is no doubt that this is a holdover from a very old mechanism that makes female primates receptive, in heat, only at one time in their cycle. But it continues to be part of our woman's evolutionary program. And it continues, as in primates, mysteriously to affect the way he behaves towards her. Somehow or other he can sense what is going on in her body. Studies have shown that men seem to want sex less during the second part of a woman's cycle, after her egg has come and gone. And though this, perhaps, can be ascribed to *external* cues —the change in a woman's attractiveness—it still does not explain some even odder things that go on between men and women. Dating a man, as we have seen—or working with male hormones, musks—alters a woman's cycle and makes it more regular. There is evidence, too, that when a man and a woman live together their base levels of testosterone—and so, perhaps, sexual desire—rise and fall in unison. The temperature changes characteristic of *her* cycle are also echoed in *him*.

It may be, then, as they sit in the restaurant, that he and she are talking together in a language they do not know they know: a pheromonal language that affects how attracted they are to each other. Within him there may still be mechanisms capable of vetting her hormonal state, seeing how close she is to producing his own reproductive goal, her egg. And within her may be mechanisms by which she can add to all the other information she is collecting about the level of his testosterone. Testosterone levels are markers in animals of their relative position in the pecking order. In human males they rise both after any success *and* when sex is anticipated. They are a good measure, then, if she can read them, of the promise or potential value of his genes, *and* of his interest in her.

And so, as they say, to bed. To the roller coaster of Masters's and Johnson's EPOR. What can science tell us about him and her at this stage? Until recently, the only sort of science that had anything to say at all was social science. And social science, after years of patient work, can tell us, according to Kinsey, that she has an eighty-nine percent chance of having more than three minutes' foreplay and a twenty-two percent chance of having more than twenty. It can tell us that their coitus will last an average of two minutes (Kinsey) or ten minutes (Hunt). And it can tell us that it will take her about eight minutes to reach orgasm, as against two minutes for him. It can also tell us that he is unlikely to be very skilled at pleasing her. Western men are by no means as good at this as the men of Mangaia in Central Polynesia, for example. There, boys at the age of thirteen or fourteen start their sexual education under the tutelage first of older men and then of older women. They learn the techniques for pleasuring a woman. And in the process they acquire a knowledge of female anatomy, according to anthropologist D.S. Marshall, superior to most western general practitioners. The result is a happily assumed responsibility for multiple female orgasms that lasts through their reproductive lives.

The difference between a Mangaian man and our western man is cultural, of course. Skills are learned, and he can always improve his performance. Again, therefore, we have to look below the surface of such cultural differences if we are to find anything fundamental to say about the sexual possibilities that exist between two hypothalamuses, two pituitaries, two lots of sixteen-square-foot skin covering and two sets of genitals. Hard science, as we have seen, can tell us something about the nervous apparatus, the hormones, the glands and the chemicals that are involved in their bedroom encounter. But it cannot answer two important questions that are basic now to the differences be-

tween them. It cannot tell us why one gaggle of human tissue
—his—reaches its peak of sexual activity at about the age of
eighteen, while the other gaggle of human tissue—hers—
reaches *its* peak much later, at around twenty-eight. And it cannot tell us why *his* orgasm is universal—a foregone conclusion
—while *hers* is various and sporadic.

This is the final fix we shall be taking on the sexual behavior
of him and her. And it leads us back to evolution, to tie together
in one bundle now their different evolutionary strategies and the
sexual mechanisms that still mediate them. First, the facts. A
man's sexual activity rises steeply immediately after puberty and
reaches its height before the age of twenty. From then on it
steadily declines towards zero, which is reached well after the
age of seventy. A woman, meanwhile, slowly increases her sexual activity after puberty and does not reach her peak until the
age of about twenty-eight. She remains at the same level of
activity until around the age of about forty-five, when a slow
decline sets in.

This is fairly easy to understand in the case of the eager male.
In the hunter-gatherer societies in which we evolved, in which
life was almost certainly nasty, brutish and short for males, there
was obviously a genetic advantage in reaching a sexual peak as
early as possible. The earlier a male started, the better the
chances his genes had of surviving. And if his genes survived,
then his male descendants would also be early starters, as men
are today. The male decline is simply a by-product of the early
peak. It is slow and very gradual. And it is the result of generations of men tending to have children earlier rather than later.
Once the children had been had, nature selected those men who
were progressively less interested in sex and more interested in
promoting the survival of the genes placed in them.

The pattern in women is at first glance more difficult to read.
But again it has to do with selection and the survival of her
offspring—her genes. One element in this is the fact that pregnancy between puberty and the late teens is associated with all
sorts of problems—her children have more difficulty surviving.

A woman does not come into full reproductive maturity until the years between nineteen and twenty-four. A second element is that a woman needs, to repeat, resources if she is to guarantee her genes' survival. So it is in her interests to wait until the right male comes along. Selection pressures now come into play, favoring those women who have the tendency to hold back until the ties of a lasting affection are established. Only then is the sexual peak of activity reached.

Given this, it would be reasonable to expect that twenty-eight-year-old women would routinely associate with eighteen-year-old men. But they do not, and for all the old protective reasons. Eighteen-year-old men are notoriously unreliable. They have little to offer in the way of resources. They are aggressive. And, equally to the point, they know very little about the complicated give-and-take of sex. If human sex were simply a branch of athletics, then of course eighteen-year-old men and twenty-eight-year-old women would be constantly in each other's company. But it is not. Contraception or no, it is about reproduction and the survival of offspring. And the considerable pleasures it offers are, in evolutionary terms, the glue that binds two humans *together* for the joint project of reproduction and the continuation of their genes. For this a woman needs intimacy, trust and consideration, precisely what a skilled older man can offer. For learning is indeed a crucial part of sex, for both him and her. Because of it, an older man can more readily understand her need for a psychological commitment—he has one of his own to give. Because of it, he knows about courtship—the foreplay before the foreplay in bed. And because of it, too, he knows something else. He knows how to produce in her the ultimate learned experience, the female orgasm.

"Orgasm," says Donald Symons, "is apparently not a common phenomenon among other female primates. And even among humans it's by no means universal. Some societies don't even have a word for it. They don't know it exists. Even in our own society, between five and ten percent of women never experience it; another thirty or forty percent experience it only intermittently. It's not tied in any obvious way, then, to reproduction, as the male orgasm is. What's so interesting is that the intense pleasure of orgasm occurs precisely when ejaculation in the male occurs. The pleasure of orgasm is the motivating force in the male, in other words, to get to the point of this crucial reproductive event. Now, there is no comparable crucial reproductive event for the female. She is the receiver. So there's no comparable reinforcing mechanism. In the female, then, orgasm is a potential, one that requires male skill and interest to be expressed. In the few societies in which all females are said to experience orgasm, there is either prolonged foreplay, in which the clitoris plays a big part, or consciously prolonged intercourse.

"Why, if it's only a potential, is it there, though? And the answer, I think, is that though it was favored by natural selection in males and not in females, it nevertheless survives in females in the same way that nipples survive in males, even though males can't normally produce milk. Ejaculation, from a vestigial prostate, can also occur in some women when they have orgasm. And I think that's the same sort of thing.

"Now this doesn't mean to say that female orgasm is not important. But it means that it's not *all*-important. The female orgasm has, I know, received a lot of press, usually linked to the idea of female insatiability. And I think it's thrown us off-track. First, I don't believe that women are insatiable. It's not what one finds cross-culturally, and it's hard to imagine how female insatiability could have been favored by natural selection. And second, orgasm is simply *not* the be-all and end-all of sex for most women. If you read *The Hite Report,* for example, an overwhelming number of women talked about affection, intimacy and love as their primary reason for liking intercourse—not orgasm. And most women considered the moment of penetration to be their favorite physical sensation."

What Symons implies is that in our culture women are being trapped into pursuing a will-o'-the-wisp—being persuaded that what is important to men is of the utmost importance to them.

This does not mean that men should not improve their performance, become much more skillful and helpful lovers than they are. But the female orgasm, remember, is most likely to be experienced in the context of a stable, loving relationship. And if a woman pursues it through variety, then she is using an essentially male strategy—playing into male hands—and probably undercutting her own satisfaction. The point is, again, that she is under evolutionary, and hormonal, constraints. Just as her vagina evolved to accommodate his penis, and vice versa, so her constraints evolved to accommodate the danger he represents. If a push-button orgasm had served her reproductive purposes in the past, then it would be with her today. Put another way, her clitoris would be in her vagina. But it is not. A woman is different from a man. She is differently programmed. She is differently arousable. And she is differently wired for pleasure. . . .

If you give a man and a woman doses of the hormones and chemical messengers that are involved in sex they tend to have quite different reactions. At one level that is obvious—the hormones in the pill do not make a man infertile. But at another level it is still extremely mysterious. Give a man testosterone, for example, and it will indeed improve his sex drive, but only up to a point. If the dose is increased, his sex life does not get any better. In a woman, though, the effect is subtly different. Given testosterone, not only does her desire for sex increase, it keeps on growing. Even though it has side effects, such as the appearance of facial hair, the rule for her is: the more testosterone, the better.

For thousands of years human beings have known instinctively about the chemistry of sex. They have used the sex scents of animals in their perfumes, as we have said. And they have also compulsively eaten not only everything that reminds them of a sex organ—bananas, avocados and oysters, for example—but also the sex organs of animals themselves—pigs' vulvas, sheep penises and bulls' testicles. What they were after was some *es-*

sence of sex to improve their performance. And especially in the case of bulls' testicles, they were on the right track. What they could not know was that the essence of bulls' testicles, testosterone, is broken down by enzymes in the stomach before it can reach the bloodstream.

They were on the right track because food does indeed contain substances from which the hormones and neurotransmitters involved in sex are made. Dopamine, for example, is manufactured from tyrosine, which is found in large quantities in cereal. And dopamine has a stimulating effect on him though not, as far as can be seen, on her. Serotonin is manufactured from tryptophan in food high in carbohydrates and seems to excite her, but depress him. Eggs should not be left out of future dietary plans, either. Eggs are high in the raw material for acetylcholine, which has a quite extraordinary effect, according to some preliminary work done at Tulane University in New Orleans, on the mating behavior of both sexes in animals.

The truth is that one would probably have to eat an enormous amount of cereal or starch or eggs to get any effect at all. But there is, of course, a simpler and more direct way of taking these and other substances—via a hypodermic or a pill. And that, inevitably, is where science is heading. For the moment it is researching something that is, on the face of it, quite harmless. And it is turning what it is finding out to important human use: the treatment of impotence and infertility and the control of conception. But what it is finding out in the process are things that, in our pill-oriented societies, could easily be put to other purposes. These are early days yet. LHRH, being tested as a contraceptive in both men and women, has a dampening effect on the male libido but, according to studies still unpublished, quite the opposite effect on women. A treated woman, in the words of one of the scientists we spoke to, "was really jumping around in bed." As for male impotence . . . A Canadian group is working with a substance from the bark of an African tree—yohimbine—with "very promising results." And there is a whole pharmacopoeia of other potential candidates with even stranger names, some derived from the human body and brain and some not. Parachlorophenylaniline (PCPA), given with or without testosterone, has aphrodisiac effects—the body seems to give up before the sex drive does. And three other substances do something of the same sort. Naloxone, according to work done at Vassar, turns sleepy male animals into Don Juans. ACTH $_{4-10}$, in the hands of an Italian group, produces in animals "dreamlike erections, copulatory movements and ejaculations." All alpha-MSH—important in animals to the production of pheromones and found at high levels in the female around the time of ovulation—vastly increases sexual behavior in both males and females.

Science has known for some time that if a rat is allowed to stimulate electrically certain areas of its brain, then it will continue to press the lever that effects this until it dies of malnutrition and exhaustion. It has known for some time that if you stimulate a certain area in the hypothalamus of a male rat it will have erections at the rate of about twenty-four an hour and will ejaculate about fifteen times during that same period of time. It is the *chemistry* of both phenomena that science is now beginning to work out. So it is time to ask: Do we want this chemistry for ourselves, for people who are *not* afflicted by sexual disorders? Should we manipulate for our own pleasure, if we can, the sexual behavior that our evolution has prescribed for us?

These, like the relationships between hormones and crime, are serious questions, questions that we will have to think about in the years ahead. For they involve the two ages we talked about at the beginning of this book. One age leads us back to nature: the place in nature, the constraints of nature, that science has recently understood us to have inherited. One age leads us, above all, perhaps, towards a technology of pleasure. And that way leads to an *ultimate* democracy of men and women, a future democracy in which we will be marooned in our own selfishness.

PART SIX

SOCIETY

19

BENEATH THE DIN

FUTURE SHOCK. PARENTS able to choose the sex of their babies by sperm separation or by sex-change operations in the womb. Genetic engineering used to eliminate in humans undesirable traits. A world controlled by a giant interlocking nervous system of computers. Population: between seven and eight billion. Information: doubling every five years. In the west, robots replace laborers and even skilled workers. Unemployment becomes not temporary but permanent. The average work week is fifteen hours. The group, the mass, the collective is now the most important social unit. Continuous cities stretch between New York and Boston, Los Angeles and San Francisco. There are pills for memory, learning, concentration and pleasure. And there are enough nuclear armaments on earth and in space to destroy our local system of planets or to light up a new sun.

That is the sort of world, say some futurists, that children now entering grade school will inherit when they leave college about the year 2000. It is a world towards which our culture is even now hurtling us. "It's as if we're in a jet plane rushing forward at gigantic speed," says Stanley Lesse, neurologist, psychiatrist and editor of *The American Journal of Psychotherapy*. "And it's no use looking out of the side windows any more, because by the time we register the scenery it's already in the past. To have a clear perspective of the present, then, we have to look ahead. We have to look at the future. For the culture is moving too fast."

The culture is moving too fast. Everywhere one looks the signs are beginning to show, especially, as Lesse and others say, in the most basic of our relations, the relations between the two sexes. In a recent, nationwide study, for example, George Serban of the New York University Medical Center found Americans to be heavily dependent on tranquilizers, sedatives and mood-changing drugs and riddled with stress, anxiety and depression. Sex, he says, lies at the root of it. Sexual permissiveness is a prime source of anxiety, in fact the most significant predictor of stress: fifty-three and eight-tenths percent of men and eighty-one and eight-tenths percent of women are disturbed by it. But close to sexual permissiveness come "the new social roles of the sexes" and "interactions with other people"—over half of single women and almost half of single men are under moderate to severe stress due to "the superficiality of their emotional relationships" and the insecurity caused by them. Marriage seems to leave Americans no better off. Loss of interest and a general resentment mean that only twenty-three percent of women and thirty-seven and nine-tenths percent of men are content with their marriages. This is not a phenomenon confined to the United States, where the divorce rate is currently running at about half of all contracted marriages. The divorce rate in Britain, for example, is about one in three. Robert Chester of the University of Hull predicts that between five and six million British adults will be involved in divorce in the last seventeen years of the century—"a town the size of Bristol every year."

The question we want to ask here is: Why? Why are men and women so dissatisfied with one another? Why are the divorce rates so high, when divorce and separation leave men and women, it seems, worse off than they were before. In the United

States—where these things are more intensively studied—the admission rate into psychiatric facilities is eight to ten times higher among separated and divorced people than it is among married people. The mortality rate is two to three times higher for a variety of diseases, including lung cancer and tuberculosis and coronary heart disease. The rate of car accidents is higher. The suicide rate is higher, as is the homicide rate, as is alcoholism.

Why? What is there about this particular, developing western culture that makes men and women so unhappy and uneasy with one another? Human beings, after all, are marvelously adaptable creatures. They are obsessive makers of cultures and civilizations. They are born into the world with an underdeveloped brain, capable of assimilating, learning and growing into virtually any sort of environment. What is it about *today,* then—and the future into which we are rushing—that makes it so special and so threatening to the relationships between us?

Throughout this book we have been exploring the biology and brain of men and women, the long evolutionary journey they have taken together and the separate evolutionary programs and constraints that are likely to influence their abilities and their behavior. Human beings, though, are both biological *and* cultural; they pass on not only genes but also knowledge and institutions from generation to generation. And we need now to take into account the different sort of evolution this involves—cultural evolution. Biological evolution, as we have seen, moves at an extremely slow Darwinian crawl. But cultural evolution—the gathering burst of knowledge that is ushering in the new age of brain science, genetic engineering, cybernation and enforced leisure—has in our recent history begun to move faster and faster. It is now moving so fast, as one scientist puts it, that seniors in college can no longer understand the attitudes and aspirations of incoming freshmen. The real question that we all must ask, then, is: Is our cultural evolution, as it flashes forward, forcing us as men and women into roles for which we are biologically ill equipped? Could it be in these, the last two decades of the twentieth century, that the culture that we have inherited and made and are accelerating towards is finally at odds with the conservative legacy of our biological evolution? Has what we are being taught to want and are being asked to become come unmoored from who we are?

This is a controversial question to ask and an extremely difficult one to answer. It is controversial because it suggests that we may not be able just to go with the flow and willy-nilly take on the shapes that the culture requires of us; we may have to pay —we may already be paying—a considerable price. And it is controversial because even to entertain such an idea strikes right at the heart of our liberal and fondly held belief that we can instantly transform ourselves into new men and new women, happy partners in some future paradise of absolute sexual equality. That, quite simply, may not be possible, without considerable personal and social upheaval, because of the basic differences in our biologies. Those differences, bred in the bone and brain and blood, can never be exorcised from the human spirit until science finally takes away from future men and women the drive to sex and reproduction that will have been responsible for their being born.

The question of whether or not there is some friction in us between culture and biology is a disturbing one, then—some will say thoroughly antiprogressive and antiliberal in the things it implies. But it is also a hard question even to begin to try to answer. And the reason is not only that our basic drives and instincts are buried deep under a welter of different individual experiences and behaviors, but also that those different experiences and behaviors are played on by so many different forces in the society—advertising, the media, the helping professions, contraception, fluctuating populations and a constantly changing industrial and economic climate.

If we are going to find anything useful to say, then, about what is going on between men and women, we are going to have to tease apart all the influences at work on us and see how they hang together to affect our current attitudes toward ourselves and each other. We think it is worth the try. For stress and anxiety are not the whole story. It is true that we have—from an army of psychologists, sociologists, market researchers, census takers and best-selling authors—convincing accounts of how times have finally, once and for all, changed. The news from the sexual front is of the rise in single-person and single-parent households and the boom in the divorce industry; of how the family is dying; and of how men and women do not trust each other and do not want commitment from each other any more. But listen again to those voices, pay closer attention to those and other reports, and a different song is playing—a song that is inimical to those who professionally auscultate human unhappiness. For all the fuss and bother that the media play up, the ideal in western society, according to work done by scientists like John Nicholson of the University of London and Theodore Caplow of the University of Virginia, is still getting married, having children and living happily with another person—against, apparently, all the well-publicized odds. Everyone is hoping for the right man or woman to appear. And neither men nor women want spontaneous, casual sex anything like as often as they are supposed to. Instead, they want integrity, sensitivity, kindness and understanding—above all, intimacy and responsibility.

Are the men and women of today simply dumb optimists, hoping aginst hope for something that is no longer available? Or is there coming through, through the static and turbulence of these changing times, a still, clear call from biology? Some scientists—a very few—are beginning to ask.

The first thing that we have to do, if we are to see through the thick mist of western culture, is to challenge several myths that are fundamental to how we think about ourselves. The first myth is that the generation that came of age in the 1960s invented a) sex and b) the problems that are today associated with it. This is simply untrue. All one has to do to prove it is to go back to the newspapers of the 1920s. "In the past fifty years," the newspapers of the time were much given to pronouncing, "the divorce rate has increased by *fifteen hundred* percent. The birthrate is falling. And men and women are marrying late, if at all. The position of women," they used to clarion, "is being radically altered. And there is today a revolution in morals, spurred by the invention of the new rubber condom. Statistics show that both premarital sex and extramarital sex are up. And the family —yes, the family—is in crisis."

It all sounds dreadfully familiar. And the bookshelves and magazine articles of the time—the learned contributions of the fledgling sciences of psychology and sociology—would be every bit as familiar, too. Self-help books and sex manuals sold extremely well in the 1920s. And the titles offered to the public by the publishers are eerily reminiscent of what we are seeing today —*What Is Wrong With Marriage?*, *Factors in the Sex Life of 2200 Women*, *The Bankruptcy of Marriage* and *Divorce and Readjustment.*

"The fact is," says Alice Rossi, professor of sociology at the University of Massachusetts at Amherst, "it was the parental generation of today's young adults that was the aberrant one. They were the ones who, after the Great Depression and the second World War, settled down to the business of peopling the suburbs and having babies. They were family-oriented and family-obsessed. And today they hold the power in the society. They control hiring policies. They complain about the young. But what they don't see is that their own parents' generation—now retired or dead—was very much like the younger generation of today. They were the Kinsey generation, the generation that was the first to tell us about sex. And what they told us was happening was very much like what's happening now."

Alice Rossi is one of those rare scientists who are today, for the first time, trying to find some common ground between the social sciences and the unfolding science of the brain. And even though she herself is a feminist she has taken much flak from her feminist colleagues. "All right," she says, sitting in her house in Amherst, "so we're not as entirely new as we think. Now we can look *beneath the surface of the similarities* between this generation and the generation of the twenties and see if we can find any important differences between them. And I think we can. Take premarital sex, for instance. In the 1920s, what was new was that women in large numbers began to have premarital sex. And though it was widespread, it meant *then* sex between couples who, by and large, knew that if pregnancy occurred they'd get married. It was limited, in other words, to couples who intended to get married and who usually did. Now, of course, the picture is quite different. So-called premarital sex today starts very early and has little to do with marriage. And a woman, by the time she comes to marriage, is likely to have had several sexual partners instead of just one. She can compare her husband's sexual performance with others she has known. And in the long run, this experience may have the effect of lowering the threshold for a woman's having sexual partners outside the marriage as well. I think this puts a strain on today's marriages that simply wasn't there before. It alters the system of checks and balances that used to operate on the sex lives of men and women in the past.

"The thing we have to remember is that women bear children and men do not. Men can be cuckolded and women cannot—a woman *always* knows that a child is hers. This is a fundamental biological imbalance. It lies at the heart of all sexual exchange between men and women. It lies at the heart of marriage. Marriage, after all, is essentially a trade-off, a consequence of this biological imbalance: the extra resources the male provides in order for the female to bear and raise children in return for a guarantee—hedged about by all sorts of social restrictions—that the children are actually his. So what happens when the social restrictions are gone and the guarantee is weakened and made less believable? You have stress, stress that affects all our sexual relations. And you have extreme, biologically rooted ambivalence in men about such issues as abortion, female sexuality and the economic independence of women."

Everyone agrees that the new pattern of premarital sex in women is, to a large degree, the result of advances in contraceptive technology. And here we come to the second myth that we want to challenge: the idea that female contraception is the best thing to happen to women since they secured the vote and that it has no social consequences except a grand new freedom for men and women.

"No one, I think, has any *real* idea of what the personal and social effects of widely available female contraception may be," says Lionel Tiger, professor of anthropology at Rutgers University, when we meet with him in New York. "Take the pill, for instance. No one knows what it means for a woman to walk around in a state of technical pseudopregnancy, which is what it is, for most of her reproductive life. Scientists are trying to find better, more effective, more long-lasting and more *powerful* pills, rather than studying the effects of the ones they have already invented. *Nor* do we know what effect this state may have on the man or men she's with. And it may have a *considerable* effect, if my and my colleagues' experiments with macaque monkeys are anything to go by. Macaques are a lot like us in many ways—they mate all year round and the males pair off with specific females. But in one of our experiments, a breeding male was simply *not* interested in his favorite females when we put them on the pill. The male was, if you like, turned off."

In a series of books written with and without his friend and colleague Robin Fox, Lionel Tiger has continually stressed that human beings are animals: Complicated animals, maybe, but, like all other animals, part of nature and subject to biological constraints. And he believes that female contraception is, in subtle and perhaps not so subtle ways, interfering with and undermining those constraints. "Look," he says, "in human evolution, in human history, the possibility of pregnancy has always been one form of control that men have exercised over women and one kind of lever by which women have gotten what they wanted from men. I don't want to be cynical about this; I just want to describe one aspect of the reality. And the reality is that the possibility of pregnancy has been the issue around which men and women have traditionally organized their sexual transactions *and* their responsibility for one another.

"Now let's look at what's happening today. For the first time in history the human female can be totally in charge of our genetic and reproductive future. For the best of medical and psychological reasons, she's been told, she's taken over a responsibility that used to be shared. How does that make the male feel? And how does it make *her* feel? Think about it. What's happened in the past two decades is that the female has taken control of the issue of whether or not she gets pregnant. As far as men are concerned, she's separated sex from reproduction and absolved them from any *responsibility* for reproduction. In effect she's liberated the male—whether he likes it or not, and that's another question—but *not* herself. Let's face it: How many men even *ask* about contraception anymore? They resist, or don't even think about, the condom.

"The irony, then," says Tiger, "is that what is seen as freeing is actually imprisoning. Women now feel a terrible guilt if they get pregnant—as if it's their *fault,* as if the man had nothing to do with it. And they often have abortions, with psychological consequences that we know little about. At the same time, because of female contraception and the freer exercise of sexual choice it allows a woman, a man really *does* have less confidence in his paternity if a pregnancy occurs. It's a vicious circle." Tiger throws up his hands. "Responsibility and guilt in women. A forced *irresponsibility,* and bravado and cruelty in men. It's no wonder that women feel angry and bitter about contraception, even though they may not know why."

The third myth we want to tackle, for the fragments of truth that may lie in the debris after it has been exploded, is related to the two we have already looked at. It is this: Given that we have been liberated by contraception (myth two) and are now able to enjoy entirely new sexual opportunities (myth one), then (according to myth three) the life of a single person today is the best possible life, because it is happy, self-contained, independent and allows for sex without the dead weight of commitment. That is what most married people in the society must believe, given their much-touted dissatisfaction with their present arrangement. And that is what most singles seem to believe, even though most of them will admit that they cannot locate this ideal for themselves.

In a recently published book, *Singles: The New Americans*, Jacqueline Simenauer and David Carroll analyzed the results of an elaborate poll and questionnaire designed to explore, through a representative sample of three thousand, the lives, emotions and attitudes of unmarried men and women in America. And some of their conclusions fairly leap off the page. Most people, for example, frankly and openly dislike the singles bars they frequent. Forty percent of women have suffered physical or mental abuse as the result of meetings made in them. And the men—the men are often very aggressive in them because, they admit, they have no respect for the sort of women who go there. They are "promiscuous," they say. Feminists, whom one would expect to object most noisily to such a blatant double standard, are given by the men a backhanded sort of praise, however. The pursuit of sexual equality, according to the male consensus, makes feminists easier to have sex with, and cheaper to court and date.

Equally interesting is what Simenauer and Carroll have to say about the intensely traditional values that singles, beneath all the supposed frolic and glitter, actually maintain. Seventy-five percent of the men questioned are indifferent or opposed to sleeping with a woman on the first date. Neither men nor women seem to like casual sex. Instead, they want commitment—in fact, marriage. About half of the women and over a third of the men think that living together is a less than satisfactory option, precisely because "lack of commitment stops it from being totally fulfilling." Singles, in other words, are not singles, by and large, because they are having such a good time of it. The largest proportion of them are singles because they haven't found the right mate. Marriage or remarriage, it seems, is almost always their ultimate goal. And the price they pay for their so-called freedom, they say themselves, is loneliness.

If the singles life, for all its freedom, is lonely, unsatisfying and incomplete—as well as dangerous to health, as we have seen—then why are so many people inexorably drawn to it? What forces are there in western society that impel people to do something that they do not seem, at bottom, to want to do—to delay or decamp from their marriages and remain alone? One underlying force is obviously the uneasiness and mistrust between men and women—the loss of checks and balances—that Alice Rossi and Lionel Tiger talk about: the stress caused in all our relationships by female sexuality, contraception, the loss of assurance in paternity and the arrogance of the liberated male. The result is that men and women find it hard to find a partner to trust, and they do not trust, and ultimately break with, the partner they have.

But to it must be added all the *other* forces in the society that have colluded to produce the climate of opinion of our times. These find their clearest and most immediate expression in the media and in advertising. As one woman in Simenauer and Carroll's book puts it: "The concept of a single's lifestyle is the invention of the 'free market' . . . purely in order to sell more useless products, for example 'natural' makeups, hair blow dryers, deodorants, singles clubs, singles vacations, bar life and so on, ad nauseam."

The media and the advertising that pays for them come together to produce the most forceful, united and persuasive voice in the society. And they have made the myth of the singles life, as well as the myths of the Brave New Worlds of sex and contraception, an uncomplicated, attractive, must-buy package. The result has been the confection of one of the most persistently peddled images in the culture: the image of the working, carefree and essentially single woman, freed from the drudgery of home and motherhood, freed from attachment to any one man and freed from any and all biological constraints on behavior. No matter that the image, once more, is one that men, deep within them, find unsettling. No matter that such a lifestyle is actually very difficult for most women to enjoy. No, what is important, as Barry Day, vice-chairman of McCann-Erickson Worldwide, says, is that "the working woman outspends her nonworking sister two to one. The working woman is the fastest growing sector of the market. In the United States, for example, she has an earning power of $115 billion a year. Thirty percent of all new insurance policies are taken out by women. Twenty-five percent of all American Express cardholders are women. And twenty percent of all airline tickets are now bought by and for women."

Women's work does guarantee their independence; it does buttress their equality with men, both of which ends the culture should indeed encourage. But it is the *image* we are talking about, not the humdrum, usually underpaid reality. The *image* of the "new" woman, continuously displayed as strong, sexually adventurous and luxuriantly self-contained, does have, like it or not, personal and social effects. Those effects strike right at the heart of the biologically defined roles of men and women and disturb the contract between them. First, the image glamorizes the singles life for both men and women, shedding over it an unreal and unsustainable glow. Second, it *devalues,* by implication, pregnancy and motherhood, as well as the cooperation and commitment necessary for the getting and raising of children. And it has helped produce a generation of women who are intensely conflicted, conflicted when working, conflicted when not working and especially conflicted, Alice Rossi says, when faced with the prospect of future childlessness in their early thirties. The singles life may have been satisfying till then. The working life may have been satisfying. But the biological drive to reproduction, which governs the sexual relations between men and women, can then be heard as an insistent voice, calling for something perhaps less glamorous than the "new" woman's life, but something a lot more central to the processes of our evolution.

Beneath all the myths we have made for ourselves, it should be remembered, evolution still works through survival to successful gene reproduction. And genes governing the urge to have offspring have always outlasted and dominated, by definition, any combination of genes governing the urge to remain childless. We are all of us children of children, going back hundreds of thousands of generations. The genes that favored an absence of children have left no progeny. It is in this sense, then, that the drive toward reproduction remains in us a fundamental one. It is in this sense, too, that the female drive to power, inasmuch as it is genetically based, can succeed only if those who have it have more children than those who do not.

This sobering thought should remind us that, beneath the clamor of modern civilization, the processes of Darwinian evolution work very, very slowly. Genetically, we are still the hunter-gatherers who roamed the thinly populated earth until fifteen thousand years ago. And our mating patterns still reflect the fact. Yes, males have a tendency to be more promiscuous, but that is because in evolution they could get away with fathering a child they did not have to take care of. No, they do not marry promiscuous women because in their *own* women they want some assurance of paternity. Yes, polygamy is still found in human cultures, but that is because women in evolution, needing resources, risked nothing by joining a wealthy man's collection of wives. And no, women are *not* as promiscuous as men because, evolutionarily speaking, and despite contraception, they still have much more to lose.

The point is that despite all our modern sexual arrangements we are still locked together in an evolutionary two-step for which we are differently primed. That does not mean, of course, that biology makes men and women socially unequal. On the contrary. In the hunter-gatherer society in which we evolved, there was a clear division of labor, but *no* lack of equality. The more expendable males—let us imagine—took care of attack and defense, protection against predators and the hunt, providing the rich stocks of protein that the mothers and growing children needed. But the females, as well as bearing and raising children, gathered the other elements in the diet—the plants and fruits, the insects and small animals. They cooked. They no doubt made clothes. And they exercised their own special power as mothers through elaborate kinship systems. When the first Christian missionaries arrived in North America they were often horrified by what they found among the "savages"—the unexpected prestige and importance of women in many of the tribes.

They were horrified because their own culture, the culture they were peddling to the Indians, had virtually enslaved women. That is the crux of this particular matter: *It is culture that produces inequality, not biology.* When agriculture took over from the earlier hunting-gathering way of life, the new system gave a fresh importance to men, since they were bigger and stronger and not tied down by child-rearing. It also meant that land and property became central to human life. With the arrival of a collective economy, the power of women began to ebb. Land and property were now passed down through the male line. A woman, then, was no longer an important part of her own kinship system. Instead, she was farmed out to her husband's family. She and her children belonged to him.

Two hundred years ago, though, human culture, as it began its continuing acceleration, took a new turn. It entered the industrial phase, and that phase, little by little, was to free Western women from their isolation and dependency. The industrial phase, as it developed, needed, not farm laborers, but educated, intelligent individual workers. Women became important as educators and mothers, preparing the generation of the future for the necessary business of work and consumption. They were seen as the providers of a vital support system. Motherhood was glorified. For the first time in fifteen thousand years, say Lionel Tiger and Robin Fox, something like the original equality of the hunting-gathering community reappeared. That brings us to today.

"The first thing we can say about today," says Stanley Lesse, "is that we're no longer primarily an industrial society at all. We're rapidly becoming a post-industrial, cybercultural society in which males no longer have any natural advantage based purely on size and strength. Their size and strength are increasingly unnecessary to industry. They're also becoming obsolete as the unique fighters of wars. They're no longer the one necessary provider. And they're no longer involved in the issue of whether a woman becomes pregnant or not. This is something that's already profoundly affecting the relationships between men and women. I think it has to do with the rise in secondary male homosexuality. I also think it has to do with the increasingly large number of male patients I see who have no respect for their maleness."

For the past twenty years, Stanley Lesse, a stocky, broad-faced man in his fifties, has been poring over the great forces at work in western society in an attempt to identify present psychological stress and the future demands that will be made of us as men and women. It is a difficult, some would say an impossible, task. "Everything, you see, hangs together with everything else. It's all interconnected. Big business, for example, no longer needs the high turnover of replacement workers that the nuclear family used to provide. So motherhood, children and the idea of family are downgraded. Work has become necessary for women, and the idea of their working has become glamorized. At the same time, though, other phenomena are appearing. Because the population is growing more slowly the industrial base faces a more limited rate of growth. And this is gradually translating into shorter work hours, which means more hours of leisure. Leisure, then, is now equated with consumption. The home is devalued. And men and women are portrayed as more and more alike, with the same needs and aspirations and desire to consume. A wedge has been driven between the working woman and the nonworking, family woman; and the latter may be looked on with disdain in the not-too-distant future.

"All of these economic and social forces—work patterns, the decline of manufacturing, the increase in leisure time, automation and advertising—hang together. And they interlock with *other* forces from which they can't really be separated. Political forces. Religious forces. The rise of feminism. Changing technology. And even the shifts in population."

Shifts in population. Demographics. With demographics we come to the final force at work in the culture, the final force that shapes our relationships. And if the word "demographics" does not inspire you, then you should know this: Demographics means that if you have recently entered the work force, you are in trouble. For by the end of the century, when you will still be working, you are going to have a massive population of old and retired people to pay for with taxes and Social Security. This is one of the most serious problems, ignored until recently by almost all politicians, facing western society today.

Demographics, too, have had a crucial part to play in the gathering uneasiness between men and women that influenced you when you were growing up. Lionel Tiger says: "Everybody knows that in the years of World War II comparatively few children were born, which means, for the purposes of our discussion, comparatively few males. And everybody knows that *after* the war *huge* numbers of children were born, which means, again for the purposes of our discussion, huge numbers of females. What were the social and sexual effects of this rise in population? I think there were several.

"Women, remember, tend to marry older men—that's rooted in our biology. The effect of this baby boom, however, is that we now have a large population of women facing a much smaller supply of these appropriate older men. So what happens? Well, the biological pattern is seriously disrupted. Women are either forced to marry *much* older men, who've been recycled by divorce—that becomes desirable and the divorce rate goes up. Or they're forced to remain in the job market for much longer than they ordinarily would. They have only two other options. They can either marry men in their own age bracket, who have inadequate resources, since lower in age means poorer—so they have to keep working. Or they can decide not to get married at all, unless the right man comes along. Chances are, though, given this demographic pressure, that he won't. So those women who wait, and face competition from younger women, have to take all their satisfaction from their careers. And if they ever wanted children, they're likely to face, in their early thirties, a considerable crisis.

"You see how quite complicated consequences can arise from something as simple as a shift in population. The rise in divorce, the stresses in marriage. Men, as the limiting resource, being spoiled, and women, against the odds, having to cope with the double demands of work and family. Women no longer trusting men to serve their reproductive interests. The rise of feminism. Now put these things together with contraceptive technology, liberalized abortion laws and economic pressures, and what have you got?" He pauses for a moment to answer his own question. "A challenge. A provocation. But not something that's easily reassuring."

Not easily reassuring, no. For we are now entering a period when the demographics of the baby boom—which peaked somewhere between 1957 and 1960—are going into reverse. There are now too many young adult males pursuing too few appropriate, younger females. What effect this shift will have in the long run no one yet knows. But if Lionel Tiger is right, then we may have to add to the mix of the future an intensified competition between males for the limited resource of young females. And if the pattern of young women's work, independence and late marriage continues, then the result may be a large population of unsatisfied, rootless and potentially violent young men. One might expect, under those circumstances, a rise in crime and an increase in all forms of violence against women.

It is a delicate balance. And it will not be improved by continuing obsessively to maintain that there are no biological differences between men and women. There *are* biological differences. And beneath all the din of the culture, the clear call from biology can still be heard coming through. Women are beginning to give up the pill, uneasy, perhaps, with the idea that the biology of their bodies is being in some fundamental way upset by it. And men are increasingly trying to exercise their rights as fathers, demanding to be involved in decisions about abortions and wanting more responsibility and more access to the children of divorce. The natural childbirth movement is growing. And the condom, which Tiger calls "the only social contraceptive we have," is making something of a comeback. Men and women, for all their confusion and indecision—for all the attacks still being mounted on the idea of the family, still strive for, it seems, the comfort of each other, the responsibility to each other and children.

The call from biology, though, has been considerably weakened by western culture; the western body has been industrialized. "We've internalized the industrial system in the psyche and body, with an arrogant antibiological attitude and with an indiscriminate use of drugs and devices," Lionel Tiger says. If the call is to be amplified in the future—as it must be, if human beings are not to be further bent out of shape—then there is one thing that we all, both men and women, have to do. We have to recognize that we are an animal species, a part of nature. We have to squarely face the fact of the differences between men and women and give back its social meaning to the joint project for which they come together—reproduction. We have to rethink our attitude toward pregnancy and motherhood. And we have to apply at a social level the lessons that brain science—the science of men and women—is beginning to teach us.

20

FOR THE SAKE
OF OUR CHILDREN

IN THE PAST five or six years various groups and societies have appeared in the west dedicated to the rights of animals and their protection from the experiments of scientists. But there is no such group designed to protect the most vulnerable experimental animals of all, perhaps—men and women. In the past twenty years science and medicine have encroached more and more on the lives of men and women. And in the years before the end of the century they will be intervening more and more purposefully in matters fundamental to our biological nature. By the end of the century, say some scientists, every gene in the human genome will be known and available in synthetic form. And when that happens our cultural evolution will be able to take charge, once and for all, of the messy, chance procedures of our biological evolution. A Brave New World is beckoning, not only of tailored genes and "Bokanovskified" eggs, but of *soma,* the pleasure pill—neurotransmitter-based, we can imagine—that is the glue that holds Aldous Huxley's imagined society together.

The future will come slowly, in small steps, to be met, as it is being met now, with an inarticulate feeling of dread, an unfocused opposition. Scientists will point, at each step, to the individual good that can be achieved: the cure in the womb, for example, of thalassemia or sickle cell anemia, the eradication of a gene predisposing to vital depression, the potential, for poor students, of a drug for memory and learning. These things, they will say, have no personal and social consequences, except good ones. The opposition will, no doubt, be forced once more into retreat. And we will be drawn, little by little, into a future none of us may want by a science that is still, for all its fine new technologies, deeply ignorant about the biological mechanisms basic to our humanity.

All this will happen unless men and women become deeply engaged in the effects science, medicine and technology have *already* had on their lives and on the lives of their children. It will happen unless the public at large forces what we might call the government-research-academic-pharmaceutical company complex to examine in detail, in the very near future, the consequences of what it has already achieved. We have talked in this book about how and why the subtle machinery of sex and reproduction evolved in males and females. We have talked about the different chemistries of their brains and bodies: the skills, strategies, disabilities, disorders and diseases to which they have differentially become heir *because* of that evolution. And we have talked about the *social* consequences of intervening in the natural processes by which our evolution, like that of all sexually reproductive animals, moves forward. Now in this last chapter we want to ask and try to answer one final question: What are the *personal* consequences of our gathering ability to interfere with and smother the natural mechanisms by which sex and reproduction are mediated? What effect do our hormonal and mechanical irruptions into the brain-body system have on the delicate interconnections between the brain, the immune system and the sexual and reproductive organs?

The answer, for the most part, is that we just do not know;

very few people in science are even looking at such questions. Or, if we do know, we often know too late—this is what makes men and women experimental animals. Take vasectomy, for example, now the fastest-growing method of contraception in America. It has recently been reported that a proportion of vasectomized men produce antibodies against their own sperm, with what further effects on their immune systems it is not yet known; and in experimental macaque monkeys vasectomy is associated with an increased incidence of hardening of the arteries. Or take the pill. For some years now it has been known that the pill is associated in women with disorders of mood and movement, problems of blood clotting and circulation, heart disease and strokes. But it wasn't until very recently that a connection was made between the pill, sexual attractiveness and libido. It was not until very recently that the pill was linked to the exacerbation of premenstrual tension and some auto-immune diseases such as SLE. Given this, it is still too early to say what *further* effects the ingestion of even tiny amounts of sex hormones will be found to have. It may be, for example, that maintaining young women for years in pseudopregnancy has a profound effect on their immune system and in the *onset* of auto-immune diseases. A recent study found that the pill may precipitate vital depression, which is rapidly rising in the west, in women who may be genetically predisposed. Vital depression may be an auto-immune disease. And the pill may well be implicated in *another* disorder which may be an auto-immune disease, another disorder which is rapidly rising in the west—anorexia nervosa. At the moment we simply do not know.

Nor do we know, with any great clarity, what effects the taking of the pill may have on a woman's children. In 1977, James Nora of the University of Colorado estimated that about ten percent of American fetuses were exposed to the hormones contained in oral contraceptives early in the pregnancy—about three hundred thousand a year—mostly because pills were prescribed *after* a woman was already pregnant. Added to this, he said, should be the progestogens still used for pregnancy testing and pregnancy maintenance even after the United States Food and Drug Administration had issued a warning *against* their use. The warning was issued as a result of Dr. Nora's own work, which in 1973 established a connection between exposure to sex hormones and an increased rate of major birth defects. His and other subsequent studies showed that babies affected by these hormones in the womb had between two and four times the normal risk of being born with malformations of heart, limbs, vertebral column, trachea, esophagus and central nervous system.

These are very clear and dramatic effects. But estrogens and progestogens also have more subtle but no less enduring effects on the reproductive function, social and psychosexual behavior of the people who have been exposed to them in the womb. These extremely powerful agents can obviously alter the chemical milieu in which the fetus develops—and change, in either small or large ways, how the normal program of maleness and femaleness unfolds. But what range of effects the persistent taking of them has had on the *personalities* of our children is still almost completely unknown. Have they affected hemisphere development? Cell migration? The available balance of neurotransmitters? And what affect have they had on *behavior?*

We will leave aside the question of male and female homosexuality—homosexuality is perfectly acceptable in most western societies. But it is entirely possible that an altered hormonal environment in the womb can produce, in later life, *other* sorts of behavior—antisocial, criminal and sexually deviant behavior, the result of changes in neurotransmitter and hormone levels and alterations in the structure and chemistry of the developing human brain. It is entirely possible, too, that the powerful and evolutionarily ancient sex hormones can draw into expression developmental and learning disorders like autism, dyslexia and hyperactivity. And their effects may not be confined to one generation. Women who have been exposed to altered levels of sex hormones in the womb may also present to their *own* fetuses a hormonal milieu that is imbalanced.

These possibilities are not simply academic musings. Little by little a general picture is beginning to emerge of just how disastrous it may be to intervene in any way in the natural mechanisms of pregnancy with a number of the drugs that medicine has in its armamentarium. June Reinisch, for example, the new director of the Alfred Kinsey Institute at Indiana University, estimates that between 1950 and 1977 over twenty-two million American fetuses were exposed to barbiturates in the womb. Barbiturates are extremely potent chemicals, with long-lasting effects on sex hormone levels—a single protective shot of phenobarbital given at birth in some cases to premature babies causes lowered levels of testosterone *six months later*. Yet preparations containing barbiturates are used in the treatment of some *seventy-seven* human diseases and disorders, everything from muscular pain to nervous tension to hay fever. They are routinely prescribed for insomnia *and* morning sickness. And fetuses continue to be exposed to them. In a study done in Edinburgh, Scotland, in the 1970s, twenty-eight percent of the pregnant women studied took barbiturates during pregnancy for an average of thirty-two days. After aspirin, they were the drugs most widely used by them.

Little is known about what effect barbiturates may have on human fetuses, except that they seem to suffer a higher rate of birth defects than normal. In a paper published in late 1982, however, June Reinisch surveyed the results of work done with animals. "The evidence derived from laboratory animal experiments," she wrote in her conclusion, "indicates that exposure to barbiturates during early developmental periods results in abnormal neural and biochemical differentiation of the central nervous system, deficits in learning, retarded attainment of developmental milestones, alteration of behavioral and physiological sex differences, increased activity, decreased responsiveness to aversive and appetitive stimuli, and interference with reproductive functioning. Thus, it is predicted that prenatal exposure to these potent substances in human subjects may lead to learning disabilities, decreased IQ, performance deficits, increased incidence of psychosocial maladjustment and demasculinization of gender identity and sex-role behavior in males." The same effects, one can predict from work done on animals, would be produced in humans by exposure to the single drug that is now being most widely prescribed in the United States—Tagamet.

This, then, is one area in which, perhaps, men, women and their families are already suffering personal consequences from the interventions of the big businesses of science and medicine that we have allowed to dominate our culture. Another, of course, is child-bearing and motherhood.

In the seventeenth century, Louis XIV wanted an unimpeded view of his mistress giving birth—so she gave birth lying horizontally. He also insisted that palace births should be attended not by a midwife, but by a male doctor. From that point on, one may say, the die was cast. Little by little all the processes of motherhood and mothering were invaded by males—first by obstetricians, then by psychologists, advertisers, nutritionists, sociologists and Dr. Spock. Mothers no longer knew best. They were drugged during childbirth, placed in the most difficult and dangerous position during labor and told that their milk was unnecessary, not nutritious enough for a growing child. And after birth they became the nervous, self-conscious prey of every expert and every child-market huckster who had a product to sell. Finally feminists—fighting for necessary rights in the workplace—delivered what was almost a *coup de grace.* Motherhood is not innate, they cried; it is just a temporary inconvenience. Have a child, but then get back to your career. Mothers, after all, are not that important. Any child-minder will do.

The problem is that this not only compounds a considerable injustice done to women. It is also patently untrue. There is now a bewildering variety of evidence that long-term, mother-child attachments were of crucial importance in the evolution of our species, and that these attachments are subserved by neural and hormonal mechanisms within every female today. They are basic to her biological design. Some of these mechanisms govern the way a woman is attracted to babies in general; the way she instinctively carries a child close to her heartbeat, regardless of her handedness; and the way a mother is automatically prepared for milking by her baby's cry. Others help control the pain of childbirth, which should take place, most naturally, with the mother standing or squatting. Still others regulate the automatic bonding of mother and child after birth—by sight, sound and smell.

During pregnancy a woman may develop extra pituitary capacity for the production of substances called endorphins ("the morphine within"). This has the double effect of producing in *her* euphoria, placidity and a relative imperviousness to pain, and in her *fetus* these things plus a depression of respiration and bowel movement. The fetus is, in effect, hibernating—and David Margules of Temple University in Philadelphia believes the endorphins are central to hibernation in animals. But it is *also* being protected from the normal immune reactions of its mother. And the endorphins have recently been found to be involved in this too in some way.

Close to term the immune protection modulated by the endorphins, perhaps, is gradually removed, probably largely due to a rapid decrease of progesterone and an accompanying rise in estrogen, resulting in the baby's rejection. The high level of estrogen seems to be important to the post-birth development of maternal behavior. And so is another hormone which produces the contractions of labor, oxytocin. Oxytocin is responsible for the nipple erection that is found in nursing mothers in response to an infant's cry. And oxytocin, injected into the brains of virgin female rats in a recent experiment at the University of North Carolina, also produces in them the full spectrum of mothering behavior.

How far this delicate chemical interplay in interfered with by cesarean births—which have tripled in the United States in the past ten years—or by the giving of pain-killing and contraction-inducing drugs—which may, again, affect the infant's chemistry —cannot be known. But there is increasing evidence that any and all interventions by doctors have damaging effects. Cesarean births, according to Edmund Quilligan of the University of California at Irvine, produce a maternal mortality rate that is thirty times higher, in some parts of the United States, than it is for normal births. The use of contraction-inducing drugs causes a high rate of neonatal jaundice, especially in boys. And two English studies have recently widened the picture. If pain-killing drugs have been used, mothers are much less likely to remember the birth experience with pleasure a year later. And if they have had Cesareans, they are twice as likely to have had post-partum depression or a psychotic episode within that year.

There is also increasing evidence that removing the newborn from its mother immediately after birth—the usual practice in most parts of the west—and allowing only restricted access thereafter may have a considerable effect on the newborn's prospects. Marshall Klaus and John Kennell at Case Western Reserve School of Medicine in Ohio have shown that if a woman is allowed to remain with her newborn infant, unclothed and in a warm room, for an hour after birth, and is allowed five more hours with it than usual on each of the three succeeding days, the results of these extra sixteen hours of interaction can be seen a year later. The children are more attentive and responsive, and the mothers more stimulating. They talk to their children more; they use more words and adjectives; they ask more questions.

This may be unsettling news for those who have been persuaded to believe that birth is an isolated reproductive event that ends with the conclusion of labor. It is not. It is a process that continues not only through mother-infant interaction but also through suckling, despite the huge efforts of big business to persuade first the women of the west, and now the women of the Third World, otherwise. In the past two or three years, it has been found that human mother's milk is essential to the development of the infant. It contains factors that cannot be found in any formula—a human growth factor, antibodies for immune protection, minerals, vitamins, hormones and proteins. What the effects of withholding it from the infant are cannot be known. As a 1982 study asked: "Does artificial feeding influence the development in later life of hypertension, obesity and auto-immune diseases?" We simply do not know. But we do know this. The provision of human milk is an automatic process under the control of its own hormone, prolactin—presumed, until 1971, to exist in animals but not in humans. If an infant is born prematurely, then its mother's milk contains two or three times the levels of antibodies and fifty percent more protein than usual. And it always contains endorphins and small quantities of plant-derived morphine, so that the infant is kept calm and happy, literally dependent on its mother.

The protein levels in human milk are characteristic of a species that gives not widely-spaced breast feedings as we do, but virtually continuous suck. And this brings us to our next theme —the patterns of infant care thought acceptable in our society. For this pattern of feeding is characteristic of the !Kung San, a tribe of primitive hunter-gatherers in southern Africa. And the !Kung, as they are known, can tell us something about a style of mothering that may be central to the biology of our species.

!Kung women, as Melvin Konner of Harvard University and others have shown, have almost constant physical contact with their newborn infants—more than seventy percent of the time, as against twenty-five percent or less in western societies. They nurse, not periodically, but virtually continuously. Lactation continues until the child is four or five. The mother-child among the !Kung is highly sensual, and their social system does everything to support it. The gap between births is about four years —by three or four !Kung children have entered a multi-age play group of both sexes—because continuous lactation and production of prolactin act as a natural contraceptive.

"I don't believe," Alice Rossi says, as we sit in her house at the end of a long afternoon, "that western women should be imprisoned by their biology in such a regimen. But I *do* think there are biological constraints on the relationship between child and mother. And I do think it's instructive to compare the !Kung style of child-rearing with our own. In our society we separate the child from the mother, in cribs and strollers, separate nurseries and child-care centers. We typically space our births at two-year rather than four-year intervals. And we isolate the child-mother unit almost completely. There's no social support for them. Motherhood, as a result, is experienced as a stressful and difficult role. And it's no wonder that it's seen less and less as an acceptable one.

"The question *must* be, then: Might we be making cultural demands of women and children that are alien to their biological needs? It's interesting that a preliminary report in a long-term study being conducted by Eleanor Maccoby and Carol Jacklin at Stanford shows that sex hormone levels were lower in second and third children than in the first, *unless* there was a gap of several years between births. And if we *are* making alien cultural demands, what might be the detectable signs of the stress that's the result? Children who are hyperactive, fear change or have problems with emotional relationships? Parents who are dissatisfied with their children and become poor role-models or even child abusers? Working women who, as it is, simply can't balance out the separate attractions and separate demands of career and motherhood?

"We don't know. But we ought to think very carefully about the problem, because if we want to achieve true equality between men and women, we may have to change some of our institutions to come in line with what may be the woman's crucial biologically inherited role. Businesses may have to be persuaded to make their job descriptions and work schedules much more flexible to accommodate the working woman and, if she's married, her husband. And it may have to confront and revise its expectations of what a full-time working mother and father can contribute to it. It may have to provide, by law, much longer maternal *and* paternal leave, because bigger and better child-care facilities may not be the only adequate answer to the problems of working parents and their children. They may make the parents' life easier, it's true, but they may mean that parents and children have to go on paying a price—a price that, as a species, we cannot afford."

These are all issues that ought to be faced by both men and women. But they will never be faced if we persist in supporting the old orthodoxy-cum-ideology that has now become our modern climate of opinion. They will only be confronted if we learn to accept, recognize and appreciate the differences between us.

From the dark continent of the human brain science is already bringing back a new psychiatry, a new understanding of and new cures for dysfunction and disorder. It is also bringing us back news about our separate inheritances as men and women that sooner or later we are going to have to heed. The news is that we are far older than we think we are. And who we are today is simply the current expression of the long, long history of our coming to this place. We were—and still are—designed by the evolutionary programs within us for the purposes of this travel, purposes that are still reflected in our strengths and weaknesses alike. Women are still protected for the purposes of motherhood—whether, as individuals, they want to have children or not. Men are still geared to be hunters and sex-seekers—whether, as individuals, they hunt and seek sex or not. Men are also less stable and more various than women; women evolved in a more balanced way.

Pluses and minuses—in the immune system, in the sex hormones, in brain organization and in social and sexual behavior: these pluses and minuses come together in packages at the heart of Freud's "special chemism" in men and women, making us complementary to one another. Neither is better, neither is worse. The making of human life requires collaboration rather than competition.

And yet competition between us seems the likeliest prospect as we enter the cybernated society towards which our cultural evolution is hurtling us, like "a jet plane rushing forward at gigantic speed"—competition in the workplace, competition for sensation and competition for the dwindling satisfactions that intimacy and the embattled family offer. This future cannot be avoided—it will be brought nearer—if women continue to fall into the trap of believing that they are the same as men. It can only be avoided, first of all, if men take to heart the terms of the original evolutionary contract by which the female transferred to the male some of her power. They must remember that in order to receive they have to give. They must remember male parenting. In this context, it does not simply mean providing resources. Nor does it mean simply taking care of children and helping with household duties. It means making sure that women in general are provided with something they need: a society flexible enough to grant them full equality of opportunity in the workplace but at the same time to give them special respect and special treatment as potential and actual mothers. It means making a space in the society in which women can begin to exercise the particular talents that men have so long ignored in them. Men are analytical and reductionist; in science, they have reduced the world to its component parts; they have torn apart the universe. Women are communicative and integrative. Perhaps they can find a way of putting the world back together.

Women too must remember the terms of the contract. They must remember that it is from their role as mother that they derive their special power. Whether or not women, as individuals, decide to be mothers, it is the value of motherhood that makes them a real community, a real sisterhood. Men have been bent out of shape by the culture they have made for themselves, as women should appreciate. And they will not easily give up their traditionally held privileges, unless women can offer them something in return. What that something may be—a fuller involvement in the processes of reproduction, new directions for the institutions that dominate men's lives, women organizing as mothers to save the planet from destruction—is not easy to predict. But women—as the continuers of the species—must take the lead.

The differences between men and women—all the differences in brain and body and inheritance, in ability, fragility and immunity—are fundamental to our human biology. They are the driving force of our biological evolution and the creators, between them, of our cultural evolution. They are what tie men and women together in such a delicate, interdependent balance. If we ignore the differences, if we pretend they do not exist, we in effect cut ourselves off from one another, and from the possibility of solving together the problems of the future. And if that happens, the battle for the family will be finally lost. Reproduction will little by little be taken over by science and industry. And we will one day arrive in a Brave New World, the only species on earth in which sex is a game and the differences between the two sexes without meaning.

"Knowledge," Jerre Levy recently wrote, "serves human welfare far better than false beliefs." This knowledge may not serve the turn of some of the entrenched institutions of our society, including big business. It may not suit the psychologized politics-for-self that is the current expression, all too often, of feminism and the other sexual liberation movements. It may not promote the idea of social justice as psychological health. But it may lead to a greater understanding, for our sake and especially for our children's sake, of the essential integrity of the male and female body and brain and the importance of the partnership of male and female in the enterprise and continuation of human life.

BIBLIOGRAPHY
AND NOTES

WHAT FOLLOWS IS a list of the books relevant to the themes and subjects covered in the text and the most important scientific papers we drew on in writing this book.

General Bibliography

Norman T. Adler (editor): *Neuroendocrinology of Reproduction* (Plenum Press, New York and London, 1981)

David Barash: *The Whisperings Within* (Harper and Row, New York, 1979)

Graham Bell: *The Masterpiece of Nature* (University of California Press, Berkeley, 1982)

Colin Blakemore: *Mechanics of the Mind* (Cambridge University Press, New York, 1977)

William Calvin and George Ojemann: *Inside the Brain* (New American Library, New York, 1980)

Bernard Campbell (editor): *Sexual Selection and the Descent of Man, 1871–1971* (Aldine, Chicago, 1972)

Napoleon A. Chagnon and William Irons (editors): *Evolutionary Biology and Social Behavior: An Anthropological Perspective* (Duxbury Press, North Scituate, Massachusetts, 1979)

Ciba Foundation Symposium: *Sex, Hormones and Behavior* (Excerpts Medica, Amsterdam, New York, 1979)

Martin Daly and Margo Wilson: *Sex, Evolution and Behavior* (Duxbury Press, North Scituate, Massachusetts, 1978)

Richard Dawkins: *The Selfish Gene* (Oxford University Press, New York, 1976)

David de Wied and Pieter A. van Keep (editors): *Hormones and the Brain* (MTP Press, Lancaster, England, 1980)

Robin Fox: *The Red Lamp of Incest* (E. P. Dutton, New York, 1980)

Michael T. Ghiselin: *The Economy of Nature and the Evolution of Sex* (University of California Press, Berkeley, 1975)

Stephen Jay Gould: *The Mismeasurement of Man* (W. W. Norton, New York, 1981)

Robert Goy and Bruce McEwen: *Sexual Differentiation of the Brain* (MIT Press, Cambridge, Massachusetts, 1980)

Fred Hapgood: *Why Males Exist* (William Morrow, New York, 1979)

Laurel Holliday: *The Violent Sex* (Bluestocking Books, Guerneville, California, 1978)

Janet I. Hopson: *Scent Signals* (William Morrow, New York, 1979)

Sarah Blaffer Hroy: *The Woman That Never Evolved* (Harvard University Press, Cambridge, Massachusetts, 1981)

J. B. Hutchison (editor): *Biological Determinants of Sexual Behavior* (John Wiley and Sons, New York, 1978)

Corinne Hutt: *Males and Females* (Penguin Books, Harmondsworth, England, 1972)

Melvin Konner: *The Tangled Wing* (Holt, Rinehart and Winston, New York, 1982)

Christopher Lasch: *Haven in a Heartless World* (Basic Books, New York, 1977)

Stanley Lesse: *The Future of the Health Sciences* (Irvington Press, New York, 1981)

Kristin Luker: *Taking Chances: Abortion and the Decision Not to Contracept* (University of California Press, Berkeley, 1975)

Sidney L. W. Mellen: *The Evolution of Love* (W. H. Freeman, Oxford and San Francisco, 1981)

Susan Michelmore: *Sex* (Eyre and Spottiswoode, London, 1964)

Ferdinand Mount: *The Subversive Family* (Jonathan Cape, London, 1982)

James C. Neeley: *Gender: The Myth of Equality* (Simon and Schuster, New York 1981)

Mariette Nowak: *Eve's Rib* (St. Martin's Press, New York, 1980)

Richard M. Restak: *The Brain: The Last Frontier* (Doubleday, New York, 1979)

Peter C. Reynolds: *On the Evolution of Human Behavior* (University of California Press, Berkeley, 1981)

Steven Rose: *The Conscious Brain* (Alfred A. Knopf, New York, 1973)

Gordon M. Shepherd: *The Synaptic Organization of the Brain* (Oxford University Press, New York, 1979)

Jacqueline Simenauer and David Carroll: *Singles: The New American* (Simon and Schuster, New York, 1982)

Sally P. Springer and Georg Deutsch: *Left Brain, Right Brain* (W. H. Freeman, San Francisco, 1981)

G. Ledyard Stebbins: *Darwin to DNA, Molecules to Humanity* (W. H. Freeman, San Francisco, 1982)

Donald Symons: *The Evolution of Human Sexuality* (Oxford University Press, New York, 1979)

Thomas Szasz: *Sex by Prescription* (Anchor/Doubleday, New York, 1980)

Lewis Thomas: *The Lives of a Cell* (Viking, New York, 1974)

Lionel Tiger: *Optimism: The Biology of Hope* (Simon and Schuster, New York, 1979)

Paul H. Wender and Donald F. Klein: *Mind, Mood and Medicine* (Farrar, Straus & Giroux, New York, 1981)

George C. Williams: *Sex and Evolution* (Princeton University Press, Princeton, New Jersey, 1975)

Rupert F. Witzmann: *Steroids, Keys to Life* (Van Nostrand Reinhold, New York, 1981)

J. Z. Young: *Programs of the Brain* (Oxford University Press, New York, 1978)

Notes

The best and most recent summaries of the work done on sexual dimorphism and sexual differentiation can be found in the Ciba Foundation Symposium and in Robert Goy's and Bruce McEwen's *Sexual Differentiation of the Brain,* both previously cited, and in a series of articles edited by Frederick Naftolin and Eleanore Butz that appeared in *Science*, March 20, 1981 (*Science* 211, pp. 1263-1324).

In what follows, we make reference only to those books and scientific articles that are most pertinent to the arguments raised in each chapter, excluding those articles which remain unpublished at the time of writing.

Introduction: The Cutting Edge

The Medawar quote is from *Plato's Republic* (Oxford University Press, New York, 1982). For the impact of science on medicine, psychiatry and society, see Colin Blakemore: "The Future of Psychiatry in Science and Society" (*Psychological Medicine*, 1981, II); Clifford Grebstein: "Coming to Terms with Test-tube Babies" (*New Scientist*, October 1982); and Paul W. Wender and Donald F. Klein: "The Promise of Biological Psychiatry" (*Psychology Today*, February 1981).

Chapter 1: The Death of the Old, the Birth of the New

An account of the rise of the social sciences and psychology, of the gradual acceptance of the all-importance of culture, can be found in Peter C. Reynolds: *On the Evolution of Human Behavior* (University of California Press, Berkeley, California, 1981); and in Christopher Lasch: *Haven in a Heartless World* (Basic Books, New York, 1977).

Chapter 2: Truth or Consequences

For an account of the effect of 19th- and early 20th-century medicine on women, see Barbara Ehrenreich and Deirdre English: *For Her Own Good: A Hundred and Fifty Years of the Experts' Advice to Women* (Pluto Press, London, 1979).

Chapter 3: The Thinking Gland

For Joseph Jastrow's work, see Joseph Jastrow: *A Statistical Study of Memory and Association* (*Educational Review*, December 1981). For a history of work done on sex hormones and animal behavior, see Frank A. Beach: "Historical Origins of Modern Research on Hormones and Behavior" (*Hormones and Behavior*, 15, 1981). For behavioral and cognitive sex differences in humans see Eleanor Maccoby and Carol Jacklin: *The Psychology of Sex Differences* (Stanford University Press, Palo Alto, 1974); Diane McGuinness: "Auditory and Motor Aspects of Language Development in Males and Females" in *The Significance of Sex Differences in Dyslexia* (editors: A. Ansara et al. The Orton Society, Inc., Towson, 1981); Diane McGuinness and Karl Pribram: "The Origins of Sensory Bias in the Development of Gender Differences in Perception and

Cognition" in *Cognitive Growth and Development: Essays in Memory of Herbert G. Birch* (editor, M. Bortner, Brunner and Mazel, New York, 1978); June Reinisch: "Fetal Hormones, the Brain and Human Sex Differences" (*Archives of Sexual Behavior*, 3, 1981); and Beatrice B. and John W. M. Whiting: *Children of Six Cultures: A Psychocultural Analysis* (Harvard University Press, Cambridge, 1975).

Chapter 4: A Tale of Two Hemispheres

The most important further reference for this chapter is to some sixty pages in two separate issues of *The Behavioral and Brain Sciences* (3, 1980, pp. 215–263 and 5, 1982, pp. 306–315). The subject of these pages was a so-called target paper by Jeannette McGlone, which was opened for criticism and review to forty-three of her peers, among them Lansdell, Inglis and Lawson, Kimura, Ojemann and Mateer. Contained within them is an account not only of their work, but of the work of Levy, Witelson, the Gurs, Flor-Henry, Buchsbaum, Hatta and Fukui. Complete references can be found there. For those keen to pursue the theme of laterality in general, of interest might be: J. L. Bradshaw and N. C. Nettleton: "The Nature of Hemispheric Specialization in Man" (*The Behavioral and Brain Sciences*, 4, 1981); V. H. Denenberg: "Hemispheric Laterality in Animals and the Effects of Early Experience" (*The Behavioral and Brain Sciences*, 4, 1981); Ruben and Raquel Gur: "Sex and Handedness Differences in Cerebral Blood Flow During Rest and Cognitive Activity" (*Science*, August 13, 1982); Jerre Levy: "Lateral Differences in the Human Brain in Cognition and Behavioral Control" in *Cerebral Correlates of Conscious Experience* (editor, P. Buser, North Holland Publishing Company, New York, 1978); Jerre Levy: a review of *Sexual Differentation of the Brain* by Robert Goy and Bruce McEwen (*The Sciences*, March 1981); and Roger Sperry: "Some Effects of Disconnecting the Cerebral Hemispheres" (*Science*, September 24, 1982).

Chapter 5: Making Connections

The more important papers referred to in this chapter are: Christine de Lacoste-Utamsing and Ralph Holloway: "Sexual Dimorphism in the Human Corpus Callosum" (*Science*, June 25, 1982); Christine de Lacoste-Utamsing and D. J. Woodward: "Sexual Dimorphism in Human Fetal Corpora Callosa" (Abstracts of the 1982 meeting of the Society for Neuroscience); Sandra Witelson: "Sex and the Single Hemisphere: Specialization of the Right Hemisphere for Spatial Processing" (*Science*,

193, 1976); Sandra Witelson: "Sex Differences in the Neurology of Cognition: Psychological, Social, Educational and Political Implications" in *Le Fait Feminin* (editor, E. Sulleret, Fayard, Paris, 1978); and Camilla Persson Benbow and Julian C. Stanley: "Sex Differences in Mathematical Ability: Fact or Artifact?" (*Science*, December 12, 1980).

Chapter 6: A Search for Clues

For Anna M., see: Edith Reske-Nielsen et al.: "A Neuropathological and Neuropsychological Study of Turner's Syndrome" (*Cortex*, 18, 1982), and Harold W. Gordon and Avinoam Galatzer: "Cerebral Organization in Patients with Gonadal Dysgenesis" (*Psychoneuroendocrinology*, 5, 1980). For an overview of the connections between sex chromosomes, hormones and brain organization and ability, see Pierre Flor-Henry: "Gender, Hemispheric Specialization and Psychopathology" (*Social Science and Medicine*, 12b, 1978). For Klinefelter's males, see Shirley G. Radcliffe et al.: "Klinefelter's Syndrome in Adolescence" (*Archives of Disease in Childhood*, 57, 1982). And for males with hypogonadotrophic hypogonadism, see Daniel Hier and William Crowley: "Spatial Ability in Androgen-deficient Men" (*New England Journal of Medicine*, May 20, 1982).

Chapter 7: The Sex Chemicals: The View from Outside

For the fullest accounts of the action and effects of the sex hormones, and for further references, see the Ciba Foundation Symposium: "Sex, Hormones and Behavior" (*Excerpta Medica*, New York, 1979) and the series of articles published in *Science* on March 20, 1981, especially Robert T. Rubin et al.: "Postnatal Gonadal Steroid Effects on Human Behavior." See also Weiert Velle: "Sex Hormones and Behavior in Animals and Man" (*Perspectives in Biology and Medicine*, 25, 2, Winter 1982).

Chapter 8: Accidents of Nature

The most complete account of Günter Dörner's work can be found in Günter Dörner: "Sexual Differentiation of the Brain" (*Vitamins and Hormones*, 38, 1980) and in Günter Dörner: "Sex Hormones and Neurotransmitters as Mediators for Sexual Differentiation of the Brain" (*Endokrinologie*, 78, December 1981). For the case of the Dominican children, see especially two papers by Julianne Imperato-McGinley, one in *Science*, 186, 1213, 1974; and the other in *The Journal of Steroid Biochemistry*, II, 637, 1979. For the case of the altered American twin, see John Money and Mark Schwartz: "Biosocial Determinants of Gender Identity Differentiation and Development" in *Biological Determinants of Sexual Behavior* (editor, J. B. Hutchison, John Wiley and Sons, New York, 1978); and for Milton Diamond's attitude and response, see Milton Diamond: "A Critical Evaluation of the Ontogeny of Human Sexual Behavior" (*Quarterly Review of Biology*, June 1965); Milton Diamond: "Human Sexual Development: Biological Foundations for Social Development" in *Human Sexuality in Four Perspectives* (editor, Frank Beach, The Johns Hopkins Press, Baltimore, 1977); and Milton Diamond: "Sexual Identity, Monozygotic Twins Reared in Discordant Sex Roles and the BBC Follow-up" (*Archives of Sexual Behavior*, II, 2, 1982). The cases of Mrs. Went and Mr. Blackwell and the remarks of Gerineldo Babilonia were drawn from a good overview of the subject again provided by the BBC, in a film and article in *The Listener* (May, 24, 1979), both entitled "The Fight to be Male."

Chapter 9: The Mechanisms of Gender: The View from Inside

For a review of the literature pertinent to this chapter, see Robert Goy and Bruce McEwen: *Sexual Differentiation of the Brain* (MIT Press, Cambridge, 1980). See also two articles in the *Science* series of March 20, 1981: Florence P. Haseltine and Susumo Ohno: "Mechanisms of Gonadal Differentiation" and Jean D. Wilson et al.: "The Hormonal Control of Sexual Development."

Chapter 10: Coming Full Circle

An important supplementary source for this chapter is, again, the Ciba Foundation Symposium: "Sex, Hormones and Behavior." A good overview is provided by Anke A. Ehrhardt and Heine F. I. Meyer-Bahlburg: "Effects of Prenatal Sex Hormones on Gender-Related Behavior" (*Science*, March 20, 1981) and by the previously cited paper by R. T. Rubin et al. that immediately follows it. See also June Reinisch's paper in the issue of *Science* immediately preceeding it (March 13, 1981). For Günter Dörner's work, see references in the notes for Chapter 7. For Lorraine Herrenkohl's work see especially John A. Meyer et al: "Stress During Pregnancy: Effect on Catecholamines in Discrete Brain Regions of Offspring and Adults" (*Brain Research*, 144, 1978); and Lorraine Herrenkohl: "Prenatal Stress Reduces Fertility and Fecundity in Female Offspring" (*Science*, 206, November 30, 1979).

Chapter 11: A Different Chemistry

It is difficult to single out particular references for the themes pursued in this chapter, since the clues come, one by one, from many sources. For a general account of the different risks faced by males and females, their different immune deficiencies and disorders, see a paper by David T. Purtilla and John L. Sullivan in the *American Journal for the Diseases of Children*, 1980. For differences between Type-A males and females, see especially Marian Frankenhaeuser et al.: "Dissociation between Sympathetic Adrenal and Pituitary-adrenal Responses to an Achievement Situation Characterized by High Controllability: Comparison Between Type-A and Type-B Males and Females" (*Biological Psychology*, 10, 1980) and David S. Holmes et al.: "Cardiac and Subjective Response to Cognitive Challenge and to Controlled Physical Exercise by Male and Female Coronary-prone (Type-A) and Non-coronary-prone Persons" (*Journal of Psychosomatic Research*, 26, 3, 1982). For a full account of depression and the phobias, see Paul H. Wender and Donald F. Klein: *Mind, Mood and Medicine* (Farrar, Straus & Giroux, New York, 1981). For post-partum blues and pre-menstrual tension, see Katharina Dalton: *Depression after Childbirth* (Oxford University Press, New York, 1980) and Katharina Dalton: *Premenstrual Syndrome and Progesterone Therapy* (William Heinemann Medical Books, London, 1977). Some interesting papers on anorexia and appetite—and on their connection to the affective disorders—are B. Timothy Walsh: "Endocrine Disturbances in Anorexia Nervosa and Depression" (*Psychosomatic Medicine*, 44, I, 1982); Harry Gwirtsman and Robert Gerner: "Neurochemical Abnormalities in Anorexia Nervosa: Similarities to Affective Disorders" (*Biological Psychiatry*, 16, 10, 1981); Walter H. Kaye et al.: "Cerebrospinal Fluid Opioid Activity in Anorexia Nervosa" (*American Journal of Psychiatry*, 139:5, 1982); Esther Eisenberg: "Toward an Understanding of Reproductive Function in Anorexia Nervosa" (*Fertility and Sterility*, 36, 5, 1981); and Katharine Blick Hoyenga and Kermit T. Hoyenga: "Gender and Energy Balance: Sex Differences in Adaptations for Feast and Famine" (*Physiology and Behavior*, 28, 1982).

Chapter 12: Of Hemispheres, Moods and Madness

For Pierre Flor-Henry's work, see Pierre Flor-Henry: "Gender, Hemisphere Specialization and Psychopathology" (*Society, Science and Medicine*, 12B, 1978); Pierre Flor-Henry: "On Certain Aspects of the Localization of the Cerebral Systems Regulating and Determining Emotion" (*Biological Psychiatry*, 14, 4, 1979); Pierre Flor-Henry and L.

T. Yeudall: "Neuropsychological Investigations of Schizophrenia and Manic-depressive Psychoses" in *Hemispheric Asymmetries of Function in Psychopathology* (editors, John Gruzelier and Pierre Flor-Henry, Elsevier, Amsterdam, 1979); and Pierre Flor-Henry: "Cerebral Aspects of the Orgasmic Response: Normal and Deviational" in *Medical Sexology: The Third International Congress* (editors, Romano Forlee and Willy Pasini, Elsevier, Amsterdam and New York, 1980). For the case of Charles Darwin Decker, see Andre Meyer and Michael Wheeler: *The Crocodile Man: A Case of Brain Chemistry and Violence* (Houghton Mifflin, Boston, 1982). And for the genetic basis of depressive disorders see Lowell Weitkamp et al.: "Depressive Disorders and HLA: A Gene on Chromosome 6 That Can Affect Behavior" (*New England Journal of Medicine*, 35, 22, November 26, 1981) and Thomas H. Maugh II: "Is There a Gene for Depression?" (*Science*, 241, December 18, 1981).

Chapter 13: The Newest Frontier

For a general discussion of handedness and a general listing of references on the subject, see Sally P. Springer and Georg Deutsch: *Left Brain, Right Brain* (W. H. Freeman, San Francisco, 1981). For an account of the pitfalls faced in development by males and females, see the paper by David T. Purtillo and John L. Sullivan referred to in the notes for Chapter 10. For natural abortion, see J. F. Miller et al. in *Lancet*, September 2, 13, 1980. For dyslexia, see Sandra Witelson: "Developmental Dyslexia: Two Right Hemispheres and None Left" (*Science*, 195, June 29, 1976). For autism, see Lorna Wing: "The Autiology and Pathogenesis of Early Infantile Autism" (*Trends in Neuroscience*, July 1978). Norman Geschwind's work with Peter Behan can be found in Norman Geschwind and Peter Behan: "Left-handedness: Association with Immune Disease, Migraine and Developmental Learning Disorder" (*Proceedings of the National Academy of Sciences*, August 1982) and Albert Galaburda's account of his first dyslexic brain can be found in Albert Galaburda and Thomas Kemper: "Cytoarchitectonic Abnormalities in Developmental Dyslexia: A Case Study" (*Annals of Neurology*, 6, 2, August 1979).

Chapter 14: The Immune System and the Brain

A useful introduction to the immune system and self-recognition is Seth Pincus: "A Sense of Self" (*Perspectives in Biology and Medicine*, 26, I, Autumn 1982). For the immune and endocrine systems in pregnancy, see Pentti K. Siiteri and Daniel P. Stites: "Immunologic and

Endocrine Interrelationships in Pregnancy" (*Biology of Reproduction*, 26, 1982). For SLE see, for example, Norman Talal: "Sex Steroid Hormones and Systemic Lupus Erythematosus" (*Arthritis and Rheumatism*, 24, 8, August 1981) and Robert G. Lahita et al.: "Alteration of Estrogen Metabolism in Systemic Lupus Erythematosus" (*Arthritis and Rheumatism*, 22, II, November 1979). A good overview of the role of the HLA major histocompatibility complex in auto-immune diseases is Charles B. Carpenter: "Autoimmunity and HLA" (*Journal of Clinical Immunology*, 2, 3, 1982). And the possibility that autism is at bottom an auto-immune disease is presented in Abraham Weizman et al.: "Abnormal Immune Response to Brain Tissue Antigen in the Syndrome of Autism" (*American Journal of Psychiatry*, 139: II, November 1982). Marian Annett's analysis of the distribution of left-handers in certain professions can be found in *Behavioral Genetics*, 8, 1979.

Chapter 15: Why Sex Exists

The quote from Porteus is from S. D. Porteus: *Porteus Maze Test: Fifty Years' Application* (Pacific Books, Palo Alto, 1965). A good account of molecular and chromosomal differences between man and his nearest relatives can be found in two articles by Jeremy Cherfas and John Gribbin: "The Molecular Making of Mankind" (*New Scientist*, August 27, 1981) and "Descent of Man—or Ascent of Ape?" (*New Scientist*, September 3, 1981). The correlation between testis weight and breeding system is in A. H. Harcourt et al.: "Testis Weight, Body Weight and Breeding System in Primates" (*Nature*, 293, September 3, 1981). Those interested in pursuing the evolution and variety of sex in nature might consult, in addition to the books mentioned in the text, Fred Hapgood: *Why Males Exist* (William Morrow, New York, 1979) and Mariette Nowak: *Eve's Rib* (St. Martin's Press, New York, 1980). For William Hamilton's work, see William D. Hamilton: "Sex Versus Nonsex Versus Parasites" (*Oikos*, 35, 1980) and William D. Hamilton: "Pathogens as Causes of Genetic Diversity in Their Host Populations" in *Population Biology of Infectious Disease Agents*, Dahlem Conference, 1982 (Verlag Chemie, Weinheim, 1983).

Chapter 16: Up the Ladder: The Sexual Two-step

For the original statement of Lovejoy's theory, see C. Owen Lovejoy: "The Origin of Man" (*Science*, 211, January 23, 1981). And for an account of John Martin's work, see Roger Lewin: "How Did Humans Evolve Big Brains?" (*Science*, 216, May 21, 1982).

Chapter 17: An Ancient Legacy

For pheromones in general, see Janet Hopson: *Scent Signals* (William Morrow, New York, 1979); J. B. Hutchinson, ed.: *Biological Determinants of Sexual Behavior* (John Wiley and Sons, New York, 1978); and Lewis Thomas: *The Lives of a Cell* (Viking, New York, 1974).

Chapter 18: He and She

For general reading, see Donald Symons: *The Evolution of Human Sexuality* (Oxford University Press, New York, 1979); Sidney Mellen: *The Evolution of Love* (W. H. Freeman, San Francisco, 1981); and James C. Neeley: *Gender: The Myth of Equality* (Simon and Schuster, New York, 1981). For a more detailed account of the mechanisms of sex and reproduction, see *Neuroendocrinology of Reproduction* (editor, Norman T. Adler, Plenum Press, New York, 1981). And for an interesting paper on the female orgasm, see R. J. Levin: "The Female Orgasm—A Current Appraisal" (*Journal of Psychosomatic Research*, 25, 2, 1981).

Chapter 19: Beneath the Din

For Alice Rossi, see Alice Rossi: "A Biosocial Perspective on Parenting" (*Daedalus*, 106, 1977) and her contribution to Robert Goy and Bruce McEwen: *Sexual Differentiation of the Brain* (MIT Press, Cambridge, 1980). For Lionel Tiger, see Lionel Tiger and Robin Fox: *The Imperial Animal* (Holt, Rinehart and Winston, New York, 1971); and Lionel Tiger: *Optimism, The Biology of Hope* (Simon and Schuster, New York, 1978). For Stanley Lesse, see Stanley Lesse: *The Future of the Health Sciences* (Irvington Press, New York, 1981) and a series of editorials and articles in *The American Journal of Psychotherapy*, especially "Factors Influencing Sexual Behavior in Our Future Society" (July 1976).

Chapter 20: For the Sake of Our Children

For a recent paper on the effects of vasectomy, see Steven S. Witkin et al.: "Sperm-related Antigens, Antibodies and Circulating Immune Complexes in Sera of Recently Vasectomized Men" (*Journal of Clinical Investigation*, 70, 1982). For a recent report on oral contraception and depression, see M. Shaarawv et al: "Serotonin Metabolism and Depression in Oral Contraceptives Users" (*Contraception*, 26, 2, August 1982). For the prenatal exposure of fetuses to drugs, see S. Anand and D. H. van Thiel: "Prenatal and Neonatal Exposure to Cimetidine Results in Gonadal and Sexual Dysfunction in Adult Males" (*Science*, 218, October 29, 1983); and, especially, June Reinisch: "Early Barbiturate Exposure: The Brain, Sexually Dimorphic Behavior and Learning" (*Neuroscience and Biobehavioral Reviews*, 6, 1982). For mother-child attachments, see Alice Rossi in Robert Goy and Bruce McEwen, as cited above. For the connection between "unnatural" birth experiences, poor recollections of birth and later problems, see, for example, Barbara Morgan et al. in *Lancet*, October 16, 1982 and P. N. Nott: "Psychiatric Illness Following Childbirth in Southampton: A Case Register Study" (*Psychological Medicine*, 12, 1982). For the contents of breast milk, see, for example, Graham Carpenter: "Epidermal Growth Factor Is a Major Growth-Promoting Agent in Human Milk" (*Science*, 210, October 10, 1980).

INDEX